RESTORATIONS

RESTORATIONS

SCHOLARS IN DIALOGUE

from COMMUNITY OF CHRIST *and*
THE CHURCH OF JESUS CHRIST
OF LATTER-DAY SAINTS

Andrew Bolton *and*
Casey Paul Griffiths
EDITORS

BYU

DESERET
BOOK

John Whitmer Books

Cover painting: *Kirtland Ohio Temple*. Courtesy of Brent Borup. www.BrentBorup.com.

Published by the Religious Studies Center, Brigham Young University, Provo, Utah, in cooperation with John Whitmer Books in Independence, Missouri, and Deseret Book Company, Salt Lake City, Utah.

Visit us at rsc.byu.edu.

Cover and interior design by Carmen Durland Cole.

ISBN 978-1-9503-0431-8

Library of Congress Cataloging-in-Publication Data

Names: Bolton, Andrew, 1950– editor. | Griffiths, Casey Paul, editor.
Title: Restorations : scholars in dialogue from Community of Christ and The
   Church of Jesus Christ of Latter-day Saints / edited by Andrew Bolton,
   Casey Paul Griffiths.
Description: Provo, Utah : Religious Studies Center, Brigham Young
   University ; Salt Lake City, Utah : Deseret Book Company, [2022] |
   Includes index. | Summary: "This book contains reflections from two
   groups of scholars who trace their beginnings to the early Saints who
   built the Kirtland Temple. These scholars come from the two largest
   branches of the Restoration movement, Community of Christ and The Church
   of Jesus Christ of Latter-day Saints, who have often found themselves on
   the opposite sides of many issues. This book is filled with honest,
   frank conversations between people of the two faiths but also
   collegiality and friendship. Centered on twelve themes, this dialogue is
   about bringing together informed scholars from the two churches working
   together, with good will, to accurately understand each other"—
   Provided by publisher.
Identifiers: LCCN 2022004234 | ISBN 9781950304318 (paperback)
Subjects: LCSH: Community of Christ—Relations—Church of Jesus Christ of
   Latter-day Saints. | Church of Jesus Christ of Latter-day
   Saints—Relations—Community of Christ. | Community of
   Christ—Doctrines. | Church of Jesus Christ of Latter-day
   Saints—Doctrines.
Classification: LCC BX8647 .R47 2022 | DDC 264/.093—dc23/eng/20220308
LC record available at https://lccn.loc.gov/2022004234

CONTENTS

INTRODUCTION

Sacred Spaces of Dialogue and Meeting

The Kirtland Temple, Ohio, built on the highest ground available, rises majestically above trees and other buildings. It was dedicated with prayer, song, and preaching in 1836 by the rejoicing Saints. Architecturally, the temple is a grand structure mixing Federal, Greek Revival, and Gothic Revival styles that creates a new fusion of beauty and reverence. It was built at great sacrifice by the early Latter Day Saints who felt they were restoring the Acts 2 church, complete with a temple and consecration of goods in the cause of Zion. Over time, the appearance of the temple has undergone many changes. According to contemporary accounts, the walls of the temple were bluish gray, the roof was red, and the doors were olive green. The doors remain the same color today, but much about the structure evolved and changed over the years. Today the temple is covered with a beautiful white stucco, allowing it to gleam brightly in the sunlight. But underneath the smooth surface created by the stucco, the actual walls of the temple consist of random-sized stones, cemented together and held in place as much by the faith of its early builders as the mortar they placed between the stones. This "House of the Lord"[1] built by the early Latter Day Saints remains a shared sacred space.² It is a place where all people can find a home for thought, contemplation, and reflection on the things of a higher and better world, including Community of Christ and The Church of Jesus Christ of Latter-day Saints. Although with a common early history, both churches, like the Kirtland Temple itself, have much more complexity beneath the surface.

This book contains reflections from two groups of scholars who both trace their beginnings to the early Saints who built the Kirtland Temple. They come from the two largest branches of the Restoration movement, Community of Christ and The Church of Jesus Christ of Latter-day Saints, who have often found themselves on the opposite sides of many issues. They may both be part of the same original family, but, like many families, find themselves at times divided with contention and bad feelings. In different eras, contention centered on the shared sacred spaces of both groups, including the Kirtland Temple itself.³ Name calling, not uncommon between the two groups, sometimes led to unkindness and unfair characterizations—unbecoming of those who call themselves Saints. Jan Shipps, a scholar not of either faith, helpfully improved things by simply labeling one group the "mountain Saints" and the other the "prairie Saints."⁴ Geography, in part, explains our differences.

Today the "mountain Saints" and the "prairie Saints" are both worldwide Saints. Now, more than two hundred years since the first revelatory experiences of Joseph Smith Jr., perhaps a family reunion of sorts is in order. The conversation between the scholars who wrote this book began tentatively in 2016. We carried many misunderstandings and misconceptions into our first conversations. Over time we gradually grew to respect each other and even became comfortable enough to engage in some good-natured teasing in our fellowship together. This book is filled with honest, frank conversations but also collegiality and friendship. From the beginning we all acknowledged that our work was not about uniting the two churches or converting each other. Each faith has a unique and vibrant character that has flourished under greatly different circumstances. This dialogue is about bringing together informed scholars from the two churches—scholars who are working together, with goodwill, to accurately understand each other. We now warmly invite you into our shared conversation on twelve themes, from Jesus Christ to Zion.

The two churches hold fourteen years (1830–44) of shared history and then nearly two centuries of separate development and growth. Yet those shared years, brief though they were, created a bond between the two churches. Like two family members who come together in their mature years to reconcile their differences and embrace shared history, we have experienced an abiding sense of fellowship and understanding in our dialogues together. Those shared, *sacred* spaces will always connect us, but we are only now finding that members from the two faiths can find connection, peace, and the grace of Jesus Christ as they create a *new* sacred space together. Perhaps oldest enemies can become respectful friends.

Notes

1. "Minutes and Prayer of Dedication, 27 March 1836 [D&C 109]," p. 274, The Joseph Smith Papers, https://www.josephsmithpapers.org/paper-summary /minutes-and-prayer-of-dedication-27-march-1836-dc-109/1.

2. Community of Christ is steward of Kirtland Temple and warmly welcomes members of all Restoration traditions, as well as those of any faith or no faith. It is a house of prayer, worship, and learning for all peoples.

3. See Roger D. Launius, "Joseph Smith III and the Kirtland Temple Suit," *BYU Studies Quarterly* 25, no. 3 (1985): 110–16.

4. See Jan Shipps, "Prophets and Prophecy in the Mormon Tradition(s): 2005 Presidential Address," *John Whitmer Historical Association Journal* 26 (2006): 1–17.

A NOTE ON TERMINOLOGY

Community of Christ and The Church of Jesus Christ of Latter-day Saints both descend from a common movement. In recent years both have also undergone significant changes in the way they prefer to be referred to by scholars and members of the media. When Joseph Smith and several close associates officially organized the church in 1830, they used the name "the Church of Christ" (LDS Doctrine and Covenants 20:1; CofChrist Doctrine and Covenants 17:1a). In May 1834, possibly to avoid confusion with other churches named Church of Christ, a conference of church leaders voted to change the name to "The Church of the Latter Day Saints."[1] A revelation given to Joseph Smith at Far West, Missouri, in 1838 gave the official name of the church, declaring, "For thus shall my Church be called in the Last days even the Church of Jesus Christ of Latter Day Saints."[2]

When the original forebears of Community of Christ formally reorganized on April 6, 1860, they also used "the Church of Jesus Christ of Latter Day Saints" as their name. In the decades following, the movement formally came to be called the Reorganized Church of Jesus Christ of Latter Day Saints, commonly abbreviated as RLDS. On April 6, 2001, the name was changed to "Community of Christ" to better reflect the church's mission to "proclaim Jesus Christ and promote communities of joy, hope, love and peace."[3] To avoid confusion, in this book we have chosen to use the name "Community of Christ" for the church, even when referring to times when the formal name of the movement was the "Reorganized Church of Jesus Christ of Latter Day Saints."

In 2018 leaders of The Church of Jesus Christ of Latter-day Saints published a statement reemphasizing the importance of using the proper name of the church as given in the 1838 revelation. Russell M. Nelson, president of the church, gave the following statement: "The Lord has impressed upon my mind the importance of the name He has revealed for His Church, even The Church of Jesus Christ of Latter-day Saints. We have work before us to bring ourselves in harmony with His will."[4] In accordance with this request, the authors in this book have generally used the full name of the church in their writing.

Proper use of terminology is a sign of respect. The authors and editors labored diligently to use the correct terms when referring to each of the churches. Even a simple term like "Latter-day Saint" was carefully used. Members of Community of Christ generally use the term "Latter Day Saint" with a capital *D*. Members of The Church of Jesus Christ of Latter-day Saints generally use the term "Latter-day Saint" with a hyphenated, lowercase *d*. We have tried to use the terms carefully, with "Latter Day Saints" referring to the entire Restoration movement and all the churches that came from those roots. "Latter-day Saints" usually refers to members of The Church of Jesus Christ of Latter-day Saints.

While the Book of Mormon remains a vital part of both faiths, we have also generally avoided the term "Mormon" to refer to either faith, since both churches feel strongly about the use of their proper names and the connections each provides to Jesus Christ and his teachings. If there are any errors or mistakes in the book regarding these terminologies, we offer our sincere apologies. We have attempted to be as sensitive as possible.

NOTES

1. "Communicated," *The Evening and the Morning Star*, May 1834, 160.

2. "Revelation, 26 April 1838 [D&C 115]," p. 33, The Joseph Smith Papers, https://www.josephsmithpapers.org/paper-summary/revelation-26-april-1838-dc-115/2; see also LDS Doctrine and Covenants 115:4.

3. "The Community of Christ Story," Community of Christ, https://www.CofChrist.org/history.

4. Russell M. Nelson, quoted in "The Name of the Church," August 16, 2018, newsroom.ChurchofJesusChrist.org.

ABBREVIATIONS AND NOTES ON SCRIPTURE

CHURCHES

CofChrist: This refers to Community of Christ.

Church of Jesus Christ: This may occasionally be used as an abbreviation for The Church of Jesus Christ of Latter-day Saints after the full name has been used.

LDS: This abbreviation, used only in scripture citations, refers to The Church of Jesus Christ of Latter-day Saints. While all efforts have been made to use the correct name of the church, this abbreviation was used in these citations for brevity and to clearly distinguish Latter-day Saint references from Community of Christ references.

SCRIPTURE

The Book of Mormon: The Book of Mormon is versed differently in the two churches, as in the following example: LDS 3 Nephi 11:7; CofChrist III Nephi 5:8. The first reference refers to The Church of Jesus Christ of Latter-day Saints edition. "CofChrist" is the abbreviation referring to Community of Christ editions and comes second.

Doctrine and Covenants: The Church of Jesus Christ of Latter-day Saints and Community of Christ use different editions. Again, the first reference refers to the Latter-day Saint edition, and the equivalent Community of Christ reference follows, as in the following example: LDS Doctrine and Covenants 89:5; CofChrist Doctrine and Covenants 86:1b.

Bible: The default Bible used by authors from The Church of Jesus Christ of Latter-day Saints is the King James Version (KJV). The default Bible used by Community of Christ authors is the New Revised Standard Version (NRSV). Any variation using another translation will be indicated.

Pearl of Great Price: If the Book of Moses is referenced, the equivalent Community of Christ reference is given in their Doctrine and Covenants, their volumes of church history, or a primary source. If the Book of Abraham is referenced, this refers only to scriptures used by The Church of Jesus Christ of Latter-day Saints.

BIOGRAPHIES OF AUTHORS

Andrew Bolton, PhD, was a British schoolteacher and college lecturer in multifaith religious education before working for Community of Christ for eighteen years, first coordinating peace and justice ministries and then coordinating the church in Asia. He has been published in *Dialogue*, the *Journal of Mormon History*, the *John Whitmer Historical Association Journal*, and *Restoration Studies*. He and his wife, Jewell, have two sons, Matthew and David, and one grandchild, Carson Breay. They live in retirement as active church volunteers in Leicester, England.

Dr. Gina Colvin is a New Zealand Māori who grew up as a Latter-day Saint. She currently worships locally with the Anglican Church and internationally with Community of Christ. She hosts the podcast *A Thoughtful Faith*—conversations about spiritual and religious life on the other side of extreme orthodoxy. Gina and her Latter-day Saint husband, Nathan, are the parents of one agnostic, one practicing Pentecostal, and four mostly Anglican—periodically Community of Christ—but sometimes Latter-day Saint—sons, who quite like Buddhism.

Eva M. Erickson works as an information specialist for the German Institute for Standardization (DIN). She is the national coordinator of Community of Christ in Germany, serves as a high priest, and has earned her master of arts in religion from Community of Christ Seminary at Graceland University. After spending several years in the United States, she now lives with her husband, John, and their two children, Daniel and Miriam, in Berlin, Germany.

Scott C. Esplin is the dean of Religious Education and a professor of church history and doctrine at Brigham Young University. Prior to joining the faculty, he earned both a doctoral and master's degree in educational leadership and foundations from BYU. His research and teaching interests include the Doctrine and Covenants, the history of Latter-day Saint education, and church historic sites. He is the author of numerous publications on these subjects, including an award-winning book on the restoration of Nauvoo.

Taunalyn Ford, PhD, is a postdoctoral research fellow at the Brigham Young University Neal A. Maxwell Institute for Religious Scholarship. For the previous seven years, she was adjunct faculty in church history and doctrine at BYU. Taunalyn received her BA and MA degrees at BYU and her PhD in history of Christianity and religions of North America at Claremont Graduate University. Her publications and current book projects focus on Latter-day Saints in India.

Matthew J. Frizzell, PhD, is currently adjunct faculty for Community of Christ Seminary at Graceland University and has been a faculty member at Graceland since 2011. Matt was dean of Community of Christ Seminary from 2015 to 2018. He currently serves as director of human resource ministries for Community of Christ International Headquarters in Independence, Missouri. Matt has served Community of Christ in full-time ministry as a pastor, campus minister, and church administrator. Matt's scholarship is in contemporary theology, Community of Christ theology, critical social theory, and social ethics.

He is married to Dr. Margo E. Frizzell and has three daughters, Katy, Kenzlee, and Kyla. They live in Chicago, Illinois.

Alonzo L. Gaskill, PhD, is a convert to The Church of Jesus Christ of Latter-day Saints, having been reared in the Greek Orthodox tradition. He has taught religion for the Church Educational System for thirty years—the last two decades at Brigham Young University, where he is a professor of world religions. His research interests lie in the fields of world religions, temple worship, symbolism, and Latter-day Saint theology. He has written more than two dozen books and numerous articles on various aspects of religious studies.

Kat Goheen grew up in Independence, Missouri, and has been active in Community of Christ her whole life. Her roles include high priest, pastor, and mission center copresident for Western Canada. She has two degrees in biblical studies from the Vancouver School of Theology. Kat also serves on various church boards and teams, teaches Hebrew Bible in weekend intensives, and is a trained spiritual director. She shares her love of music and laughter with her husband, Jon, and two wonderful daughters in Vancouver, British Columbia, Canada.

Casey Paul Griffiths is an associate teaching professor of church history and doctrine at Brigham Young University. He holds a bachelor's degree in history, a master's degree in religious education, and a PhD in educational leadership and foundations. He lives in Saratoga Springs, Utah, with his wife, Elizabeth, and their four adorable children.

Maclane E. Heward, PhD, has been teaching in the Seminaries and Institutes of Religion system for twelve years. He earned his bachelor's and master's degrees from Brigham Young University in public relations and religious education, respectively. His PhD is in the history of Christianity and religions of North America from Claremont Graduate University. His research interests focus primarily on evangelism among Protestants and Latter-day Saints. He and his wife, Maria, have five children and currently reside in Cedar Hills, Utah.

Katherine Hill is a sixth-generation member of Community of Christ and a professional historian. She grew up attending World Church events at the Community of Christ Temple in Independence, Missouri. She received a BA in history and international studies from Graceland University and an MA in history from Georgia Southern University. She was a summer intern in both Kirtland and Nauvoo. She is the *Restoration Studies* journal editor and has served on the John Whitmer Historical Association Board.

David J. Howlett, PhD, is the Mellon Visiting Assistant Professor of Religion at Smith College. He is the author of *Kirtland Temple: The Biography of a Shared Mormon Sacred Space* and a coauthor of *Mormonism: The Basics*. An elder in Community of Christ, David serves as one of its World Church historians. He and his wife, the Reverend Anna Woofenden (Episcopal Church), reside with their infant daughter in Easthampton, Massachusetts.

Lachlan Mackay serves in Community of Christ's Council of Twelve Apostles and oversees the Northeast USA Mission Field. He also manages Community of Christ historic sites and is the Church History and Sacred Story Ministries team lead. He is a past president of the John Whitmer Historical Association and has published articles on the Kirtland Temple and the Smith family in the *Journal of Mormon History*, the *John Whitmer Historical Association Journal*, and *Latter-day Saint Historical Studies*.

Robert L. Millet is professor emeritus of religious education at Brigham Young University, where he taught for thirty-one years. There he served as chair of the Department of Ancient Scripture and dean of Religious Education. Since 1997 he has been engaged in interfaith dialogues with scholars from evangelical Christianity, the Church of the Nazarene, and Community of Christ. He and his wife, Shauna, are the parents of six children and twelve grandchildren and reside in Orem, Utah.

Richard G. Moore was raised in Salem, Utah. He received a master's degree in history from Brigham Young University and a doctorate in education from the University of the Pacific. He was an instructor for the Latter-day Saint Church Educational System for thirty-eight years, teaching seminary and institute and teaching classes at BYU. He is the author of several books, including *A Comparative Look at Mormonism* *and Community of Christ*. He and his wife, Lani, have three children, Adam, Travis, and Asia, and nine grandchildren. They live in Orem, Utah.

Barbara Morgan Gardner, PhD, is an associate professor of church history and doctrine at Brigham Young University. She serves as the chaplain-at-large in higher education for The Church of Jesus Christ of Latter-day Saints. She is the author of *The Priesthood Power of Women in the Temple, Church, and Family*. Barbara and her husband, Dustin, live in Highland, Utah, and have two daughters, Alli and Jane.

Joshua M. Sears is an assistant professor of ancient scripture at Brigham Young University. He has a PhD in Hebrew Bible from the University of Texas at Austin and writes on Israelite prophecy, marriage, and families in the ancient world and on the publication history of Latter-day Saint scripture. He and his wife, Alice, live in Lindon, Utah, with their five children.

Christie Skoorsmith, MA, is a third-generation Community of Christ member and an ordained elder who has worked and volunteered for the church in Africa, Central America, and Europe. Currently she is an international business manager for a medical device company in Seattle, Washington. She has been published in various peace studies journals, as well as in a book about Gandhi's relevance in the twenty-first century. She and her husband have three children, ages twelve, ten, and ten, and two cats. She enjoys gardening, sustainable living, and painting.

John Taylor, PhD, is a pastor of Community of Christ, Drummoyne Congregation, and has published articles on theology, policy, and mission in the *Australian Herald* and the *Saints' Herald*. John was a legal practitioner for seven years and then a tax law academic for thirty-five years. He is currently an emeritus professor in taxation law at the University of New South Wales in Sydney, Australia. He and his wife, Janine Wood, live in Sydney, Australia, and have two adult children, Hannah and Colin.

Jordan T. Watkins received his PhD in American history from the University of Nevada, Las Vegas. His book, *Slavery and Sacred Texts:*

The Bible, the Constitution, and Historical Consciousness in Antebellum America, examines the ways in which biblical and constitutional debates over slavery brought awareness to the historical distances separating Americans from their hallowed biblical and revolutionary pasts. Before joining the faculty in Religious Education at BYU, Jordan was a volume editor of the Documents series of *The Joseph Smith Papers*.

Dr. Keith J. Wilson hails from Ridgecrest, California. He is an associate professor of ancient scripture at Brigham Young University, where he regularly teaches a variety of scripture courses. In 2008 he spent a year at the BYU Jerusalem Center. He received bachelor's and master's degrees from BYU. He also received a PhD in educational administration from the University of Utah. His educational specialty is institutional change, and he researches and publishes about the fundamental changes in Community of Christ.

A Brief History of the Dialogue

Richard G. Moore

Richard G. Moore, EdD, was employed for thirty-eight years as an instructor for the Church Educational System of The Church of Jesus Christ of Latter-day Saints, and he has authored several books and articles on theology and church history.

O n a warm day in August 2016, a small group of individuals met at the campus of Graceland University in Independence, Missouri. This was the first meeting of a proposed semi-annual assembly of people composed of members of Community of Christ (formerly the Reorganized Church of Jesus Christ of Latter Day Saints [RLDS Church]) and members of The Church of Jesus Christ of Latter-day Saints from Brigham Young University's Office of Religious Outreach. Considering the many years of "bad blood" between these two organizations, it seemed an unlikely gathering.

Dialogues between religious institutions are not uncommon. A Latter-day Saint and evangelical dialogue has been taking place for nearly twenty years. A dialogue between several Latter-day Saint and

Jewish scholars has also been established. Community of Christ has a long history of ecumenical efforts and cooperation, including membership in the National Council of Churches.[1] What made The Church of Jesus Christ of Latter-day Saints / Community of Christ dialogue unique was the organizations' shared history. Both groups trace their origins to the church organized by Joseph Smith in 1830.

Joseph Smith didn't speak of creating a new church or reforming Christianity. Rather, he spoke of a "restoration" of the ancient church established by Jesus Christ during his mortal ministry. Focused efforts at evangelization resulted in the dramatic growth of the restored church, initially known as the Church of Christ, then the Church of the Latter Day Saints, and later The Church of Jesus Christ of Latter-day Saints.[2]

The Latter-day Saints faced opposition in every part of the United States in which they tried to establish themselves.[3] Eventually, they gathered to Illinois, on the banks of the Mississippi River, where they built a city they named Nauvoo. However, during the Nauvoo era, the church once again faced bitter opposition, resulting in the murders of Joseph Smith and his brother Hyrum while they were incarcerated in Carthage, Illinois.

Following the death of Joseph Smith, division and confusion arose as to who should take the reins of leadership in Joseph's place. This period of uncertainty is often referred to as a succession crisis.[4] Brigham Young (with the Quorum of the Twelve Apostles), Sidney Rigdon, James J. Strang, and several others each claimed to be the rightful heir to the leadership of the church. Based on these assertions, various churches emerged, each claiming (in one way or another) to be the continuation of the church restored by Joseph Smith.

Within a few years of Joseph Smith's death, most of the Saints left the Nauvoo area, either by choice or by force. Most followed Brigham Young and the Twelve, though many joined other factions, and still others chose not to unite with any organization. Eventually, the two groups that became the largest and most thriving (of the schisms resulting from the succession crisis after the death of Joseph Smith) were The Church of Jesus Christ of Latter-day Saints and the Reorganized Church of Jesus Christ of Latter Day Saints.

Brigham Young and his group traveled west and established their church headquarters in what would become Salt Lake City, Utah. Some who did not accept Brigham Young's leadership remained in the Midwest, still believers in the Restoration but unsure whose leadership to follow. Many former followers of Joseph Smith united with the several factions led by various individuals, such as Sidney Rigdon, James Strang, and William Smith, only to become disillusioned with these new churches, their leaders, and their doctrines. Jason W. Briggs received a revelation in which he learned that a descendant of Joseph Smith would rise up and take his rightful place as the prophet of the restored church. A loosely organized group of branches—consisting of Saints who had refused to join any of the post-Joseph-era factions and others who had followed one claimant or another but then had withdrawn from those movements—coalesced around Briggs's prediction, awaiting the time when its promise would be fulfilled. A conference of these congregations met in the summer of 1852 to consider the revelation that had been received by Briggs. Community of Christ historian Roger D. Launius wrote of this conference: "It was united only in its opposition to other Mormon factions, in its acceptance of the Briggs document as divine revelation, in its belief that Mormonism as set forth in the Scriptures was correct, and in its affirmation that the proper successor to the prophetic office was growing to maturity in Nauvoo and would one day step forth to accept his calling."[5]

This "New Organization" of the Church of Jesus Christ of Latter Day Saints selected presiding officers and made efforts to persuade Joseph Smith III to accept the role of leader of their church. After several years of what young Joseph considered to be humbling, preparatory experiences, he agreed to take leadership of the "New Organization." At a church conference held in Amboy, Illinois, on April 6, 1860, Joseph Smith III was unanimously accepted as the "prophet, seer, and revelator of the church of Jesus Christ, and the successor of his father."[6] In 1872, this organization took on the name of the Reorganized Church of Jesus Christ of Latter Day Saints.

From the time of Joseph Smith's death, there were disagreements and hard feelings among the various factions that arose. Between the two largest organizations, The Church of Jesus Christ of Latter-day Saints and the Reorganized Church of Jesus Christ of Latter Day Saints, there was much distrust and even some animosity. Harsh things were said and put into print from each of the two churches about the other.[7] In those early days, polygamy was a significant issue between the two churches, with sharp exchanges about the origins and practice of plural marriage.

However, in more recent decades, much of the rancor that defined the early relationship between the two main Restoration churches has dissipated. There are several reasons behind this change of attitude. First, with a fourteen-year history shared by the two churches, historians from both camps have become acquainted with one another and have even worked together on some projects. These connections have facilitated the development of a comradery between historians of the two organizations, the effects of which have improved relationships. Community of Christ members also began to participate in the Mormon History Association, and Latter-day Saint scholars became involved in the John Whitmer Historical Association.[8]

Another circumstance that has led to closer relationships is, strangely enough, changes within both faith traditions that have resulted in fewer issues between the formerly hostile Restoration relatives. The Reorganized Church of Jesus Christ of Latter Day Saints aligned themselves more with the Kirtland-era church and doctrine, whereas The Church of Jesus Christ of Latter-day Saints theology was based more on the doctrine and practices of the Nauvoo era. Though early on there were certainly doctrinal differences between the two branches, such as polygamy and lineal successions of the presidency versus succession through the Quorum of the Twelve, these are not considered major issues today.[9]

A move toward more mainstream Protestantism has effected changes in doctrinal focus and resulted in a new name for the Reorganized Church of Jesus Christ of Latter Day Saints—now known as Community of Christ. While The Church of Jesus Christ of Latter-day Saints moved toward the conservative American mainstream, it has maintained many of its early distinctive beliefs, although plural marriage (or polygamy) is no longer practiced. Similarly, lineal succession is no longer perceived as a requisite for succession in Community of Christ.

In light of improved relationships between individuals within Community of Christ and The Church of Jesus Christ of Latter-day Saints, people in both groups began to consider the possibility of improving communication and understanding through an organized dialogue. Identifying all the events that created an environment for the Latter-day Saint / Community of Christ dialogue to take place is not possible; however, a few experiences can be cited as being foundational for the dialogue.

The John Whitmer Historical Association (JWHA), created primarily by members of the then Reorganized Church of Jesus Christ of Latter Day Saints, is an independent scholarly society composed of individuals of various religious faiths who share a lively interest in the history of the Restoration movement. The annual JWHA conference in 2014 was held in Lamoni, Iowa, where the main campus of Community of Christ's Graceland University is located. Several members of The Church of Jesus Christ of Latter-day Saints attended that conference, including Scott Esplin from Brigham Young University. Esplin related the following:

> After the awards ceremony on Friday night of that conference, I found myself seated at a table at the back of the room. A conversation began with Andrew and Jewell Bolton (from Community of Christ) about our respective life experiences and beliefs. I wanted to better understand the Community of Christ and to represent them properly when questions arise (as they often do) in my classes, and it quickly became clear that they had questions about our teachings as well. A lengthy, productive conversation emerged, followed by a lasting friendship. As we talked, others gathered at our table until there were several together, asking and answering questions in a spirit of genuine understanding. . . . In his kindly way, Andrew sent a nice note upon our respective return to our homes following the conference, thanking me for our time of sharing together and for answering so many questions. The friendship, and the spirit of open discussion, has remained. He has since visited my classes at BYU, we toured Temple Square and the Church History Library together, visited the open house for the Jordan River Temple, and continue to have meaningful discussions.[10]

Another influential experience took place during the annual Book of Mormon in Zion Conference in Independence, Missouri.[11] Andrew Bolton had made arrangements for a small group of individuals from Brigham Young University to meet with the president of Community of Christ, Stephen M. Veazey. At a luncheon that day, Robert L. Millet (emeritus dean of Religious Education at BYU) and Andrew Bolton (then an apostle in Community of Christ) sat together and visited. The topic of interfaith relationships came up, and Millet commented about how enjoyable the dialogue with evangelicals had been since their first meeting in 2000. Millet recalled, "Andrew asked if I thought that a Latter-day Saint / Community of Christ dialogue would be something worth doing. I expressed a desire to investigate the possibilities."[12]

Of this discussion, Bolton wrote, "I had been impressed by the kindly, insightful, and personable reasoning of Bob[,] who had been involved in that interchange [the Latter-day Saint / evangelical dialogue] over perhaps a decade. In addition, Bob Millet had inspiringly introduced me to the concept of 'infinite atonement' for which I will be forever grateful. There were already blessings of Latter-day Saint / Community of Christ conversations happening."[13]

Over the next few weeks, Bolton and Millet communicated by email regarding what such a dialogue would look like. Principles that had guided the Latter-day Saint / evangelical dialogue were sent to Bolton, and he agreed that those principles should guide the proposed dialogue. There were some initial concerns that the dialogue might become argumentative, each side pointing out the flaws in beliefs and practices of the other, or that the dialogue was simply an attempt by Latter-day Saints to proselytize Community of Christ members. In one email response, Millet "expressed what a worthwhile experience [they] had with Evangelicals, and . . . felt [they] (Latter-day Saints and Community of Christ) could learn many things about the 'other' and also disabuse [themselves] of false or inaccurate perceptions about each other." A few weeks later, Bolton contacted Millet and said he had received approval from Community of Christ's First Presidency to move ahead with the dialogue.[14]

Not long after that, Millet was at the headquarters for The Church of Jesus Christ of Latter-day Saints in Salt Lake City, where he visited with Elder Jeffrey R. Holland of the Quorum of the Twelve Apostles. Of this conversation Millet wrote:

> We chatted for a few minutes and then [Elder Holland] asked, "How's the interfaith work going?" I spoke for a bit about our most recent experiences with our Evangelical friends. I then asked him how he perceived the Brethren would view an interfaith dialogue with Community of Christ. I specifically asked if he could foresee any problems in doing so. He was quiet for a few seconds and then said, "No, I don't see any problems there." He then added, "I think Brother Joseph and Hyrum would be very pleased."[15]

The first meeting of the newly created Latter-day Saint / Community of Christ dialogue was scheduled for August 10, 2016, and a small group of people was invited to attend—based on their interest in, experience with, and understanding of the other church and their interfaith work. Community of Christ participants in the inaugural meeting included Andrew Bolton (former member of the Council of Twelve Apostles),[16] Lachlan Mackay (member of the Council of Twelve Apostles), Shandra Newcom (mission center president for the Rocky Mountain Mission Center), and Matt Frizzell (dean of the Community of Christ Seminary at Graceland University). Representing BYU's Office of Religious Outreach were Robert Millet (former dean of Religious Education), Keith Wilson (BYU professor), and Lani and Richard Moore (authors of a book about Community of Christ). Representing Restoration branches was Richard Neill (a Seventy in the RLDS Church from 1982 to 1989 and currently a Seventy in a Restoration branch).[17] Invited to be members of the group but unable to attend the first meeting were David Howlett (member of Community of Christ and visiting professor at Smith College) and Casey Paul Griffiths (member of The Church of Jesus Christ of Latter-day Saints and BYU professor).

Ground rules for the dialogue were established during the first meeting. As noted, Bolton and Millet chose to follow some of the guidelines used for the Latter-day Saint / evangelical dialogue. A few of the most significant principles for the dialogue were the "Three Rules for Religious Understanding" created by Krister Stendahl, emeritus dean of the Harvard Divinity School and Church of Sweden Bishop of Stockholm:

1. When you are trying to understand another religion, you should ask the adherents of that religion and not its enemies.
2. Don't compare your best to their worst.
3. Leave room for "holy envy."[18]

Other ideas for respectful dialogue came from Richard Mouw's book *Uncommon Decency: Christian Civility in an Uncivil World*.[19] A template for the exchange was discussed and agreed on during that first meeting. Participants agreed to be respectful of one another's perspectives and to avoid arguing or seeking to "prove" their own church's position or point of view. Participants also agreed to uphold strict confidentiality, with no one reporting or publishing what another person in the group said without permission. In addition, participants agreed that they would avoid saying *anything* about another participant that they would not say to that person in kindness, face to face.

Before beginning the dialogue, participants were aware that there would be differing views and beliefs, some of them substantial. They would not be in total agreement on some very basic issues: the nature of God, the Apostasy, the nature of the Restoration, the First Vision, scripture, revelation, priesthood, gender and sexual orientation, and many other issues. Participants were all cognizant of the fact that this dialogue was not an effort to merge the two groups together but, rather, to better understand one other, dispel misconceptions, and develop friendly relationships.

By the conclusion of those first meetings, a spirit of cooperation and a feeling of optimism grew within the group so that an honest, friendly dialogue was possible and would be a positive endeavor. The group decided to meet twice each year. Two people, one from each of the faith traditions, would be selected to lead future meetings, with reading assignments suggested by each of the leaders to help prepare participants for the subject to be discussed. Topics for future dialogues were recommended, and the next gathering was scheduled for February 2017 to discuss the topic "What Is the Restoration?"

In September 2017, the group met in Nauvoo, Illinois, to exchange views on the topic "The History of Nauvoo," not an easy subject to tackle because of the vastly different perspectives about the Nauvoo period of the organizations' shared history. While in Nauvoo, the group toured historical sites sponsored by both churches. In March 2018, the group met in Utah for several days to discuss the topic "Ordinances and Sacraments." The Provo get-together provided opportunities in addition to the actual dialogue, including a tour of the newly renovated but not yet rededicated Jordan River Utah Temple, a visit to the Latter-day Saint Church History Library and Museum, and attendance at a performance by the Tabernacle Choir at Temple Square.

Six months later, participants met in a conference room in the Community of Christ Temple in Independence, Missouri, and visited the Community of Christ archives, where they viewed fascinating historical items. The archives and meeting in the Temple were both unique and thrilling experiences for the Latter-day Saint participants. The topic for this dialogue was "Zion." In the fall of 2019, the group met in Fairport, New York, in conjunction with the John Whitmer Historical Association Conference. The focus for that meeting was "The Person and Work of Jesus Christ." Some meetings have been held online, with participants from various parts of the globe, as was necessary during the COVID-19 pandemic. Topics for these meetings included "The First Vision" and "Gender."

Additional people were added to the group after the initial dialogue. Also, depending on the topic, special guests were invited to attend specific dialogues because of their particular expertise or interest in the subject.[20] Plans are being made for future meetings of the Latter-day Saint / Community of Christ dialogue, with the intention of meeting twice annually.

Looking back at the origin and history of the Latter-day Saint / Community of Christ dialogue, it is not difficult to see that to some degree the organizations were taking a risk in starting the whole venture. There have likely been members of both The Church of Jesus Christ of Latter-day Saints and Community of Christ who, after becoming aware of the dialogue, have questioned the value of the endeavor. Some of the

Latter-day Saints who have participated in the dialogue have been asked, "Have any of the Community of Christ members been converted and baptized into our church?" After they respond, "That is not really the purpose of the dialogue," the reply has sometimes been "Then if you are not getting any baptisms, what's the point of meeting with them?"

Some Community of Christ participants have heard from a few members of their church, "Is this a productive use of your time—should this be a priority?" The assumption of Community of Christ members who have asked these questions is that members of The Church of Jesus Christ of Latter-day Saints are extremely conservative, fixed in their views, and not serious about the equal worth of all people. In response to those who doubt the value of the dialogue, Community of Christ participants have reminded their coreligionists that Community of Christ is serious about peacemaking and reconciliation. Also, even if The Church of Jesus Christ of Latter-day Saints is considered by some to be their oldest enemy, shouldn't the admonition of the Savior to "love your enemies" (Matthew 5:44) be followed? The dialogue is important for many reasons.

Critics might be suspicious of motives for the dialogue, citing the "missionary mindedness" of the Latter-day Saint people as the real purpose for their participation, or perhaps a Community of Christ desire to correct what they perceive as non-Christian errors found in the Latter-day Saint faith. The Latter-day Saint / Community of Christ dialogue might not be regarded as a valid ecumenical effort according to some critics' definition of what that should look like. The dialogue might be viewed as what John-Charles Duffy refers to as "conservative pluralism" or what Matthew Bowman calls "pragmatic pluralism," in which the groups are involved for a common cause or political ends.[21] Considering the conservative and liberal natures of the two religions and that neither group has plans to change its beliefs or unify the institutions, the dialogue appears to be simply an effort to eliminate the negative feelings of the past and strive for clearer understanding and better relationships.

Those who have been involved in the dialogue have considered it a positive effort to put away old animosities, gain a better understanding of one another, correct misconceptions,[22] and develop positive relationships and sincere friendships. To be sure, there have been some disagreements and uncomfortable moments during dialogue meetings, even what might be considered mild clashes. But there have also been enlightening and even view-changing insights during each of the meetings. All of the participants would likely readily agree with declarations from Joseph Smith's "Articles of Faith" or "Epitome of Faith," in which he stated, "We claim the privilege of worshipping Almighty God according to the dictates of our conscience, and allow all men the same privilege let them worship how, where, or what they may," and "If there is any thing virtuous, lovely, or of good report or praise worthy we seek after these things."[23]

After eight meetings of the Latter-day Saint / Community of Christ dialogue, what are the feelings of participants concerning its value? What are some of the results? Comments have included the following:

"I have a greater appreciation for the early history that we shared."

"Sometimes I have changed my view for the better in light of more information and deeper sharing."

"It has not been hard to like each other and for some of us to become really close friends."

"I have invited Community of Christ friends to make presentations and participate in question/answer sessions in the religion classes I teach at BYU. Students have expressed how much they enjoyed those classes."

"I experienced holy envy when I attended the classes at BYU and spent time with so many students who had the courage and conviction to serve lengthy LDS missions."

"I feel that this experience has strengthened my faith in God and has helped me gain a greater feeling of love for all of God's children."

"What have I appreciated as a Community of Christ participant about our times and discussions together? Meeting in each other's sacred space has been illuminating. It has been lovely to eat in each other's homes. There has been laughter and teasing, like when Community of Christ bishop Carla Long said she was the only pregnant bishop in Utah. There have been deep and serious conversations where we have found hidden treasures in our shared tradition that bring us both joy and a sense of closeness."

The initial plan was to meet twice each year for five years and then to review the value of the dialogue to determine whether or not to continue. From what participants are saying, it appears that they would like to see the Latter-day Saint / Community of Christ dialogue proceed for years to come.

NOTES

1. See Mark S. Diamond and Andrew C. Reed, eds., *Understanding Covenants and Communities: Jews and Latter-day Saints in Dialogue* (Provo, UT: Religious Studies Center, Brigham Young University, in cooperation with the Central Conference of Rabbis, 2020); Craig L. Blomberg, "Mormon-Evangelical Dialogue," *Religious Educator* 13, no. 2 (2012): 27–33; Mark Scherer, *The Journey of a People: The Era of Worldwide Community, 1946 to 2015* (Independence, MO: Community of Christ Seminary Press, 2016), 390–92.

2. The name of the church was changed in an 1838 revelation to Joseph Smith, originally published in "An Extract of Revelation," *Elders' Journal of the Church of Latter Day Saints*, August 1838, 52–53. This revelation was added to the Latter-day Saint Doctrine and Covenants in 1876. It is not included in the Community of Christ Doctrine and Covenants.

3. They also had opposition in Canada in 1833 and in the British Isles in 1837.

4. See Benjamin E. Park and Robin Scott Jensen, "Debating Succession, March 1846: John E. Page, Orson Hyde, and the Trajectories of Joseph Smith's Legacy," *Journal of Mormon History* 39, no. 1 (Winter 2013): 181–205.

5. Roger D. Launius, *Joseph Smith III: Pragmatic Prophet* (Chicago: University of Illinois Press, 1988), 88.

6. Conference minutes, April 6, 1860, as quoted in Richard P. Howard, *The Church through the Years*, vol. 1, *RLDS Beginnings, to 1860* (Independence, MO: Herald Publishing House, 1992), 375.

7. For examples, see Joseph Fielding Smith, *The Origin of the "Reorganized Church" and the Question of Succession* (Salt Lake City: Deseret News, 1909); and W. C. Cather, *Salt Land Heresies: An Investigation of Truth and Error, or the Path of Right and Where Found* (Atchison, KS: Lawless and Morgan, 1897).

8. See Richard P. Howard, "The Mormon-RLDS Boundary, 1852–1991: Walls to Windows," *Journal of Mormon History* 18, no. 1 (Spring 1992): 1–18.

9. See William D. Russell, "The LDS Church and Community of Christ: Clearer Differences, Closer Friends," *Dialogue* 36, no. 4 (Winter 2003): 177–90.

10. Scott Esplin, personal correspondence with author, April 9, 2021.

11. The Book of Mormon Festival was created by Patrick and Jim McKay in 2009. In 2012 Keith Wilson and Richard Moore from Brigham Young University

were invited to speak at the festival. Since that time, the annual event has become known as the Book of Mormon in Zion Conference, jointly planned by the McKay brothers and several faculty members from BYU, with speakers from various Restoration churches.

12. Robert Millet, personal correspondence with author, February 26, 2021.

13. Andrew Bolton, personal correspondence with author, January 14, 2021.

14. Bolton, personal correspondence, January 14, 2021.

15. Millet, personal correspondence, February 26, 2021.

16. Andrew Bolton, in the normal tradition of Community of Christ, retired from the Council of Twelve in June 2016.

17. In the latter part of the twentieth century, the Reorganized Church of Jesus Christ of Latter Day Saints began moving to a more liberal Protestant view of Christianity. A substantial number of its members did not agree with the changes. Some withdrew their membership from what would become Community of Christ, while others retained their membership but pulled back their involvement. Independent Restoration branches that no longer affiliated with Community of Christ were created. Andrew Bolton felt that the views of the earlier RLDS Church should be represented. Richard Neill and later Danny Hight, members of Restoration branches, were invited to be part of the dialogue to represent RLDS beliefs.

18. An account of Stendahl's 1985 press conference at which he gave his three rules for religious understanding is found in Barbara Brown Taylor, *Holy Envy: Finding God in the Faith of Others* (San Francisco: HarperOne Publishers, 2019), 64–67. By "holy envy," Stendahl meant that we should be willing to recognize aspects of another's religion or faith tradition that we admire and seek to emulate. Interestingly, the press conference was in response to opposition to the Latter-day Saint temple being built in Sweden.

19. See Richard J. Mouw, *Uncommon Decency: Christian Civility in an Uncivil World*, rev. and exp. ed. (Downers Grove, IL: InterVarsity Press, 2010).

20. Up to this time, the members of the group and special guests have included the following: Community of Christ—Andrew Bolton, Jewell Bolton, David Howlett, Matt Frizzell, Lachlan Mackay, Shandra Newcom, Katherine Hill, Carla Long, John Taylor, Barbara Walden, Christie Skoorsmith, Katie Harmon-McLaughlin; Restoration branches—Richard Neill, Danny Hight; The Church of Jesus Christ of Latter-day Saints—Robert Millet, Keith Wilson, Richard Moore, Lani Moore, Barbara Morgan Gardner, Casey Griffiths, Alonzo Gaskill, Scott Esplin, Carter Charles, Steven Harper, Taunalyn Ford, Josh Sears, Maclane Heward, J. Devn Cornish (General Authority); Church of Jesus Christ of Latter Day Saints (Strangite)—Bill Shepard; Church of Jesus Christ (Bickertonite)—Daniel Stone.

21. John-Charles Duffy has examined various views and criticisms of the Latter-day Saint / evangelical dialogue, some of which could also be applicable to the Latter-day Saint / Community of Christ dialogue. See John-Charles Duffy, "Conservative Pluralists: The Cultural Politics of Mormon-Evangelical Dialogue in the United States at the Turn of the Twenty-First Century"

(PhD diss., University of North Carolina at Chapel Hill, 2011). See also Matthew Bowman, "The Evangelical Countercult Movement and Mormon Conservatism," in *Out of Obscurity: Mormonism Since 1945*, ed. Patrick Q. Mason and John G. Turner (New York: Oxford University Press, 2016), 259–77.

22. For examples of common misconceptions that Latter-day Saints often have about Community of Christ, see Richard G. Moore, "LDS Misconceptions about the Community of Christ," *Mormon Historical Studies* 15, no. 1 (Spring 2014): 1–23.

23. Joseph Smith, "Church History," *Times and Seasons*, March 1, 1842, 710.

JESUS CHRIST

Andrew Bolton and Alonzo L. Gaskill

JESUS CHRIST IN COMMUNITY OF CHRIST

ANDREW BOLTON

Andrew Bolton, PhD (Wales), worked for eighteen years for Community of Christ in Independence, Missouri, and has published essays on theology, the mission of Community of Christ, and church history.

"[Jesus] asked them, 'But who do you say that I am?' Peter answered him, 'You are the Messiah.'" (Mark 8:29)

When I was baptized at the age of twenty-three in South Wales, I knew three things. First, I wanted to make the world a better place—I wanted to commit my life to the cause of Zion. Second, I knew I needed to change for the sake of Zion. Third, I felt God calling me to be baptized and to join with others in seeking first the kingdom of God—Zion—in this world.

What does this empty picture of Jesus mean in the old Community of Christ joint council room in which the First Presidency, the Twelve, and the Presiding Bishopric met? We cannot in the end define Jesus. As members of a noncreedal church, Community of Christ members are open to one another's personal journeys in discovering who Jesus is. The Holy Spirit has yet more light and truth to illuminate who Jesus is. Photo by Andrew Bolton.

But who was Jesus? I didn't have a clue. That was my next quest: to find out. Jesus asks those who follow him as disciples the same question he asked Peter and the other first disciples: "But who do you say that I am?" Now Jesus was prompting me, although I did not know it—"Who are you, Jesus? How do you fit in?" About a year later, the answer dawned on me like a revelation, helped by reading the Bible and the Book of Mormon.[1] I understood both intellectually and spiritually at the same time: "Jesus, you are God become human." I was stunned. Uplifted. Awed. At the same time, I felt humbled and stupid. Why was I so slow to understand this? I also felt grateful to have a profound answer to my question, thankful for God's grace and patience with this slow disciple.

God is patient, though, with all of us, as we can see with the early disciples. Peter and Andrew, Mary and Martha, followed Jesus as the first disciples, thinking Jesus was just a rabbi. Then Peter understood that Jesus was the Messiah, God's special king. A few days later, Peter, James, and John saw Jesus in glory with Moses on one side and Elijah on the other, and Jesus was greater than either. Andrew missed out completely. Doubting Thomas was the "scientist," needing sense evidence before he believed. When Thomas touched the resurrected Jesus for himself, he confessed, "My Lord and my God!"[2] (John 20:28). Jesus was ordinary, smelled like anyone without deodorant after a day's work, and got tired, thirsty, and hungry. But in Jesus, God sneaks up on you and me little bit by little bit as we hang out in his stories and in the fellowship of other followers.

Jesus also asks Community of Christ together as a people, "But who do you say that I am?" This is our answer. We begin with the One "who meets us in the testimony of Israel," who "is revealed" to us in the person and life of Jesus Christ, and who begins and "moves through all creation as the Holy Spirit." We affirm three as one God, the Trinity, "mystery beyond understanding and love beyond imagination." The triune God "alone is worthy of our worship."[3] We join with other Christians over two thousand years who have also confessed this faith.

"WE PROCLAIM JESUS CHRIST . . ."

The Community of Christ mission statement begins, "We proclaim Jesus Christ"![4] Why proclaim Jesus Christ? Jesus is "the Son of the living God, the Word made flesh, the Savior of the world," and as the Council of Chalcedon concluded in 451 CE, he is fully human and fully divine.[5] In the life of Jesus, we see what God is really like. Jesus reveals a God who heals, has compassion on the hungry, and has equal regard for both women and men. When Jesus hugs and blesses children, he reveals

God's great love for eager, energetic, giggling little ones and tells us that we must become like them in trusting faith. In Jesus's tortured body on the cross, God suffers the evil of the world and absorbs the pain, violence, and injustice infinitely to give everyone a fresh new beginning.[6] God does not take revenge; God loves God's enemies and forgives all of us, including Peter and Judas, and calls us to do the same. Infinite grace floods the universe with new possibilities. And in the early light of Easter morning, we see the power of God's love bringing new life, healing, and resurrection wholeness. In the early-morning surprise of an empty tomb, justice may still take its time, but Zion is coming.

Why proclaim Jesus Christ? Jesus is the human window into God's infinite, loving divinity. Jesus is God with skin on, the human face of God. Jesus is the perfect translation of divinity into a human life. Jesus is the Word, greater than scripture, whose kindness and love can be especially understood by children of every gender and race. The One God, Creator of the universe that Jesus reveals, is truly good, wonderful news. This is the gospel! But there is more . . .

"WE . . . PROMOTE COMMUNITIES OF JOY, HOPE, LOVE, AND PEACE"

Community of Christ's mission statement in full reads, "We proclaim Jesus Christ and promote communities of joy, hope, love, and peace."[7] We believe in the salvation of individuals, societies, and the earth.[8] We proclaim Jesus Christ as "the Savior of the world."[9] We declare God's big salvation through Christ in our troubled times. This salvation includes ending oppressive systems, whether slavery in Egypt, the brutal Roman Empire, or racism, sexism, homophobia, or militarism; confronting ideologies like nationalism, fascism, or neoliberalism; or addressing the present climate emergency. "Through Jesus' life and ministry, death and resurrection, God reconciles the world and breaks down the walls that divide. Christ is our peace."[10] Seeking Zion means becoming one family, all humans becoming brothers and sisters, with Christ as our head. We think globally and work out Zion locally in our neighborhoods and villages, one street or footpath at a time.

THE SPIRIT OF JESUS

A new life is possible through the continuing presence of the Spirit of Jesus, the Holy Spirit:[11] "The Spirit moves through and sustains creation; endows the church for mission; frees the world from sin, injustice, and death; and transforms disciples. Wherever we find love, joy, peace, patience, kindness, generosity, faithfulness, gentleness, or self-control, there the Holy Spirit is working."[12] Every Communion service, I am reminded by the prayers on bread and grape juice that in remembering Jesus, in taking his name on myself again, and in keeping his commandments, I will always have his Spirit to be with me.[13] I remember both the darkness of his Crucifixion and the hope of his Resurrection. Evil, injustice, and death do not have the last word. I also love the first account of Joseph Smith's First Vision in 1820, written in his own hand in 1832. Young Joseph saw the crucified Lord, heard his sins were forgiven him, and for many days afterward felt a great love and joy.[14] Jesus Christ is present for all people, from youth to old age; for every gender, ethnicity, and race; and for every century. Jesus is alive and can be found today by those who seek him; he is the one in whom Zion, shalom on earth, is possible. This is our testimony of Jesus in Community of Christ.

JESUS CHRIST IN THE CHURCH OF JESUS CHRIST OF LATTER-DAY SAINTS

ALONZO L. GASKILL

Alonzo L. Gaskill, PhD, has taught religion for more than thirty years—twenty of which have been at Brigham Young University, where he is a professor of world religions.

The theological term *Christology* comes from two Greek words— Χριστός (meaning "Christ") and λογία (meaning "words" or "discussion"). Thus, the literal meaning of the term *Christology* is "words or discussion about Christ."

The Christology of the early Christian Church—particularly in the postapostolic era—was not very united. Much of the theological discussion about Jesus was focused less on how to be like Christ, or how to apply his teachings in one's life, and more on his nature (for example, was Jesus "half man and half God" or "fully man and fully God"?).[15] Of course, the typical Christian (the nontheologian) was heavily focused on the application of Christ's teachings and example—as is evidenced by the thousands who were willing to die a martyr's death.[16] However, in those early years, the application of Christ's teachings and salvific atonement was sometimes overshadowed by the vigorous theological debates surrounding lingering Christological questions.

Just as the early Christian Church had shifts in its understanding of Jesus and his nature leading up to and even provoking events like the Council of Nicaea (AD 325), The Church of Jesus Christ of Latter-day Saints has had at least one significant shift in its Christology—and that shift took place on a "beautiful, clear day, early in the spring of eighteen hundred and twenty" (LDS Joseph Smith—History 1:14).[17] We know that when Joseph Smith entered the Sacred Grove, he held a Sabellian, or modalistic, view of the Holy Trinity, presuming the Father and Son to be a singular being.[18] However, following that sacred encounter, his understanding of the personhood of Christ evolved quite dramatically. Thus, Joseph spoke of his surprise at learning that God the Father and God the Son were wholly and completely two separate and distinct beings, though they "exactly resembled each other in features, and likeness."[19]

The Church of Jesus Christ of Latter-day Saints certainly has a systematic theology, particularly surrounding Christological issues. However, the *Encyclopedia of Mormonism* is correct in noting that "the term 'Christology' is not frequently used by Latter-day Saints."[20] Not only is the term not frequently employed, but questions about whether Jesus was "fully God and fully man" as opposed to "half God and half man" remain largely unasked in the church.[21] Even the Book of Mormon seems unconcerned about some early Christological issues.[22] Rather, leaders of the church, and the majority of the denomination's members, seem much more focused on the practical side of Jesus and what he taught. Thus, our theology is less "Christological"—in the proper, academic sense of the term—and more "practical" in its discussion of

"Jesus Christ, and him crucified" (1 Corinthians 2:2). Thus, the Prophet Joseph once explained, "The fundamental principles of our religion [are] the testimony of the apostles and prophets concerning Jesus Christ, 'that he died, was buried, and rose again the third day, and ascended up into heaven;' and all other things [pertaining to our religion] are only appendages to these."[23] Note that Joseph's definition is void of any focus on the more nuanced questions of Jesus's "nature." Rather, the Prophet's 1838 statement seems more interested in defining Jesus's sacred and salvific mission, not his "divine DNA," per se.

For me, this "practical" Christology—this focus on Jesus's love, holiness, and unique way of living and being—has made him more real. Focusing on the lived religion that Jesus taught, not only in his sermons but also in how he lived his life, has shown me how to live a peace-filled, purposeful, and holier existence. Thus, when I converted from Greek Orthodoxy, one of the things that most attracted me to the Restoration was its ability to transition me from a belief in Christ to an actual relationship with him; that relationship, for the first time in my life, included an awareness of the many ways in which I needed Jesus and the many ways in which I could rely on him. Thus, the Christology of the Church of Jesus Christ focuses little on nuanced theological arguments about his personal being and more on how followers of Jesus should personally be. Consequently, the Book of Mormon speaks of "the doctrine of Christ" (LDS 2 Nephi 31; 32; CofChrist II Nephi 13:2), which, in essence, it defines as the path to the celestial kingdom. This doctrine means living as Christ lived and incorporating into our lives the tools he has given us in order to overcome Satan, the world, and all sin and temptation.

With all of that said, there are three theological teachings in The Church of Jesus Christ of Latter-day Saints that I would like to highlight as important for those seeking to understand who Jesus is and what he should mean *to* and *for* us.

First, the church takes quite literally the scriptural declaration that Jesus Christ was "begotten of the Father" (John 1:14; see also John 3:16; Hebrews 1:5; LDS 2 Nephi 25:12; CofChrist II Nephi 11:21). He is the firstborn Son of an Eternal Father and a Heavenly Mother. He is our

"Elder Brother"—as Brigham Young[24] was wont to call him—and thus "all human beings—male and female—are created in the image of God [just as Jesus was]. Each is a beloved spirit son or daughter of heavenly parents."[25] This doctrine lays the greatest possible foundation for our belief in eternal families—all of us, including Jesus, being part of the eternal family of our heavenly parents.

Second, Jesus is our exemplar in all things (see John 13:15; 1 Peter 2:21; LDS 3 Nephi 27:27; CofChrist III Nephi 13:5).[26] Indeed, he commanded us to "follow" him—to "deny [ourselves]" and "take up [our] cross" (Matthew 16:24; see also Matthew 19:21; Mark 8:34; 10:21; Luke 9:23; 18:22; John 21:22). Jesus was the epitome of self-denial, self-sacrifice, and love, and he invites all who profess discipleship to do as he has done. In an increasingly irreligious world—a world that is seldom selfless but so often self-serving—Jesus calls those who truly believe in him to follow him through doing their best to live and love as he lived and loved.

Third, and most important of all, Jesus is our Savior and Redeemer. As the Book of Mormon so aptly testifies, "By the law no flesh is justified. . . . Wherefore, redemption cometh in and through the Holy Messiah; for he is full of grace and truth. . . . No flesh . . . can dwell in the presence of God, save it be through the merits, and mercy, and grace of the Holy Messiah" (LDS 2 Nephi 2:5, 6, 8; CofChrist II Nephi 1:69, 71, 73). The words of William Sloane Coffin echo these words of Father Lehi. Coffin wrote, "There is more mercy in God than sin in us."[27] That is the testimony repeated over and over again in the Book of Mormon (see LDS 2 Nephi 25:20; 31:21; Mosiah 4:8; 5:8; Alma 21:9; 38:9; CofChrist II Nephi 11:39; 13:31; Mosiah 2:12; 3:10–11; Alma 13:13; 18:11–12), and it is the belief, the hope, and the witness of all who have placed their lives and salvation in the hands of Jesus.

The Church of Jesus Christ of Latter-day Saints is often perceived as unique among Christian denominations because of its temple ordinances, including its associated covenant relating to eternal families, and because of its doctrine of *theosis*, or divinization. Importantly, each of these intertwined ordinances and doctrines has Jesus at its center, and each highlights the need for us to strive to be Christians—not just in name but in how we think, live, interact, and love. The three doctrinal principles previously mentioned—being part of God's eternal family, earnestly seeking to follow Jesus's way of living, and sincerely repenting through the Atonement of Christ—are at the core of what is taught in the temple endowment, the sealing ordinances, and the doctrine of deification. Each is *entirely* about Christ.

Because Jesus is central to *all* the Church of Jesus Christ teaches and does, not surprisingly, in their January 1, 2000, proclamation to the world—"The Living Christ"—the First Presidency and Quorum of the Twelve Apostles declared sacred truths such as these: "None other [than Jesus] has had so profound an influence upon all who have lived and will yet live upon the earth." His was "a message of peace and goodwill," and he "entreated all to follow his example" of propagating peace and kindness. "He gave His life to atone for the sins of all mankind," and "His life . . . is central to all human history." In a coming day, "every knee shall bend and every tongue shall speak in worship before Him. . . . He is the light, the life, and the hope of the world. His way is the path that leads to happiness in this life and eternal life in the world to come. God be thanked for the matchless gift of His divine Son."[28]

As a summary of Jesus's most precious gift, I would point the reader to the words of the ancient prophet Alma, who spoke of Christ as choosing to suffer not just for our sins or our unavoidable eventual death but also for our "pains and afflictions . . . and [our] sicknesses" and our "infirmities." Alma informs us that Jesus did this "that his bowels [might] be filled with mercy," that he might "succor his people according to their infirmities" (LDS Alma 7:11–12; CofChrist Alma 5:20–22). Jesus felt a need—no, a desire—to know you and me so intimately that he would perfectly understand what it was like to be us, to be tempted almost beyond the ability to withstand while having our personal history, our health, our upbringing, our situation in life, and so on. Jesus truly understands our challenges because he personally experienced them and suffered for them—and this personal understanding has filled him with mercy and the ability to succor us in all things. Remarkable! Unfathomable! As the old hymn says, "What a friend we have in Jesus."[29]

This is the Christ whom we *worship* and *adore*!

RESPONSE TO ALONZO L. GASKILL

I love Alonzo's mention of the quote by William Sloane Coffin: "There is more mercy in God than sin in us."[30] Alonzo writes about Jesus Christ with elegance, scholarship, and sincere personal conviction. I am grateful that he has opened up new insights and perspectives on The Church of Jesus Christ of Latter-day Saints that are interesting and thoughtful. I especially appreciate his final paragraph, which sings of Jesus as a real and personal Savior who loves us more fully, deeply, and completely than we can know.

It is again important for me to say that Jesus is both as human as we are and much more. I know I will never fully understand Jesus. Jesus is more than I can conceive and greater than I can fathom or understand. "We see through a glass, darkly," the apostle Paul wrote (1 Corinthians 13:12, KJV). For me, all language about God is provisional, metaphoric. The commandment against creating idols pushes me away from being literal about God. That is why we believe in continuing revelation; God's Holy Spirit has more to share or to reveal. So humility in seeking to define or discuss Jesus is an important quality in a scholar disciple. That is why creeds are inadequate and why, in the end, we simply are drawn to worship in both praise and profound silence, moved too deeply to find words to express the wonder of Jesus Christ. If smartphones had been around two thousand years ago, we could have photographed Jesus, but we would not have captured at all Jesus's divine depth. So in responding to Alonzo's understanding of Jesus, who am I in my limited humanity to be sure I am right? If the first apostles were around Jesus for three years and still struggled to really understand him, I need to be very humble in my conclusions.

So, what are my humble reflections about Alonzo's account?

First, we agree that in the first three hundred years after Jesus's death, the early church was rigorous in teaching discipleship. As Alonzo states, early Christianity was a movement that suffered persecution and martyrdom. I would add that the Sermon on the Mount was central to discipleship formation at this time.[31] It took at least three years of teaching and being an apprentice Christian, including serving the poor, before a candidate was baptized.[32] Alan Kreider, an outstanding early Christian Church scholar, wrote, "It was not Christian worship that attracted outsiders; it was Christians who attracted them, and outsiders found the Christians attractive because of the Christian habitus, which catechesis and worship had formed."[33] I think the Restoration was about recovering high-commitment discipleship and the journey of sanctification after justification through faith in Christ's grace. After Constantine, the first Christian emperor (306–37), this purpose was often lost, except in the monastic traditions. So for the early Christians, rigorous, faithful discipleship was important. And this kind of discipleship is important for us in the Restoration. I find it beautifully significant that Jesus teaches a version of the Sermon on the Mount in all its demanding radicality to the Nephites. So if we are serious about following Jesus, we should be serious about living the Sermon on the Mount.[34]

Second, who did Joseph really see in the First Vision? Joseph's own first account of the 1820 First Vision says he simply saw the crucified Lord, a single personage. This account was written in Joseph's own hand in the summer of 1832.[35] This initial theology is also evident in the Book of Mormon (LDS 2 Nephi 31:21; CofChrist II Nephi 13:31; LDS Mosiah 15:1–4; CofChrist Mosiah 8:28–32). Did Joseph continue to reflect theologically on the profound experience of the 1820 First Vision? Yes, his reflections are clear in later accounts, including the 1838 account of two personages, canonized by The Church of Jesus Christ of Latter-day Saints in the Book of Moses. So I would suggest that seeing two personages is a later reflection, not an initial understanding.

It is important to know who Jesus is as well as what it means to follow Jesus as a student disciple. For Community of Christ, Jesus is the One, infinite God of the universe, Creator of all things—become human. The human, finite Jesus is also the infinite, eternal God. Christ's Atonement is thus infinite and personal, which is why we can agree that "there is more mercy in God than sin in us." The infinite and personal nature of the Atonement means Zion is possible. Thus, in the mercy of God in Christ, there is hope for Alonzo, me, and you. Blessed as we are with mercy, we should also be merciful to others and love our enemies as the Savior did.

RESPONSE TO ANDREW BOLTON

Right out of the gate, Andrew lays the foundation for the remainder of his essay by defining what it means to be a Christian. Andrew speaks of what he wanted when he converted to Community of Christ (back then the Reorganized Church of Jesus Christ of Latter Day Saints) at the ripe old age of twenty-three. He hoped to become the type of disciple of Jesus who (1) had a *desire* to do good, (2) had a *willingness* to conform his life to the image and pattern of the Savior's life and teachings, and (3) had a *sense* of calling or mission wherein he knew his life had purpose and divine direction. What a beautiful summary of the true Christian life.

At times in his essay, Andrew's language feels creedal and thus may be a bit unfamiliar to those of The Church of Jesus Christ of Latter-day Saints, in which formal creeds are not utilized. For example, he writes that Jesus was "God become human." Then he adds, "We affirm three as one God, the Trinity, 'mystery beyond understanding and love beyond imagination.' The triune God 'alone is worthy of our worship.'" While Andrew's wording will feel foreign to those who are members of the Utah-based church, setting language aside, I think there is much in Andrew's statement that members of The Church of Jesus Christ of Latter-day Saints would agree with. For example, the oneness of the three "persons" or "members" of the Godhead is repeatedly attested to in scripture,[36] though it is a spiritual and purposeful oneness, not a metaphysical oneness. Also, Alma testified that "there are many mysteries which are kept, that no one knoweth them save God himself" (LDS Alma 40:3; CofChrist Alma 19:31). For the most enlightened among us, God is beyond our full understanding, and his love is beyond our imagination. As to the focus of our worship, surely no Latter-day Saint Christian (of any branch of the Restoration movement) would challenge the assertion that the only beings worthy of our worship would be the members of the Godhead (or, as Andrew refers to them, the "triune God"). The *Encyclopedia of Mormonism* points out the following:

> Latter-day Saints center their worship in, and direct their prayers to, *God the Eternal Father*. This, as with all things—sermons, testimonies,

prayers, and sacraments or ordinances—they do in the name of Jesus
Christ (2 Ne. 25:16; Jacob 4:4–5; 3 Ne. 18:19; D&C 20:29; Moses 5:8).
The Saints also worship Christ the Son as they acknowledge him as the
source of truth and redemption, as the light and life of the world, as
the way to the Father (John 14:6; 2 Ne. 25:29; 3 Ne. 11:11).[37]

Thus, while we certainly have disagreements in how we speak of
and potentially understand the Godhead or Trinity, there is more in
common here than I think there is distinctiveness—all language aside.

I think the most important aspect of Andrew's essay is his description of God's nature and how you and I should respond to who God
is at his core. Andrew speaks of God as a "compassionate . . . healer"
who has concern and love for *all*. He describes God not as a vengeful
God but instead as one who "loves His enemies and forgives all of us"
through his "infinite grace." That grace and love brings "new life, healing, and . . . wholeness," Andrew wisely points out.

Having offered these descriptors of the character and nature of God
and Christ, Andrew then makes what I feel are the most important
statements in his essay and gives the most important invitations for you
and me as disciples of Jesus Christ. He writes, "Jesus is . . . the human
face of God," and he is "present for all people, from youth to old age;
for every gender, ethnicity, and race; and for every century." Reflecting
on these ideas, he adds, "Every Communion service, I am reminded by
the prayers on bread and grape juice that in remembering Jesus, [I am]
taking his name on myself again." Of course, taking upon us the name
of Jesus implies being wedded to our Bridegroom (see LDS Doctrine
and Covenants 33:17; CofChrist Doctrine and Covenants 32:3e), yoked
fully with him (see Matthew 11:29), and striving to be one with him
while living and acting like him (see 1 Corinthians 2:16). This important
point reminds me of a comment made by Elder Dieter F. Uchtdorf, a
member of the Quorum of the Twelve Apostles in The Church of Jesus
Christ of Latter-day Saints, paraphrasing a statement often attributed to
Saint Francis of Assisi: "'Stand as witnesses' of the power of the gospel
at all times—and, when necessary, use words."[38] That famous statement
is at the heart of Andrew's essay. As disciples of Jesus Christ, we must
live our lives as more than a verbal attestation that there is a God and
Jesus is his Christ. True discipleship has, at its heart, a living, breathing,

loving imitation of the words, walk, and ways of the Lord Jesus Christ. I think Andrew and I would both agree—that is the teaching and message of Community of Christ, and it is the message of The Church of Jesus Christ of Latter-day Saints as well. And, in the end, it *must* be the message that *all* our lives send to the world, if we truly do love the Lord.

CONCLUSION

We are denominations with a common Restoration origin but have been separate for nearly 180 years. For the first time in our histories, we are engaging in authentic dialogue, listening and seeking to understand each other. This is significant.

We agree about the nature of true discipleship—we must follow the grace-filled Jesus. We both believe that Jesus is the *only* true manifestation of God in the flesh. Jesus's life is the road map for salvation. We both believe that only in and through Jesus Christ is salvation possible. While sacraments and ordinances have their place as potential avenues to God's grace, Christ is always the source of grace. To follow Jesus also means to be committed to the equal worth of all people and "the cause of Zion"—the transformation of the world into the kingdom of God on earth. Finally, we both rejoice in William Sloane Coffin's statement that "there is more mercy in God than sin in us." This mercy, revealed in and through Jesus Christ, is how our personal salvation and the realization of Zion—so necessary for the redemption of the world—are possible.

As to our dissimilarities, our two traditions differ on the relative weight we each place on the importance of the Prophet Joseph Smith and Christian tradition. The Church of Jesus Christ of Latter-day Saints leans heavily on scripture (ancient and modern) and the Prophet's revealed teachings and sacramental ordinances (and their grounding in Christ) for its understanding of the nature of Jesus and his relationship with the Father. For Community of Christ, on the other hand, the Bible, especially the New Testament, and two thousand years of Christian tradition are foundational to how Jesus's nature and relationship to the Trinity are understood.

NOTES

1. See John 1:1–18; 14:8–11; Colossians 1:15–20; and Philippians 2:5–11. Additionally, the introduction to the Book of Mormon reads in part, "To the convincing of the Jew and Gentile that Jesus is the Christ, the Eternal God, manifesting himself unto all nations." Echoes of the high Christology found in the Gospel of John ("Whoever has seen me, has seen the Father. . . . The Father who dwells in me does his works" [John 14:9–10, NRSV]) can also be found at least fourteen times in the Book of Mormon (e.g., CofChrist Mosiah 8:28–32; LDS Mosiah 15:1–5). Jesus is the incarnation of the God of Israel, the Creator of the universe (CofChrist III Nephi 5:11–17, 27; LDS 3 Nephi 11:10–17, 27). Incarnation is beautifully clear in many passages of the Book of Mormon.

2. "Jesus is Lord" is the first and simplest creed of the New Testament and early church (see 1 Corinthians 12:3, NRSV). This confession of Jesus as Lord and Savior is also important for the World Council of Churches, which "is a fellowship of churches which confess the Lord Jesus Christ as God and Saviour according to the scriptures." "What Is the World Council of Churches?," World Council of Churches, https://www.oikoumene.org /about-the-wcc. *Lord* is frequently used to refer to Jesus in Joseph Smith Jr.'s early revelations in the Doctrine and Covenants.

3. "Basic Beliefs," Community of Christ, https://www.CofChrist.org/basic-beliefs. Trinitarian formulations are found throughout the New Testament, including the baptismal scene of Jesus (Matthew 3:16–17; Luke 3:21–22), the Great Commission (Matthew 28:19), and endings to the apostle Paul's letters (clearest in 2 Corinthians 13:13). The Trinity was taught in the early church and formulated clearly in the Nicene Creed in 325 CE and in the First Council of Constantinople in 381 CE. Trinitarian formulations can also be found in the Book of Mormon (e.g., CofChrist II Nephi 13:31–32; LDS 2 Nephi 31:21) and in the Doctrine and Covenants (CofChrist Doctrine and Covenants 17:5g–h; LDS Doctrine and Covenants 20:27–28). Baptism in both churches is in the trinitarian tradition (CofChrist Doctrine and Covenants 17:21c; LDS Doctrine and Covenants 20:73).

4. Community of Christ, *Sharing in Community of Christ: Exploring Identity, Mission, Message, and Beliefs*, 4th ed. (Independence, MO: Herald Publishing House, 2018), 20.

5. "Basic Beliefs."

6. The following references are teachings on infinite atonement that I find very moving: CofChrist II Nephi 6:11–19; LDS 2 Nephi 9:6–7; CofChrist II Nephi 11:26; LDS 2 Nephi 25:16; CofChrist Alma 16:207–17; LDS Alma 34:8–16.

7. Community of Christ, *Sharing in Community of Christ*, 20.

8. See Community of Christ, *Sharing in Community of Christ*, 34–35.

9. "Basic Beliefs."

10. "Basic Beliefs," in the paragraph on Jesus Christ. See also the paragraph on salvation.

11. For example, references to the Spirit of Jesus are found in Acts 16:6–7 and in Paul's letters in Philippians 1:19 and Galatians 4:6. Jesus sends or gives the Holy Spirit: see Luke 24:49; John 15:26–27; and John 20:22.

12. "Basic Beliefs."

13. See CofChrist Doctrine and Covenants 17:22a–23b; LDS Doctrine and Covenants 20:75–79.

14. See Joseph Smith, "History, circa Summer 1832," https://www.josephsmith papers.org/paper-summary/history-circa-summer-1832/2.

15. For example, in the years following the death of Jesus and the apostles, there were different Christological "schools," which have been referred to as the "Heretical Left" (those who exaggerated the *humanity* of Jesus) and the "Heretical Right" (those who exaggerated the *divinity* of Christ). On the "left" were groups like the Arians (and other subordinationist schools), the Ebionites, the *Logos-Anthropos* school (also known as the "Word-Man" school), and the Nestorians. On the "right," however, were Gnostics (and various branches of Gnosticism, like Docetism), Apollinarians, Monophysites, and Monothelites. Jesus's exact nature when he walked the earth was not universally agreed on in the first centuries of the Common Era, nor is it agreed on by all Christian denominations today—including the various denominations of the Restoration.

16. See David B. Barrett and Todd M. Johnson, "The Demographics of Christian Martyrdom, AD 33–AD 2001," in *World Christian Trends, AD 30–AD 2200: Interpreting the Annual Christian Megacensus*, ed. Christopher R. Guidry and Peter F. Crossing (Pasadena, CA: William Carey Library, 2001), 228, graphic 4-1.

17. See also Richard P. Howard, *The Church through the Years*, vol. 1, *RLDS Beginnings, to 1860* (Independence, MO: Herald Publishing House, 1992), 94.

18. *Modalism*, also called *Sabellianism* (after the third-century theologian Sabellius), in essence holds that the Father, Son, and Holy Spirit are the same singular divine being, who appears in different "modes" or forms to humankind. Thus, contrary to the doctrine of the Holy Trinity, wherein the Father, Son, and Holy Spirit are three distinct "persons" (or "hypostases"), modalists hold that there is only one divine "person," but that "person" or deity chooses to reveal himself sometimes in the form of the Father, at other times in the form of the Son, and at other times in the form of the Holy Spirit.

19. Joseph Smith, "Church History," *Times and Seasons*, March 1, 1842, 707.

20. Gary P. Gillum, "Christology," in *Encyclopedia of Mormonism*, ed. Daniel H. Ludlow (New York: Macmillan, 1992), 1:272. Not only is the term *Christology* uncommon in the church, but for some time after Joseph Smith's death, the term *Trinity* lingered before the church officially rejected that term, replacing it with the New Testament descriptor *Godhead*. As an example, Brigham Young would sometimes use *Godhead* and other times use *Trinity* when referencing the Latter-day Saint heavenly presidency. See *The Complete Discourses of Brigham Young*, 5 vols., comp. Richard S. Van Wagoner (Salt Lake City: Smith-Pettit Foundation, 2009), 1:46; 3:1377; 3:1838; 5:2818.

21. Of our Christology, the 1992 *Encyclopedia of Mormonism* states the following:

The doctrine of the Church can be described in the following manner: Jesus Christ descended from his high pre-existent station as a
God when he came to earth to die for mankind's sins. . . . He was
Jehovah come to earth in a physical body as the Only Begotten of
the Father in the flesh. . . . While on earth he was still God, but he
received from his Father "grace for grace," as do God's other children [Doctrine and Covenants 93:12]. The Book of Mormon and
Doctrine and Covenants speak forcefully of the divine sonship of
Christ and also of his humanity (Mosiah 15:2–3; Alma 6:8; 11:38;
13:16; 34:2; 3 Ne. 11:7, 28:10; D&C 93 . . .). (Gillum, "Christology,"
1:272)

22. Indeed, that sacred text is inconsistent in its Christology, contingent on which
of the ancient prophetic witnesses speak of Jesus. At times, the Book of Mormon
sounds rather modalistic in its description of the Father and Son (e.g., LDS
2 Nephi 11:7; CofChrist II Nephi 8:14; LDS Mosiah 7:27; CofChrist Mosiah
5:44–45; LDS Mosiah 13:28, 34; CofChrist Mosiah 8:5, 13; LDS Mosiah
15:1–4; CofChrist Mosiah 8:28–31; LDS Mosiah 16:15; CofChrist Mosiah 8:91;
LDS Mosiah 17:8; CofChrist Mosiah 9:11–12; LDS 3 Nephi 11:27; CofChrist
III Nephi 5:27; LDS 3 Nephi 11:36; CofChrist III Nephi 5:38; LDS Mormon
7:7; CofChrist Mormon 3:29; LDS Mormon 9:12; CofChrist Mormon 4:71;
LDS Ether 3:14; CofChrist Ether 1:77–78; LDS Ether 4:7; CofChrist Ether
2:101). At other times, it is quite clear that the Father and Son are distinct
and separate personages (e.g., LDS Alma 12:33–34; CofChrist Alma 9:54–55;
LDS 3 Nephi 9:15; CofChrist III Nephi 4:44; LDS 3 Nephi 11:7; CofChrist
III Nephi 5:8; LDS 3 Nephi 19:29; CofChrist III Nephi 9:30; LDS Mosiah
3:8; CofChrist Mosiah 1:102; LDS 3 Nephi 20:31; CofChrist III Nephi 9:69;
LDS 3 Nephi 27:28; CofChrist III Nephi 13:5–6; LDS Ether 4:12; CofChrist
Ether 2:107). For at least two reasons, this inconsistency actually supports the
argument that Joseph Smith is not the author of the Book of Mormon. First,
Joseph's own Christology shifted after the First Vision, and yet there are still
seemingly modalistic views of the Godhead in the Book of Mormon—a text
Joseph translated *after* his First Vision. Second, were Joseph the author of
the text (as a work of nineteenth-century fiction), it is hard to imagine him
consciously vacillating in his Christology as he wrote. Indeed, it would make
fabricating the text much more challenging, as one would have to keep the
various Christological and theological views distinct and unique, based on
which "character's" voice the novelist is seeking to convey. That said, Professor
Roy Doxey suggested that the seeming contradiction in the Christology of the
Book of Mormon is a result of stripping the passages cited as "evidence" of
modalism from their context. See Roy W. Doxey, "Some Passages in the Book
of Mormon Seem to Indicate That There Is Only One God and That He Is a
Spirit Only. How Can We Explain This?," *Tambuli*, May 1986.

23. Joseph Smith, *Elders' Journal of the Church of Jesus Christ of Latter Day Saints*,
July 1838, 44.

24. See Brigham Young, in *Journal of Discourses* (London: Latter-day Saints' Book Depot: 1854–86), 1:91, 6:332, 7:283, 8:137, 8:339, 11:273, 12:69, 14:71, 18:77, etc.

25. "The Family: A Proclamation to the World," ChurchofJesusChrist.org.

26. "The Restoration of the Fulness of the Gospel of Jesus Christ: A Bicentennial Proclamation to the World," ChurchofJesusChrist.org.

27. William Sloane Coffin, "Our Resurrection, Too," in *The Riverside Preachers*, ed. Paul H. Sherry (New York: Pilgrim Press, 1978), 163.

28. See "The Living Christ: The Testimony of the Apostles," ChurchofJesusChrist.org. See also Gospel Topics, "Jesus Christ," topics.ChurchofJesusChrist.org.

29. Joseph Medlicott Scriven, "What a Friend We Have in Jesus," https://hymnary.org/text/what_a_friend_we_have_in_jesus_all_our_s.

30. Coffin, "Our Resurrection, Too," 163.

31. See Alan Kreider, *The Patient Ferment of the Early Church: The Improbable Rise of Christianity in the Roman Empire* (Grand Rapids, MI: Baker Academic, 2016), 161. See also Ronald J. Sider, ed., *The Early Church on Killing: A Comprehensive Sourcebook on War, Abortion, and Capital Punishment* (Grand Rapids, MI: Baker Academic, 2012), 168, 171. Sider compiled, read, and analyzed all the relevant early church documents on killing. He found that Matthew 5:38–48 is probably the most frequently cited biblical text in the writings collected. At least ten different writers in at least twenty-eight different places cite or refer to this biblical passage and note that Christians love their enemies and turn the other cheek. One can also note that the Sermon on the Mount was central to Jesus's teaching of the Nephites.

32. See Kreider, *Patient Ferment*, 177.

33. Kreider, *Patient Ferment*, 135.

34. In the "New Testament" of the Book of Mormon, Jesus teaches a version of the Sermon on the Mount, and later the disciples of Jesus live in peace for two hundred years in an expression of Zion. By seeking to live nonviolently and obey the law of consecration in communal forms of Zion, the early Saints were seeking to live bold and faithful discipleship. They embarked on the journey of sanctification, not deification.

35. See Smith, "History, circa Summer 1832."

36. See, for example, John 10:30; 17:22; 1 John 5:7; "The Testimony of the Three Witnesses"; LDS Mosiah 15:1–4; 3 Nephi 11:27, 36; 20:35; 28:10; Mormon 7:7; Doctrine and Covenants 20:28; 50:43; 93:3–4; CofChrist Mosiah 8:28–31; III Nephi 5:27, 38; 9:73; 13:21; Mormon 4:29; Doctrine and Covenants 17:5h; 50:8f; 90:1b.

37. Robert L. Millet, "Jesus Christ," in *Encyclopedia of Mormonism*, ed. Daniel H. Ludlow (New York: Macmillan, 1992), 2:726; emphasis added.

38. Dieter F. Uchtdorf, "Missionary Work: Sharing What Is in Your Heart," *Ensign*, May 2019, 17.

SCRIPTURE

Kat Goheen and Joshua M. Sears

SCRIPTURE IN COMMUNITY OF CHRIST

Kat Goheen, ThM, is an academic, a minister, a mother, a musician, and a spiritual director serving in Vancouver, British Columbia, Canada, in Community of Christ.

Scripture evokes so much for me, yet never did I imagine as a young person that I would pursue being a biblical scholar. I remember memorizing verses of the Bible as a young girl and learning the chronology of the events in I and II Nephi by heart in our Community of Christ church basement in summer Sunday School. Moving from Missouri to Vancouver, British Columbia, Canada, as a young adult was a culture shock in more ways than one. Perhaps it was the flexibility with which my new community held scripture that pulled me to seminary to study the Hebrew Bible and New Testament.

Scripture is essential to the life of Community of Christ. It is our witness of Jesus Christ, the basis of our worship services, and the way we understand our identity and mission in the world. Our scripture statement explains our relationship with scripture:

> With other Christians, we affirm the Bible as the foundational scripture for the church. In addition, Community of Christ uses the Book of Mormon and the Doctrine and Covenants as scripture. We do not use these sacred writings to replace the witness of the Bible or improve upon it, but because they confirm its message that Jesus Christ is the Living Word of God.[1]

The foundational book of scripture in Community of Christ is the Bible. While there are different translations favored in different areas, the most common is the New Revised Standard Version because of its excellent scholarship and the interpretive principle of inclusion that guides its work. Jesus Christ is the lens for all our interpretation because Jesus is our Good News, so the Bible is our primary witness. Scripture guides our discernment as it did for Joseph Smith Jr., who took James 1:5 seriously when it counseled him to ask God for wisdom.

The beauty of worshipping in a noncreedal church is diversity, and I suppose if you visited with five Community of Christ members about their relationship with scripture, then you would receive five different flavors of response! There is no better example of this than the Book of Mormon. While it is an official book of scripture in Community of Christ, for many of us it is silent because of issues around its provenance and content and because in some areas it precludes us from joining ecumenical organizations. For others, it is beloved. Some hold the Book of Mormon as a record of ancient peoples who traveled to North America, while some believe it is a product of the nineteenth century.[2] The fact that there is room at the table for all who hold these beliefs is testament to our Enduring Principle of Unity in Diversity.[3]

The Doctrine and Covenants shows us God's interaction with our movement from 1830 to the present. We added section 114 to the Doctrine and Covenants in 1861 and have continued to receive direction from God through to our adoption of section 165 in 2016, which counsels us, "Beloved Community of Christ, do not just speak and sing of

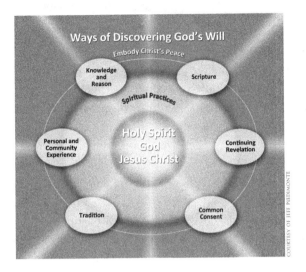

Zion. Live, love, and share as Zion: those who strive to be visibly one in Christ." The Doctrine and Covenants helps us shape our sacramental life, understand our history, and imagine our future through poetic prophecy.

There are golden threads that run through our relationship with scripture. These six lenses describe how we discern and interpret textual meanings for today. Community of Christ president Stephen Veazey explains: "This model guides exploration of God's will based on the Wesleyan Quadrilateral with additional elements drawn from the Community of Christ expression of the Restoration Movement."[4]

We use all of these lenses to interpret and receive scripture. For example, Doctrine and Covenants 163:7 teaches us, "Scripture is an indispensable witness to the Eternal Source of light and truth, which cannot be fully contained in any finite vessel or language." It continues: "Scripture is not to be worshiped or idolized. Only God, the Eternal One of whom scripture testifies, is worthy of worship." This passage saves us from a literalism that would trap us in false dualisms such as "true or false" and "faithful or unfaithful."

Reason is also a firm basis of our relationship with scripture. If all our vessels are limited in containing and describing the holy, then we are called on to use our intellect to discern the wisdom and instruction contained therein. Community of Christ has a tradition of informal educational opportunities through Temple School and various seminar offerings, and it now has a seminary through Graceland University focused on stimulating the faith and reasoning of all who study there.[5] Most exciting, many different tools are encouraged for understanding scripture, from historical criticism to theologies of liberation. God is truth and so is not threatened by vigorous inquiry. In the same way, we believe that our relationship with scripture is not harmed by inquiry but is enhanced. All scripture is translation—between languages or from experience into words—so we bring our best selves to this work of translation.

Tradition is a lens that holds us in our relationship with scripture, from the writings of the ancient church fathers all the way through the long development of Christian theology and to the Restoration testimonies of Joseph Smith Jr. and the faithful who started this movement. All those seekers and settlers who lived into the truth of those initial sparks of brilliance have brought us where we are today. Our tradition includes the wisdom of the larger ecumenical church. Our use of the Revised Common Lectionary in our worship services, along with the Christian year that includes Advent and Lent, shows our participation in this larger experience of tradition. Our spirit of the Restoration follows the currents of aliveness of the Holy Spirit wherever they lead, so tradition serves as both a balancing and destabilizing agent in our work of interacting with scripture.

Experience touches our relationship with scripture as well. Our spiritual practice of *lectio divina*, practiced in many parts of Community of Christ, takes us into the world of scripture.[6] We are Bartimaeus, standing by the road, feeling sight return to our eyes (see Mark 10:46–52). We become the woman reaching for the hem of Jesus's robe, feeling our faith bloom into heath in our bodies (see Mark 5:25–34). We read the prayers of Enos in the Book of Mormon and remember our own history of intercessory prayer. The stories of scripture serve the function of testimonies at prayer meetings, edifying each of us with examples of courage and obedience. And sometimes serving as cautionary tales! We engage with scripture with the senses of our own bodies and feel God's redeeming work in our discipleship.

Experience also helps us navigate the many challenges of responsibly interpreting scripture. Since we accept that scripture is not infallible, when we encounter passages that give us pause, we look to our experience and ask, "Does this portrayal of God fit with what I have experienced in my life, or is it more a product of a specific time and place?" We look inward and outward in our journey with scripture.

Experience with scripture is related to our experience with hymns. We sing many of our scriptures in our hymn texts, and our hymnal is often revered as a fourth book of scripture, since it has a similar level of influence in our discipleship. Our hymns help us focus our interpretive lenses (such as the song "We Limit Not the Truth of God"); they remind us that we worship God in many different languages and cultures ("Kanisa Litajengwa"); and they sing us into new understandings of scripture and mission: "For Everyone Born, a Place at the Table."[7] Our hymns offer us a meditative and challenging engagement with our core beliefs, along with the entrainment of sharing the gospel message with our beloved brothers and sisters in real time, in full harmonies.

An important lens for us is that of continuing revelation. There are times when God calls us to live into new understandings of the gospel through revelations we receive in our Doctrine and Covenants. These new interpretive principles call us to change our hearts and our behaviors. For example, Doctrine and Covenants 163:7c proclaims: "It is not pleasing to God when any passage of scripture is used to diminish or oppress races, genders, or classes of human beings." This passage becomes a new lens to use in reading about women in some New Testament letters, about race in I and II Nephi, and about the emergence of the Israelite people in Canaan. It prevents us from reacting against perceived differences and challenges us to question our implicit biases and complicity in structures of oppression in the world.

A final lens is that of common consent. We live in the beautiful tension of a hierarchical church structure that simultaneously values the voice of each member: a theocratic democracy. There is a dynamic interaction and dialogue when we encounter new revelation that calls forth the best interpretation of each person. Common consent has been described as "open consideration of issues, in a spirit of worship, during which all opinions may be voiced."[8] This lens reminds us of the prayer-ful attention given to receiving our modern revelations, which is so similar to the careful reception over time of the tradition that transmits the Bible to us. It is a caution against individualistic Christianity or atomistic interpretations that break down the body of Christ. We have been drawn together, and we are in it together: the good, the bad, and the interesting.

Scripture tells us who we are in Community of Christ. It shows us where we have been and where we might dream to go. It awakens our best selves and draws us into community with all those who also work for the good. It brings us into relationship with the One who loves and gives so freely and teaches us how to follow the leadings of the Holy Spirit, always with our hearts focused on Jesus Christ. We give thanks for the richness and complexity of scripture and bring our best selves to journey with it.

SCRIPTURE IN THE CHURCH OF JESUS CHRIST OF LATTER-DAY SAINTS

JOSHUA M. SEARS

Joshua M. Sears, PhD, is an assistant professor of ancient scripture at Brigham Young University.

As Joseph Smith experienced his First Vision of the Father and the Son, he "found the testimony of James to be true." Deciding that a passage from the Bible was "true" was not a particularly surprising interpretation for a believing Christian, but the visit from the heavenly messenger three years later would sow the seeds of a dramatically different use of scripture. First, that messenger "said there was a book deposited written upon gold plates, . . . [and] that the fullness of the everlasting Gospel was contained in it." New, extrabiblical scripture was coming. Second, the messenger quoted biblical texts, "though with a little variation from the way it reads in our Bibles." The Bible was not just insufficient, it was subject to revision. Third, the messenger declared that these biblical prophecies were "about to be fulfilled" and were "soon to come in."[9] Ancient scripture was crashing into the modern world, with urgent and immediate relevance. For Latter-day Saints today, understanding our relationship with scripture requires exploring these seeds and how they have grown, as well as the productive tensions they create.

Joseph Smith's prophetic career was saturated with the production of scripture and scripture-related texts, including his translation and publication of the Book of Mormon, his new translation of the Bible, his work on the Egyptian papyri, and the publication of numerous revelations in the Doctrine and Covenants. After Joseph's death in 1844, Brigham Young and other church leaders who immigrated to Utah saw themselves as custodians of Joseph's scriptural legacy. A new edition of the Doctrine and Covenants in 1876 added twenty-six new sections, one of which contained a Brigham Young revelation, marking the first expansion of the canon beyond Joseph's work.[10] In 1880 the church canonized the Pearl of Great Price, an anthology of Joseph Smith texts. Among other items, it contained extracts from the Prophet's new translation of the Bible (covering Genesis 1:1–6:13 and Matthew 23:39–24:51), the texts of the Book of Abraham that had been published during Joseph's lifetime, extracts from his personal history, and thirteen statements of belief he had penned for a newspaper article.[11]

The twentieth century saw two major periods of canonical development. In a rare example of decanonization, the 1921 edition of the Doctrine and Covenants removed the Kirtland-era *Lectures on Faith*,[12] while the Pearl of Great Price dropped several short texts. Wilford Woodruff's 1890 manifesto ending plural marriage, which had appeared as an appendix since 1908, was also definitively added to the Doctrine and Covenants as an "Official Declaration." The late 1970s saw the canonization of three texts—Joseph Smith's 1836 vision of the celestial kingdom, Joseph F. Smith's 1918 vision of the redemption of the dead, and the 1978 announcement that all worthy men could be ordained to the priesthood "without regard for race or color." In 1979 the church published the first-ever Latter-day Saint edition of the Bible, which paired the traditional King James text with interpretive chapter headings, cross-references to Restoration scripture, explanatory footnotes, and appendices, all of which provided Bible readers with a uniquely Latter-day Saint reading experience.[13] Most significantly, and thanks to the generosity and support of President W. Wallace Smith and other leaders of the Reorganized Church of Jesus Christ of Latter Day Saints, this edition included hundreds of quotations from Joseph Smith's Bible revision (now dubbed "the Joseph Smith Translation"), bringing that work into serious use by Latter-day Saints for the first time since Joseph's lifetime.[14]

Scriptural publication in the twenty-first century has thus far focused on helping more people feast upon the testimony of Christ found in the scriptures. Digital versions are freely available online and in apps. Latter-day Saint editions of the Bible have been published in Spanish and Portuguese, with additional foreign languages in development. Apostles constantly encourage a habit of daily scripture study: "The Lord is telling us that our need for constant recourse to the scriptures is greater than in any previous time."[15]

This history of the Latter-day Saint scriptural canon allows us to now explore various tensions that exist because of it. To say that different principles are in "tension" is not to suggest that something is wrong. Harvard Divinity School professor David Holland argues that, like the individual brushstrokes of a painting, Latter-day Saints' numerous and often contradictory impulses with regard to revelation actually produce cohesion *because of,* not *in spite of,* their differences. Lines and colors that are at odds in isolation produce masterful, even beautiful complexity when one steps back and takes in the whole canvas.[16] I will highlight three such productive tensions that emerge from our approach to scripture.

The first tension is the relative authority of the established, written word of God and the contemporary, charismatic voice of living prophets. Church leaders have varied in their approach to this issue. Brigham Young recalled that after Hyrum Smith preached the sufficiency of the published revelations, a distraught Joseph Smith urged Brigham to stand and speak. "I would not give the ashes of a rye straw for these 3 books [the Bible, the Book of Mormon, and the Doctrine and Covenants] for the salvation of any man," Brigham had told the assembly, declaring that "if we had not living oracles in our midst we had nothing."[17] Brigham continued to prioritize the "living oracles" over written scripture throughout his life, although other contemporary leaders, such as Orson Pratt, showed different propensities in this regard.[18] In the twentieth century, Joseph Fielding Smith notably advocated that "it makes no difference what is written or what *anyone* has said, if what has been said is in *conflict* with what the Lord has revealed [in the scriptures], . . . then every member of the Church is duty bound to reject it."[19] In the twenty-first century, church leadership has usually tipped the scales in favor of living apostles. "The scriptures are *not* the ultimate source of knowledge for Latter-day Saints," Elder Jeffrey R. Holland declared, stressing the primacy of "living, vibrant, divine revelation" communicated from "the living God."[20] A 2013 compendium of Joseph Fielding Smith's teachings left out his views of scripture vis-à-vis prophets,[21] and when the church published a new history in 2018, it tellingly included the story of Brigham's correction of Hyrum.[22]

A second area of tension is the relative priority that Latter-day Saints place on different books in the scriptural canon. Although the Book of Mormon played an important role in shaping priesthood organization and ordinances in the early church,[23] Joseph Smith overwhelmingly preferred to use and quote from the Bible throughout his life, and this same preference for traditional Christian scripture continued with other church leaders throughout the nineteenth century.[24] Although the Book of Mormon served as an important missionary tool—a sign that God had restored his covenant (see 3 Nephi 21:1–7)—it was relatively neglected by Latter-day Saints as a source for doctrine and inspiration until the second half of the twentieth century.[25] Perhaps the single greatest catalyst for renewed focus on the Book of Mormon was the emphatic attention it received under the leadership of Ezra Taft Benson in the 1980s.[26] Since then, church members have responded to this call from their leaders, such that "in LDS worship services, Sunday Schools, and family devotionals, the Book of Mormon is [now] fully central."[27] So far has the pendulum swung that some have claimed that "Mormons have developed a kind of amnesia towards the Bible,"[28] with even an apostle counseling that we must do better to "help all people, including our own members, understand the power and importance of the Holy Bible" and calling on members to "balance" their study "in order to love and understand *all* scripture."[29] Regardless of what "balance" individual members find in their private devotion, church curriculum remains committed to taking time for each part of the canon, with classes and the family study curriculum rotating through the Old Testament, the New Testament, the Book of Mormon, and the Doctrine and Covenants every four years.

A third tension is the pull of traditional approaches to scripture set against the pull of modern academic interpretations. In recent years, the church has modified its approach on some issues. For example, in light of the fact that no text from the Book of Abraham can be located on any of the surviving Joseph Smith papyri, a church essay from 2014 presented—as two alternative possibilities to explain the text's origin— both the traditional idea that Joseph translated directly from (now missing) papyri and the newer theory that the papyri simply served as a "catalyst" for revelation.[30] The Joseph Smith Papers Project has demonstrated that, contrary to popular notions of a prophet transcribing God's voice like a stenographer, Joseph's revelations often came as a *process* of inspiration, with corrections and expansions possible as new understanding came.[31] Church-sponsored editions of the Bible in foreign languages have updated archaic language and incorporated non-KJV readings based on the results of textual criticism.[32]

With other issues, however, Latter-day Saint approaches remain rooted in tradition. Despite the proliferation of modern Bible translations and the declining use of the King James Version among English-speaking Christians, the KJV remains the official Bible of English-speaking Latter-day Saints.[33] Church curriculum has striven to update Doctrine and Covenants manuals to align with current scholarship, but manuals on the Old and New Testaments remain conservative in their approach (Moses wrote the Pentateuch, the Flood covered the earth, Paul wrote all the epistles attributed to him, and so forth).

The church has remained institutionally committed to the historicity of the Book of Mormon, and relatively few members find theories of nineteenth-century pseudepigrapha to be compatible with their faith.[34]

Notwithstanding the occasional complexity of these tensions, we turn to the scriptures because through them we find God. As a young missionary in southern Chile, I was walking down the street with my companion one day when a woman suddenly burst out of her home sobbing that her father was dead. We joined her in her home, but as I watched her tears and trembling frame I felt completely inadequate to address her unexpected bereavement. Suddenly a thought came into my mind (I identify it as the Holy Spirit) to "read Abinadi's testimony." I flipped open my Libro de Mormón and read her these words in Spanish:

> If Christ had not come into the world, . . . there could have been no redemption. And if Christ had not risen from the dead, . . . there could have been no resurrection. But there is a resurrection, therefore the grave hath no victory, and the sting of death is swallowed up in Christ. He is the light and the life of the world; yea, a light that is endless, that can never be darkened; yea, and also a life which is endless, that there can be no more death. (Mosiah 16:6–9)

As I read, scripture succeeded where my own efforts fell short. She felt peace; her weeping ceased. We talked at length about God's plan for his children. As happens to Latter-day Saints across the globe every day, I found that "the word of God is quick, and powerful" (Hebrews 4:12), leading us "to . . . the love of God" (1 Nephi 11:25), because in his word we find "the power of God unto salvation" (Doctrine and Covenants 68:4).

RESPONSE TO JOSHUA M. SEARS

It is a deep work to consider together the ways in which Community of Christ and The Church of Jesus Christ of Latter-day Saints live with scripture. What is obvious from a first read is that scripture forms and influences both traditions in an important way, while we have different ways of interacting with our sacred books. There is no easy way to summarize this difference, other than to suggest that Latter-day Saints use scripture often and are quite familiar with it, while Community of Christ members appreciate the critique and encouragement scripture offers us.

We have been offered a candid view of the use of scripture over time among the Latter-day Saints. The movement from their near amnesia of the Book of Mormon to their prioritizing its use over the Bible in one lifetime is fascinating. This causes me to reflect on the Community of Christ relationship with scripture. I would observe that the informal scriptural authority for Community of Christ today, at least in Western countries, leans toward the narratives and wisdom writings in the Hebrew Bible, the Gospels of the New Testament, and the most recent revelations in the Doctrine and Covenants. There are other parts of our scriptures, such as the more Deuteronomistic texts of the Hebrew Bible, the Book of Mormon, and the beginning of the Doctrine and Covenants, that are in shadow for us. Like all shadow content, they hold gifts as well as stumbling blocks when held to the light in love.

The question of the balance of authority between written scripture and living oracles is an interesting one for Community of Christ. Charisma was one of Joseph Smith Jr.'s gifts, and Community of Christ has an ambivalent relationship with parts of his legacy. We love charisma, yet we are wary of it. For this reason, written scripture appears to hold more sway than the spontaneous offerings of our leaders, perhaps because of the safeguard of the church's Enduring Principle of Common Consent.

I do admire the cherishing of Restoration history evidenced in Josh's essay. There is a beauty in honoring your mothers and fathers evidenced there and in the solidity that comes from embracing your roots. However, I don't believe that this cherishing is an ideal model for Community of Christ, because of our outlook on the history we share. We are still living through our relationship with the past, much as individuals work through painful chapters of their growing-up phase. I believe we carry a healthy perspective, aided by distance, that allows us to look to the present and to the future as we continue to come to terms with our past.

An area in Josh's chapter that is helpful for Community of Christ is the strong value that Latter-day Saint leadership places on scripture. From President Ezra Taft Benson's emphasis on the Book of Mormon to the current exhortation their apostles offer to spend time reading scripture, these words from leadership show that scripture is highly valued in their church. In Community of Christ, scripture is also valued, but I believe experience is a more privileged lens overall, evidenced in part by the size of the experience-lens section in my article! Another way of saying this is that scripture becomes important to us where it intersects with our experience. While we acknowledge and appreciate the gifts of rational arguments, scripture, and tradition, in the end we trust more what we and others have witnessed.

There is so much life in this conversation about the importance of scripture in The Church of Jesus Christ of Latter-day Saints and in Community of Christ. We have gone in different directions from our shared beginnings, but we honor those beginnings in our own ways and show signs of following the Holy Spirit in good faith. May we seek to live from the best we know, and may there always be more light and truth in our explorations and understanding.

RESPONSE TO KAT GOHEEN

I enjoyed so much learning from Kat's experience with scripture in Community of Christ. Her story, and the experience of Community of Christ more broadly, resonates deeply with my love for the Savior and the ways I have drawn closer to him through scripture. It is apparent that Community of Christ and The Church of Jesus Christ of Latter-day Saints share several fundamental uses of scripture, even with a few important differences.

Classifying extrabiblical books as "scripture" sets us both apart from many of our fellow Christians, for whom the Bible is categorically unique. We can certainly relate to the difficulty this can sometimes create for ecumenical relations! I also loved Kat's description of the hymnal as a somewhat official book of scripture, and given the role that sacred music plays in our worship, I'm sure we could say the same. And while the contents of our respective versions of the Doctrine and Covenants obviously took different paths some time ago, it is beautiful to see how for each community that volume manifests God's continued involvement in our lives.

One difference that has emerged between us is the conceptualization of the Book of Mormon. Kat celebrates the diversity in Community of Christ, where some maintain that the Book of Mormon is a record of ancient people and some look for an origin in the nineteenth century. In principle I admire this commitment to diversity, but I do not believe it would work for our approach to the Book of Mormon. Church leaders have consistently linked the Book of Mormon's spiritual and historical claims, and when our missionaries bear testimony that the Book of Mormon is "true," they similarly imply no distinction. A recent intensified refocus on early church history has only affirmed the significance in our founding narratives of the visit of Moroni, the existence of the gold plates, and the witnesses who supported Joseph's account of each. As Latter-day Saints have studied the Book of Mormon in greater depth, we have also been struck by the book's own remarkable self-referential awareness—its clear vision of its own role in preserving the ancient words of Jesus so that those words could come forth in the latter days to restore lost truth, confirm the testimony of the Bible, enact the gathering of Israel, and turn Christianity away from secularization and back toward a "God of miracles."

I also find it interesting that Kat's survey omits any role for Joseph Smith's new translation of the Bible, which for more than a century was published and used only by Community of Christ, with the title "Inspired Version" suggestive of its role. During that same period, most Latter-day Saints had no idea Joseph had even produced such a work, notwithstanding the two canonized excerpts in the Pearl of Great Price. But ever since thousands of excerpts were incorporated into the Latter-day Saint Bible in 1979, Joseph's work has become extremely influential in Latter-day Saint readings of the Old and New Testaments, and Brigham Young University continues to turn out articles and books on its production, textual history, and theological value. It appears our two communities have swapped places on this issue.

One principle that Kat emphasized that I believe we could learn from is the openness to different ways of approaching biblical scripture.

There are certain reasons why the King James Version will always remain embedded in our biblical praxis, but even supplementary use of additional translations would provide the additional benefits of modern scholarship and inclusive language that Kat mentioned. And while certain true/false dualisms and literalistic readings are important for our faith, there are no doubt some traditional interpretations for which a lens of knowledge and reason would serve us well without sacrificing significant theology (something like the Mosaic authorship of the entire Pentateuch comes to mind).

It is clear that despite some significant differences in how our approaches to scripture have developed, our communities share a dedication to Jesus Christ, to whom all scripture points us.

CONCLUSION

We both appreciate the opportunity to learn from each other, to learn about each other's traditions, and to have a fresh appreciation for our own. Both of our churches share a fundamental lens of seeing Jesus as the sum of all scripture, and in our canon that includes books beyond the Bible. Our open canon also is a distinctive similarity. One key difference between us is the relative weight given to the Book of Mormon. The contents of our canon of scripture from Joseph Smith are different, like the Book of Abraham and specific inclusions from the Doctrine and Covenants. We also interpret what we have received in these books differently, such as the ways we use the Inspired Version of the Bible given by Joseph Smith. Ultimately, we both agree with John 20:31 that scripture is written so that we can believe Jesus is the Son of God and that through believing we can have life in him.

NOTES

1. "Scripture in Community of Christ," Community of Christ, https://www.CofChrist.org/scripture-in-community-of-christ.

2. Some Community of Christ members look for themes of peace and justice in the Book of Mormon's pages to inform their identity, regardless of the book's provenance. For example, see Andrew Bolton, "Utopian Vision and

Prophetic Imagination: Reading the Book of Mormon in a Nineteenth-Century Context," *Restoration Studies* 10 (2009): 142–53.

3. Our Enduring Principles are explored at https://www.CommunityofChrist.ca /enduring-principles.html.

4. Stephen Veazey, email to author, January 28, 2021. For an explanation of the Wesleyan Quadrilateral, see "Glossary: Wesleyan Quadrilateral, the," United Methodist Church, May 26, 2015, https://www.umc.org/en/content/glossary -wesleyan-quadrilateral-the.

5. The Community of Christ Seminary offers a two-year master of arts in religion degree.

6. For more on how *lectio divina* is used in Community of Christ, see "Lectio Divina," https://www.CofChrist.org/lectio-divina/.

7. *Community of Christ Sings* (Independence, MO: Herald Publishing House, 2013), hymn nos. 69, 338, and 285.

8. Stephen M. Veazey, "Ways of Discovering God's Will," script of video presentation, https://www.heraldhouse.org/products/ways-of-discovering-gods -will-listening-guide-pdf-download.

9. Joseph Smith, "History, 1838–1856, volume A-1 [23 December 1805–30 August 1834]," pp. 4–6, The Joseph Smith Papers, https://www.josephsmithpapers.org /paper-summary/history-1838-1856-volume-a-1-23-december-1805-30-august -1834/.

10. See Richard E. Turley Jr. and William W. Slaughter, *How We Got the Doctrine and Covenants* (Salt Lake City: Deseret Book, 2012), 80–89.

11. See Terryl L. Givens with Brian M. Hauglid, *The Pearl of Greatest Price: Mormonism's Most Controversial Scripture* (New York: Oxford University Press, 2019).

12. See Noel B. Reynolds, "The Case for Sidney Rigdon as Author of the *Lectures on Faith*," *Journal of Mormon History* 32, no. 3 (2005): 1–41.

13. See Fred E. Woods, "The Latter-day Saint Edition of the King James Bible," in *The King James Bible and the Restoration*, ed. Kent P. Jackson (Provo, UT: Religious Studies Center, Brigham Young University; Salt Lake City: Deseret Book, 2011), 260–80.

14. See Thomas E. Sherry, "Robert J. Matthews and the RLDS Church's Inspired Version of the Bible," *BYU Studies* 49, no. 2 (2010): 93–119. The published version of Joseph Smith's work had been known as the "Inspired Version" in the Reorganized Church, but the editors of the 1979 Latter-day Saint Bible coined the term "Joseph Smith Translation" (JST) because they believed the abbreviation "IV" would be mistaken for a Roman numeral.

15. D. Todd Christofferson, "The Blessing of Scripture," *Ensign*, May 2010, 35.

16. See David F. Holland, "Revelation and the Open Canon in Mormonism," in *The Oxford Handbook of Mormonism*, ed. Terryl L. Givens and Philip L. Barlow (Oxford: Oxford University Press, 2015), 149–63.

17. Brigham Young, discourse, October 8, 1866, as found in shorthand notes in the George D. Watt Papers, https://catalog.ChurchofJesusChrist.org/assets /ec6e5ce5-c41a-4a9d-8d7c-ed1feb903321/0/0#ChurchofJesusChrist.

18. See Philip L. Barlow, *Mormons and the Bible: The Place of the Latter-day Saints in American Religion*, Religion in America (New York: Oxford University Press, 1991), 77–94.

19. *Doctrines of Salvation: Sermons and Writings of Joseph F. Smith*, ed. Bruce R. McConkie (Salt Lake City: Bookcraft, 1954–56), 3:203–4.

20. Jeffrey R. Holland, "My Words . . . Never Cease," *Ensign*, May 2008, 93.

21. See *Teachings of Presidents of the Church: Joseph Fielding Smith* (Salt Lake City: The Church of Jesus Christ of Latter-day Saints, 2013).

22. See *Saints: The Story of the Church of Jesus Christ in the Latter Days*, vol. 1, *The Standard of Truth, 1815–1846* (Salt Lake City: The Church of Jesus Christ of Latter-day Saints, 2018), 484–86.

23. See Gerald E. Smith, *Schooling the Prophet: How the Book of Mormon Influenced Joseph Smith and the Early Restoration* (Provo, UT: Neal A. Maxwell Institute for Religious Scholarship, Brigham Young University, 2016).

24. See Barlow, *Mormons and the Bible*, 43–46, 74–102.

25. See Noel B. Reynolds, "The Coming Forth of the Book of Mormon in the Twentieth Century," *BYU Studies* 38, no. 2 (1999): 6–47.

26. See Casey Paul Griffiths, "The Book of Mormon among the Saints: Evolving Use of the Keystone Scripture," in *The Coming Forth of the Book of Mormon: A Marvelous Work and a Wonder*, ed. Dennis L. Largey, Andrew H. Hedges, John Hilton III, and Kerry Hull (Provo, UT: Religious Studies Center, Brigham Young University; Salt Lake City: Deseret Book, 2015), 199–226.

27. Terryl L. Givens, *Feeding the Flock: The Foundations of Mormon Thought; Church and Praxis* (Oxford: Oxford University Press, 2017), 269.

28. Philip Barlow, as quoted in Peggy Fletcher Stack, "And It Came to Pass, One Day the Book of Mormon Overtook the Bible—in LDS Eyes," *Salt Lake Tribune*, February 10, 2015, https://archive.sltrib.com/article.php?id=2139857 &itype=CMSID.

29. M. Russell Ballard, "The Miracle of the Holy Bible," *Ensign*, May 2007, 82; emphasis added.

30. Gospel Topics Essays, "Translation and Historicity of the Book of Abraham," https://www.ChurchofJesusChrist.org/study/manual/gospel-topics-essays /translation-and-historicity-of-the-book-of-abraham.

31. See Steven C. Harper, "'That They Might Come to Understanding': Revelation as Process," in *You Shall Have My Word: Exploring the Text of the Doctrine and Covenants*, ed. Scott C. Esplin, Richard O. Cowan, and Rachel Cope (Provo, UT: Religious Studies Center, Brigham Young University; Salt Lake City: Deseret Book, 2012), 19–33.

32. See Joshua M. Sears, "Santa Biblia: The Latter-day Saint Bible in Spanish," *BYU Studies Quarterly* 54, no. 1 (2015): 42–75.

33. See Daniel O. McClellan, "'As Far as It Is Translated Correctly': Bible Translation and the Church," *Religious Educator* 20, no. 2 (2019): 52–83.

34. See Terryl L. Givens, *By the Hand of Mormon: The American Scripture That Launched a New World Religion* (Oxford: Oxford University Press, 2002).

SALVATION

Robert L. Millet and John Taylor

THE PROCESS OF SALVATION IN THE CHURCH OF JESUS CHRIST OF LATTER-DAY SAINTS

ROBERT L. MILLET

Robert L. Millet is professor emeritus of religious
education at Brigham Young University.

I t is not uncommon for a member of The Church of Jesus Christ of
Latter-day Saints to be asked the following questions by a caring or
curious Christian: "Are you a saved Christian?" or "Have you been
saved?" While we may stumble over their words and wrestle with how
to respond, we generally associate salvation with the life to come and
believe that being saved has to do with gaining eternal life following
death and eventual resurrection.

Here, as in other theological matters, we use the same or similar words as our Community of Christ neighbors to describe a Christian concept but discover on more serious investigation that what we mean is at least slightly different. In that vein, I would suggest that for members of the Church of Jesus Christ, being saved is a *process*, one that has something to do with what has been accomplished in the past, what is going on now, and what will yet take place in the future. Thus, our hesitation to respond to a rather straightforward question about being saved derives not from any effort to avoid the issue or to suggest that we do not believe in the saving role of Jesus Christ, but rather from the fact that the question is not easily answered.

To be sure, Joseph Smith taught that we are eternal beings. He declared that a person's spirit "is not a created being: it existed from eternity, and will exist to eternity. Anything created cannot be eternal."[1] Subsequent church leaders have explained that the attributes, powers, and capacities possessed by our Father in Heaven reside in men and women in rudimentary and thus potential form. There is a sense, then, in which we might say that men and women, being spiritual heirs to godliness, are good by nature; that is, they are good because they are related to and products of the Highest Good, a spark of divinity from the Father of lights (see James 1:17). As the scriptures declare, men and women are created in the image and likeness of God (see Genesis 1:26). God is good, even the embodiment and personification of all that is noble, upright, and edifying, and we are from him.

Fundamental to the plan of God is moral agency, the divine right and capacity to choose. Agency is a gift of God, one that comes through the blessings of the Atonement of Jesus Christ. A Book of Mormon prophet explained that "the Messiah cometh in the fulness of time, that he may redeem the children of men from the fall. And because that they are redeemed from the fall they have become free forever, knowing good from evil; to act for themselves and not to be acted upon. . . . Wherefore, men are free according to the flesh; . . . and they are free to choose liberty and eternal life, through the great Mediator of all men, or to choose captivity and death, according to the captivity and power of the devil" (LDS 2 Nephi 2:26–27; CofChrist II Nephi 1:116–20).

Jesus did what no other man or woman has ever done, could do, or will do—he lived a perfect life. He was tempted in all points just as we are, but he did not yield (see Hebrews 4:15; 1 Peter 2:22). Jesus was the Truth; he taught the truth, and his teachings stand as the formula for happiness and the guide for personal, interpersonal, and world peace. His words are timely and timeless; they are a treasure house of wisdom and divine direction for our lives. But other men and women have spoken the truth, have offered wise counsel for our lives, and have even provided profound insight as to who we are and what life is all about. However, Jesus did what no other person could do—he atoned for our sins and rose from the dead. Only a god, only a person with powers over life and death, could do such things.

How this took place is unknown. We believe in Christ and trust in his redeeming mercy and grace. We accept the word of scripture, both ancient and modern, in regard to the ransoming mission of Jesus the Christ. We know from personal experience—having been transformed from pain to peace, from darkness to light—of the power in Christ to renew the human soul. But like the rest of the Christian world, we cannot rationally comprehend the work of a god. We cannot grasp how one person can assume the effect of another person's error and especially how one person, even someone who possessed the power of God, can suffer for another's sins. The Savior's Atonement, the greatest act of mercy and love in all eternity, though real, is incomprehensible and unfathomable for now.

Though salvation is available to all through the goodness and grace of Christ, there are certain things that must be done in order for divine grace and mercy to be activated in the lives of Christians. People must come unto him, accept him as Lord and Savior, and have faith on his name. The products of that faith include repentance, baptism, reception of the Holy Spirit, and dedicated discipleship until the end of one's life. Eternal life comes to those who believe and obey. Christ is "the author of eternal salvation unto all them that obey him" (Hebrews 5:9).

We believe that all men and women have the capacity to be saved. "We believe," Joseph Smith wrote in 1842, "that through the Atonement of Christ, all mankind may be saved, by obedience to the laws and ordinances of the Gospel" (LDS Articles of Faith 1:3). Stated another way, there is no person who comes to earth who is outside the reach of Christ's power to save, no soul beyond the pale of mercy and grace. God is no respecter of persons, as Peter pointed out, "but in every nation he that feareth him, and worketh righteousness, is accepted with him" (Acts 10:35). Thus, Latter-day Saints do not believe in predestination, that men and women are chosen or elected unconditionally to salvation or damnation. Joseph Smith taught that "unconditional election of individuals to eternal life was not taught by the apostles. God did elect or predestinate, that all those who would be saved, should be saved in Christ Jesus, and through obedience to the gospel; but he passes over no man's sins, but visits them with correction, and if his children will not repent of their sins, he will discard them."[2]

We believe that the gospel is a gospel *covenant*. The Lord agrees to do for us what we could never do for ourselves—forgive our sins, lift our burdens, renew our souls and re-create our nature, raise us from the dead, and qualify us for glory hereafter—whereupon we strive to do what we *can* do: have faith in Christ, repent of our sins, be baptized, love and serve one another, and do all in our power to put off the natural man and deny ourselves of ungodliness. In short, we believe that more is required of men and women than a verbal expression of faith in the Lord, more than a confession with the lips that we have received Christ into our hearts. Without question, the power to save us, to change us, to renew our souls, is in Christ. True faith, however, always manifests itself in *faithfulness* (see John 14:15; James 1:22; 2:17–20). Thus, the real question is not whether one is saved by grace or by works but rather whom we trust and rely on. To exercise true faith in Christ is to have total trust in him, complete confidence in him, and a ready reliance on him.

As early as February 1832, Joseph Smith declared that the life beyond consists of more than heaven and hell. He recorded a revelation known as the vision of the three degrees of glory (see LDS and CofChrist Doctrine and Covenants 76). This vision serves as a type of commentary on the Master's declaration that "in my Father's house are many mansions" (John 14:2) and on the apostle Paul's passing comment to the Corinthians about types of bodies in the Resurrection (see 1 Corinthians 15:40–42). The Prophet Joseph stated that God revealed to him the concept of three main divisions in the afterlife—in descending order (in terms of the greatest eternal reward), the celestial kingdom, terrestrial kingdom, and telestial kingdom, each of which is a kingdom of glory.

As for the fate of those who do not obey, in our faith we use the term *hell* to mean two things: (1) the division of the postmortal spirit world where those who lived wickedly and spurned morality and decency reside until the time of their resurrection; and ultimately (2) the final abode of those called the "sons of perdition," people who deny and defy the truth, who come to know God and then fight against him and his plan of salvation (see LDS Doctrine and Covenants 76:31–35; CofChrist Doctrine and Covenants 76:4). Only the sons of perdition face the second death (meaning the second or final spiritual death). They inherit a kingdom of no glory. Everyone else will come forth from the grave to inherit a kingdom of glory.

In that sense, we believe in a type of universal salvation—not in the sense that everyone will one day dwell with God and be like God, but rather that all who do not defect to perdition will enjoy a measure of God's goodness and grace through inheriting a heaven of some type.[3] For one thing, all people who have had a physical body will be resurrected, "for as in Adam all die, even so in Christ shall all be made alive" (1 Corinthians 15:22; see also LDS Alma 11:41; CofChrist Alma 8:97–98). As stated in the vision of the degrees of glory, "And this is the gospel, the glad tidings, . . . that he came into the world, even Jesus, to be crucified for the world, and to bear the sins of the world, and to sanctify the world, and to cleanse it from all unrighteousness; that through him all might be saved whom the Father had put into his power and made by him; who glorifies the Father, and saves all the works of his hands, except those sons of perdition who deny the Son after the Father has revealed him" (LDS Doctrine and Covenants 76:40–43; CofChrist Doctrine and Covenants 76:4g–h).

Once while I was sitting with a group of religious scholars, they commented to me that the problem with the Latter-day Saint conception of heaven is that *everyone* is saved. I thought of that conversation as I later read the following from Richard John Neuhaus, a Roman Catholic scholar: "The hope that all may be saved . . . offends some Christians. It is as though salvation were a zero-sum proposition, as though there is only so much to go around, as though God's grace to others will somehow diminish our portion of grace. . . . If we love others, it seems that we must hope that, in the end, they will be saved. We must hope that all will one day hear the words of Christ, 'Today you will be with me in paradise.' Given the evidence of Scripture and tradition, we cannot deny that hell exists. We can, however, hope that hell is empty. We cannot know that, but we can hope it is the case."[4]

While our faith and conduct in this mortal experience are vital, learning and growth and redemption continue well beyond the grave. "When you climb up a ladder," Joseph Smith explained only two months before his death, "you must begin at the bottom, and ascend step by step, until you arrive at the top; and so it is with the principles of the gospel—you must begin with the first, and go on until you learn all the principles of exaltation. But it will be a great while after you have passed through the veil [of death] before you will have learned them. It is not all to be comprehended in this world; it will be a great work to learn our salvation and exaltation even beyond the grave."[5]

I sat at lunch some time ago with a dear friend of mine who is an evangelical minister. On many occasions we have met to chat, to reflect on each other's faith, to ask and respond to hard questions, to seek to better understand each other. On this particular occasion, we were discussing grace and works. I had assured my friend that Latter-day Saints do in fact believe in, accept, and rely on the saving mercy of Jesus. "But, Bob," he said, "you folks believe you have to do so many things to be saved!"

"Like what?" I asked.

"Well," he continued, "let's just take baptism, for example. You believe that baptism is what saves you."

"No, we don't," I responded.

"Yes, you do," he followed up. "You believe baptism is essential for entrance into the celestial kingdom."

"Yes," I said, "while baptism and other ordinances are necessary as channels of divine power and grace, they are not what saves us. *Jesus* saves us!"

While Latter-day Saints believe and teach that the highest form of salvation comes to those who receive the blessings of our temples (see LDS Doctrine and Covenants 131:1–4), we do not in any way believe that it is the temple, or the ordinances contained there, that saves us. Salvation is in Christ.

We come to the earth to take a physical body, to be schooled, and to gain experiences that we could not have in the "first estate" (see Jude 1:6), the premortal life. We then strive to keep the commandments and grow in faith and spiritual graces until we are prepared to go where God and Christ are. The Doctrine and Covenants says, "That which is of God is light; and he that receiveth light, and continueth in God, receiveth more light; and that light groweth brighter and brighter until the perfect day" (LDS Doctrine and Covenants 50:24; CofChrist Doctrine and Covenants 50:6b). That "perfect day" is the Resurrection, the day when spirit and body are inseparably united in immortal glory. That is, those "who are quickened by a portion of the celestial glory [in this life] shall then [in the Resurrection] receive of the same, even a fulness" (LDS Doctrine and Covenants 88:29; CofChrist Doctrine and Covenants 85:6d). The Doctrine and Covenants also instructs that those who come unto Christ, follow his path to the Father, and thus realize the fruits of true worship are empowered to "come unto the Father in my name, and in due time receive of his fulness" (LDS Doctrine and Covenants 93:19; CofChrist Doctrine and Covenants 90:3b). This is what we fondly call gaining eternal life.

All men and women, like Christ, are made in the image and likeness of God (see Genesis 1:27; Moses 2:27), so we feel it is neither audacious nor heretical for the children of God to aspire to be like God (see Matthew 5:48; 1 John 3:2–3). Acquiring the attributes of godliness comes through overcoming the world through the Lord's Atonement (see 1 John 5:4–5; Revelation 2:7, 11; LDS Doctrine and Covenants 76:51–60; CofChrist Doctrine and Covenants 76:5b–h); becoming heirs of God and joint heirs with Christ, the natural heir (see Romans 8:17; Galatians

4:7); becoming partakers of the divine nature (see 2 Peter 1:4); and thus inheriting all things, just as Jesus inherits all things (see 1 Corinthians 3:21–23; Revelation 21:7; LDS Doctrine and Covenants 76:55, 95; 84:38; 88:107; CofChrist Doctrine and Covenants 76:5f; 83:6e; 85:33b). In that glorified state, we will be conformed to the image of the Lord Jesus (see Romans 8:29; 1 Corinthians 15:49; 2 Corinthians 3:18; 1 John 3:2; LDS Alma 5:14; CofChrist Alma 3:28), receive his glory, and be one with him and with the Father (see John 17:21–23; Philippians 3:21).

To summarize, the doctrine of our church teaches that through the cleansing and transforming power of the blood of Jesus Christ, men and women may mature spiritually over time. That is, by and through his blood, they

> have a forgiveness of sins, and also a sure reward laid up for them in heaven, even that of partaking of the fullness of the Father and the Son through the Spirit. As the Son partakes of the fullness of the Father through the Spirit, so the saints are, by the same Spirit, to be partakers of the same fullness, to enjoy the same glory; for as the Father and the Son are one, so, in like manner, the saints are to be one in them. Through the love of the Father, the mediation of Jesus Christ, and the gift of the Holy Spirit, they are to be heirs of God, and joint heirs with Jesus Christ.[6]

It is glorious and heartwarming to know that God our Father has a plan for his children, a plan of recovery, a plan of renewal and reconciliation, a plan of salvation, a plan by which those who wander—and that includes all of us—can pick themselves up, dust themselves off, and through the cleansing and enabling power of the Savior's Atonement, return home. None of us is bright enough or powerful enough to do it alone; we must have help. And were it not for divine assistance, each of us would falter and fail, would lose the battle of life. "But thanks be to God, [who gives] us the victory through our Lord Jesus Christ" (1 Corinthians 15:57). Our God offers us "so great salvation" (Hebrews 2:3) through the infinite intercession of the only completely pure and perfect being to walk the earth, and we would be foolish and seriously shortsighted to refuse such an offering.

SALVATION IN COMMUNITY OF CHRIST

JOHN TAYLOR

John Taylor, PhD, is pastor of the Community of Christ
Drummoyne Congregation in Sydney, Australia, and an emeritus
professor of taxation law at the University of New South Wales.

In 1965, when I was in my thirteenth year, I was baptized into Community of Christ. In that same year my maternal grandmother died. She was the first close relative of mine to die in my lifetime (an uncle had died a year or two before, but I had not known him well). I had been in prebaptismal classes for several years before I was baptized but made the decision to be baptized only after a local elder conducted a series of prebaptismal classes in my home. Looking back, I suspect that the death of a close relative and involvement in personalized classes on church doctrine before baptism made me think about questions concerning the meaning of life and eternity.

My maternal grandmother was a second-generation member of Community of Christ. Her parents had been early converts in Australia, having been baptized around 1880. Her brother had been mission president[7] and had written several books for the church. She had received what was then called her patriarchal blessing from Alexander H. Smith.[8] I remember her as someone not to argue with but do not remember deep and meaningful theological conversations with her. I do remember, though, my mother saying that my grandmother held the strong view that we are saved by our works, probably citing the letter of James to the effect that "faith without works is a dead thing"[9] and "I will show you my faith by my works."[10]

My maternal grandfather had died six years before I was born, so I never knew him. He had been a builder and then a house painter and decorator. My mother told me that he used to preach the gospel to his customers (which probably accounted for his lack of success in business). One of his emphases was that the Community of Christ doctrine (in contrast to Catholicism and most of Protestantism) was that little children were born innocent and were "saved" without baptism. This, of course, was consistent with a view of salvation as deliverance from sin and death and eternal punishment. This view defined salvation as being achieved through compliance with the gospel plan, involving faith, repentance, and baptism once you had reached the age of accountability.

During the 1960s, a Basic Beliefs Committee was developing a Statement of Belief that, along with a commentary, was published in book form as *Exploring the Faith* in 1970. As paragraphs of the statement and commentary were developed, they were progressively published in the *Saints' Herald*. Before this publication, Community of Christ used the document known as the Epitome of Faith, derived from Joseph Smith's "Wentworth Letter," as its official statement of belief. The paragraph on "The Gift of Salvation" in the 1970 statement clearly showed a significant shift in the church's thinking. It read:

> We believe that man [*sic*] cannot be saved in the Kingdom of God except by the grace of the Lord Jesus Christ, who loves us while we are yet in our sins, and who gave his life to reconcile us unto God. Through this atonement of the Lord Jesus Christ and by the gift of the Holy Spirit, men receive power to choose God and to commit their lives to him [*sic*]; thus are they turned from rebellion, healed from sin, renewed in spirit, and transformed after the image of God in righteousness and holiness.[11]

Thus, during a period when some living church members continued to see salvation as a product of works, here was a committee of church leaders stating that salvation was by the "grace of the Lord Jesus Christ." The shift had begun earlier and can be detected in some of the writings of church leaders like F. Henry Edwards and Arthur Oakman, where there is sometimes a message both of God's love and forgiveness and of the necessity for repentance and baptism.

All the earlier thinking tied in with the church's exclusive claims to authority through the restoration of the priesthood. The period when Community of Christ theology shifted from a theology of works to a theology of grace was accompanied by an effective abandonment of exclusive claims to authority and a consequent reduction in emphasis on ordinances and sacraments as being essential to salvation. Over time, church thought saw authority as not being in the exclusive possession of Community of Christ and saw baptism as an expression of discipleship rather than as a passport to celestial glory. This was most clearly evident in the decision of Community of Christ to accept and confirm people as members who had been baptized as responsible believers by another faith.

Community of Christ thinking has shifted away from personal salvation and afterlife questions to an emphasis on salvation as the present and ongoing transformation of human beings and human society by the love of God. Just as discipleship has been seen increasingly as servanthood, so too has salvation been seen in the transformed lives of disciples in community. The origins of this development may be deeper and older than is sometimes supposed. The churches of the Joseph Smith Restoration movement have historically seen "the cause of Zion" and "the New Jerusalem" as a key focus of their mission. All things were seen as spiritual (see CofChrist Doctrine and Covenants 28:9; LDS Doctrine and Covenants 29:34–35). Personal and historical eschatologies were linked through Joseph Smith's "millennialism of place," which required the building of a "righteous" city to which Christ would return in glory.[12] The righteous city would be peopled by disciples who had been saved through compliance with the ordinances and sacraments of the restored faith.

Arguably the kingdom was always seen both as a present worldly reality and as a future hope both in and beyond time. The consummation of history was envisaged but so too was the present reality of an afterlife with kingdoms of glory. Joseph Smith sought guidance on eternal judgment because of his concern at the apparently arbitrary features of evangelical Calvinist personal eschatology and the experience of the Smith family with the death of Alvin.[13] The resulting revelations in Doctrine and Covenants section 76 (for both churches), LDS Doctrine and Covenants section 88, CofChrist Doctrine and Covenants section 85, and later Joseph's 1836 vision of the celestial kingdom[14] amounted to something close to a universal salvation position with the possibility opened for further education and salvation after death.

Although I do not think that it has been explicitly stated, I do believe that Community of Christ has now moved to a position of universal salvation. This can be regarded as consistent with the move away from exclusive claims to authority and the shift from a works-based theology to a theology of grace. In one sense this is consistent with and an extension of the kingdoms-of-glory eschatology of Doctrine and Covenants section 76. More importantly, this position is a product of the emphasis on the love of God for all as revealed in the life, death, and Resurrection of Jesus Christ. An implicit belief in universal personal salvation through reliance on the love of God as revealed in Jesus Christ enables focus to be shifted from proselytizing based on the fear of eternal judgment to a mission focused on transforming human lives and human society into the peaceable kingdom of God. This shift is clearly evident in the current Community of Christ Statement of Belief on Salvation:

> The gospel is the good news of salvation through Jesus Christ: forgiveness of sin, and healing from separation, brokenness, and the power of violence and death. This healing is for individuals, human societies, and all of creation. This new life is the loving gift of God's grace that becomes ours through faith and repentance. Baptism is how we initially express our commitment to lifelong discipleship. As we yield our lives to Christ in baptism we enter Christian community (the body of Christ) and have the promise of salvation. We experience salvation through Jesus Christ, but affirm that God's grace has no bounds, and God's love is greater than we can know.[15]

Section 163, a recent revelation in Community of Christ Doctrine and Covenants, speaks of "all of the dimensions of salvation" (2a) and then calls for responses indicating that salvation involves personal, social, cultural, political, and ecological dimensions. Community of Christ proclaims a big on-this-earth salvation, far more than just heaven when we die.

RESPONSE TO JOHN TAYLOR

In our conversations about salvation, two things have stood out to me about the differences between The Church of Jesus Christ of Latter-day Saints and Community of Christ. First, in the last fifty years both churches have taken a serious look at their approach toward grace and works; consequently, both have given more emphasis to the importance of the grace of Jesus Christ in the salvation of all people. This is an encouraging point of harmony. Second, in the last few decades the two churches have followed different directions when it comes to the question of life after death. This is a point where the current directions of each faith will continue to diverge.

First, let's address the role of grace. There is no question that the Latter-day Saints have been hesitant, even slow, to reflect on and teach what the Book of Mormon and latter-day revelation say about the grace of God. This is understandable when we remind ourselves that the early Saints viewed the restored gospel and church as major correctives to a Christian world that had gone off course. More especially, since the Restoration occurred in a largely Protestant America, it ought not surprise us that the Saints strongly emphasized the need to perform righteous works to qualify for salvation. Many early church members would have responded to any kind of "easy believism" or the accompanying antinomianism in much the same way the apostle Paul did: "What shall we say then? Shall we continue in sin, that grace may abound? God forbid" (Romans 6:1–2).

Striking the delicate balance between grace and works, between faith and discipleship, is a formidable challenge in today's complex world. It seems to me that the Latter-day Saint way is quite different from monergism: our approach is called *synergism*—God and humanity are working together for the salvation of souls. Is this not what the apostle Paul wrote to the Philippian Saints? "Wherefore, my beloved, as ye have always obeyed, not as in my presence only, but now much more in my absence, work out your own salvation with fear and trembling" (Philippians 2:12). If we stop there, it appears that salvation is something that man himself is to "work out," a process over which we as mortals have the greatest control. But we dare not stop there, for Paul adds, "For it is God which worketh in you both to will and to do of his good pleasure" (Philippians 2:13). Now it sounds like God is the principal, the initiator, the prompter and motivator, the conductor of our soul's symphony.

Second, John mentioned that thinking in Community of Christ has shifted away from personal salvation and afterlife questions to an emphasis on salvation as the present and ongoing transformation of human beings by the love of God. Latter-day Saints feel that the grace of Christ is seen not only in this life and the joy we gain from it right now but also in the next life. All people must confront death, so why ignore that simple fact of life? In a world gripped by cynicism and strangled by hopelessness, the scriptures and revelations of the Restoration bear witness of a God of mercy and vision, of an Omnipotent One whose reach to his children is neither blocked by distance nor dimmed by death. And so, after the doctrinal foundation had been laid, God made known through the Prophet of the Restoration those ennobling truths that pertain to life and salvation, both here and hereafter. As Joseph Smith explained, "It is no more incredible that God should *save* the dead, than that he should *raise* the dead."[16] Surely no work could represent a more noble cause, a more valiant enterprise. And no labor in time could have more eternal implications. The emphasis on the afterlife in our scriptures, ordinances, and temples is a further extension of the grace of Jesus Christ and the central position it occupies in our teachings and our practices.

Response to Robert L. Millet

Reading Brother Millet's "The Process of Salvation" reminded me of Winston Churchill's remark that the United Kingdom and the United States were divided by a common language. We use many of the same terms and refer to some of the same scriptures but appear to mean somewhat different things by them.

Some years ago, my late mother was invited by Latter-day Saint friends to a service featuring a member of their church's First Presidency as a speaker. The service reminded my mother, then in her eighties, of Community of Christ services from her childhood. Perhaps the differences in understanding might not have been so apparent in the 1920s. My response tries to identify the core of the current differences and to explain why they have become more extreme. I believe that one key understanding is both the core and the explanation of the differences.

That key is the change in how Community of Christ has understood and emphasized Christ. The change is usually dated to the opening of the first Community of Christ mission in the Orient in 1960. Community of Christ found that distinctives relevant in a Western cultural and religious context were neither of interest nor meaningful in non-Christian cultures. This led to a de-emphasis on what had been seen as the five basic principles of the gospel and "distinctives." The core of the faith was found to be the proclamation of Christ.[17]

Another 1960s influence was enrollment of Community of Christ paid ministers in the Methodist Saint Paul School of Theology programs. This led to greater awareness among the priesthood and membership of critical approaches to scripture, of the limitations of human understanding of God, and of attempts to record that understanding. Community of Christ had historically been suspicious of the integrity of records of Joseph Smith's sermons at Nauvoo in the 1840s but largely had literally interpreted the Book of Mormon and the revelations in the Doctrine and Covenants up to the Nauvoo editions. The critical approach understood these and other scriptures as having been influenced by the culture of their time and place.[18]

The understanding of Christ that developed is primarily concerned with the historical Jesus. What we, members of Community of Christ, have come to appreciate is Jesus's spirituality, his concern for the poor and oppressed, and his sacrificial love. We have seen in "the crucified God"[19] the suffering and forgiving God. We share with our Latter-day Saint friends a belief in universal or near-universal salvation but draw different implications. This assurance of universal salvation has led us to be less concerned with questions about the afterlife and more concerned with finding our true selves and with disciples' responsibilities to humanity and for nature. We now describe this process as taking "the path of the disciple." We see atonement and sanctification in the lived experience of disciples as a way of life rather than a doctrine.[20] The passionate and just Jesus that Community of Christ sees in current research of New Testament scholars resonates with its historic sense of mission as expressed in gathering and the building of Zion.

The usual explanations are not quite sufficient, though. Other Western churches did not rework their whole approach to mission when they encountered non-Christian cultures. Many sects of equivalent size have neither embraced a critical approach to scripture nor been so concerned with current research into the historical Jesus.

Another explanation may be in the key differences in The Church of Jesus Christ of Latter-day Saints and Community of Christ that arose from their respective origins. Community of Christ emerged from a collection of small branches in the Midwest containing independent thinkers like Jason W. Briggs and Zenas H. Gurley. They needed to live alongside their other Christian neighbors. Local autonomy and independent critical thinking remain characteristics of many Community of Christ congregations. Church leaders are the products of this culture, and the leadership both influences it and is influenced by it. By contrast, a key formative experience for the Latter-day Saints was the pioneer trek and establishment of church headquarters in the Rocky Mountains. This required organization and a unified message expressed in logical propositions that could be understood and adhered to. Utah was remote, and the establishment of Deseret was seen as the literal expression of the kingdom of God on earth. There was less need to interact with and accommodate the beliefs of other Christians.[21]

A belief that we share with our Latter-day Saint friends is that God still speaks, but our processes for sharing new revelations with the membership differ. The ongoing process of canonizing of revelations received by prophet-presidents of Community of Christ has deepened our understanding of revelation and of the nature of Christ and of mission. Both traditions see salvation as a process.

Both the Church of Jesus Christ and Community of Christ genuinely seek to understand and do the will of God as expressed in Christ. We both seek to be followers of what we see as "the way of Jesus

Christ."[22] Our divergent histories necessarily mean that, at present, we express the product of that seeking differently.

CONCLUSION

From our exchange, it is clear that both churches have widely different approaches to the concept of salvation. However, an encouraging development is the increased focus in both churches on the faith that "redemption cometh in and through the Holy Messiah; for he is full of grace and truth" (LDS 2 Nephi 2:6; CofChrist II Nephi 1:71). The amplified emphasis on the grace of Jesus Christ as a transformative factor in our lives in both religions is an overwhelmingly positive development. Members of The Church of Jesus Christ of Latter-day Saints demonstrate this faith in Christ through their ongoing efforts to bring salvation to both the living and the dead, emphasizing a robust theology of the afterlife. Members of Community of Christ focus primarily on the here and now, emphasizing the joy and power of encountering the saving grace of Christ in this life. Both agree that Jesus Christ is central to our salvation. Expressions of how Christ carries out this great work of salvation differ greatly, but at the heart of both our faiths is a loving Savior, ready to offer his grace to us at every moment.

NOTES

1. Joseph Smith, in *Journal of Discourses* (London: Latter-day Saints' Book Depot, 1859), 6:238. See "Account of Meeting and Discourse, 5 January 1841, as Reported by William P. McIntire," The Joseph Smith Papers, https://www .josephsmithpapers.org/paper-summary/account-of-meeting-and-discourse-5 -january-1841-as-reported-by-william-p-mcintire/1; and Joseph Smith, "Discourse, 7 April 1844, as Reported by *Times and Seasons*," The Joseph Smith Papers, https://www.josephsmithpapers.org/paper-summary/discourse-7-april-1844 -as-reported-by-times-and-seasons/1. See also "Accounts of the 'King Follett Sermon,'" The Joseph Smith Papers, https://www.josephsmithpapers.org/site /accounts-of-the-king-follett-sermon.
2. Joseph Smith, *Times and Seasons*, June 1, 1841, 430.
3. See John A. Widtsoe, *Evidences and Reconciliations* (Salt Lake City: Bookcraft, 1960), 198–201.

4. Richard John Neuhaus, *Death on a Friday Afternoon: Meditations on the Last Words of Jesus from the Cross* (New York: Basic Books, 2000), 57, 61.

5. *Teachings of Presidents of the Church: Joseph Smith* (Salt Lake City: The Church of Jesus Christ of Latter-day Saints, 2007), 268.

6. *Lectures on Faith* (Salt Lake City: Deseret Book, 1985), 61.

7. At the time, Community of Christ was organized into fields, each supervised by an apostle. Each field could contain several missions, each presided over by a mission president. Australia was one mission. Within the mission were several districts, each presided over by a district president. Within each district were several branches, each presided over by a branch president. The mission president was usually a full-time church employee. District presidents were often full-time church employees. Australia and French Polynesia, at that time, were the largest Community of Christ missions outside North America.

8. The office of evangelist dates to Community of Christ Doctrine and Covenants 104:17 and Latter-day Saint Doctrine and Covenants 107 in 1835. Joseph Smith Sr. was the first person ordained to this office, and following his ordination he blessed his sons Joseph and Hyrum. Following the death of Joseph Smith Sr., Hyrum Smith was designated as patriarch to the church in Latter-day Saint Doctrine and Covenants 124 (formerly Community of Christ Doctrine and Covenants 107). The office was continued and expanded in Community of Christ with explanation of the role and function of the office being provided in Community of Christ Doctrine and Covenants 125:3–6 in 1901 and sub-sequent sections. The functions specified in section 125 included "lay[ing] on hands for the conferment of spiritual blessing." These blessings were referred to as patriarchal blessings. Following the ordination of women in 1984, the terminology for the office was changed from "patriarch-evangelist" to "evangelist," and the term for the blessing was changed to "evangelist blessing." Alexander H. Smith was one of Joseph Smith Jr.'s sons and, at the time, was presiding patriarch of the church.

9. My grandmother would have been familiar with both the King James Version of the Bible and with the Joseph Smith Revision published at that time under the title "Holy Scriptures." The King James Version references are James 2:17 and 2:20. The references to the equivalent passages in the Joseph Smith Revision are James 2:17 and 2:18. James 2:18 in the Joseph Smith Revision is the equivalent to James 2:20 in the King James Version but, importantly in the context of the issue discussed here, reads, "Faith without works is dead *and cannot save you.*" The words in italics are an addition in the Joseph Smith Revision.

10. The reference in the King James Version is James 2:18; the reference in the Joseph Smith Revision is James 2:15. It is likely that in conversation, and in writing, my grandmother, like the Joseph Smith Revision, would have modern-ized the "shew" of the King James Version to "show."

11. *Exploring the Faith: A Series of Studies in the Faith of the Church Prepared by a Committee on Basic Beliefs* (Independence, MO: Herald Publishing House, 1970), 11, 104.

12. Robert Flanders made this observation in his article "Dream and Nightmare: Nauvoo Revisited," in *The Restoration Movement: Essays in Mormon History*, ed. F. Mark McKiernan, Alma R. Blair, and Paul M. Edwards (Lawrence, KS: Coronado Press, 1973), 141–66. See also CofChrist Doctrine and Covenants 36:12c–14c; LDS Moses 7; and CofChrist Genesis 7:67–75, Joseph Smith Revision. I thank Matt Frizzell for drawing the Doctrine and Covenants, Pearl of Great Price, and Joseph Smith Revision references to my attention.

13. Richard L. Bushman makes this argument in *Joseph Smith: Rough Stone Rolling* (New York: Vintage Books, 2007), 195–214.

14. The vision and the revelation concerning the presence of Alvin Smith in the celestial kingdom are recorded in Joseph Smith, "Journal, 1835–1836," p. 134, The Joseph Smith Papers, https://www.josephsmithpapers.org/paper-summary/journal-1835-1836/135#full-transcript. See also Joseph Smith III and Heman C. Smith, *The History of the Reorganized Church of Jesus Christ of Latter Day Saints* (Lamoni, IA: Herald Publishing House, 1897), 2:16; and B. H. Roberts, ed., *History of the Church of Jesus Christ of Latter-day Saints*, 2nd rev. ed. (Salt Lake City: Deseret Book, 1978), 2:380.

15. "Basic Beliefs," Community of Christ, https://www.CofChrist.org/basic-beliefs.

16. "Minutes and Discourse, 1–5 October 1841," p. 577, The Joseph Smith Papers, https://www.josephsmithpapers.org/paper-summary/minutes-and-discourse-1-5october-1841/2; emphasis in the original.

17. This standard explanation is arguably oversimplified. President Frederick Madison Smith was said to be "big on the Christ," and earlier church leaders such as F. Henry Edwards and Arthur Oakman were significantly influenced by William Temple and other Protestant theologians.

18. Again, the standard explanation is probably oversimplified. As early as the 1870s, Apostle Jason W. Briggs (who had been president pro tem of Community of Christ from 1852 to 1860) published articles reflecting a critical understanding of scripture.

19. Jürgen Moltmann, *The Crucified God* (London: SCM Press, 1974). The phrase comes from the title of the book.

20. Apologies to the late C. H. Dodd. I have a clear memory of reading in one of his writings, "Atonement was a way of life before it became a doctrine." I have been unable to locate the precise reference, which may mean that I will have to read some of his books again.

21. See the persuasive analysis to this effect in Douglas D. Alder and Paul M. Edwards, "Common Beginnings, Divergent Beliefs," *Dialogue* 6, no. 1 (Spring 1978): 18, 25–26.

22. Jürgen Moltmann, *The Way of Jesus Christ* (London: SCM Press, 1990; Minneapolis, MN: Fortress Press, 1993). The phrase comes from the title of the book.

ORDINANCES AND SACRAMENTS

Eva M. Erickson and Casey Paul Griffiths

SACRAMENTS IN COMMUNITY OF CHRIST

EVA M. ERICKSON

Eva M. Erickson has served as the national coordinator for Community of Christ in Germany since 2013 and enjoys exploring the faith and culture of other communities.

"The God who acts and the Christ who is present in the sacraments sustains the church and its members so that they in turn can reach out to others."[1]

A s a minister, I think that some of the most exciting and sacred moments can happen while administering a sacrament (or ordinance, a term perhaps better known to some readers). My favorite sacramental experience is probably the baptism of a young man a few years ago. We were at our church campground in Germany, and the campground did not have a baptismal font. Because of that, we used a local outdoor pool for the baptisms that day. It was pouring rain! But that did not deter the candidate. Baptisms often are somber, reflective moments, but after the young man came back up from the waters, he jumped and shouted with joy! What an experience that was, not just for me as the minister but for all in attendance, to see how this young man had been touched by the presence of God's Spirit and by the story of Jesus as witnessed through this baptism.

Sacraments have been an integral part of church life in Community of Christ from the very beginning. Initially the term *ordinance* was used alongside the term *sacrament.* It is not clear exactly when or why Community of Christ moved away from using the term *ordinance.* In 1962 the authors Charles E. Brockway and Alfred H. Yale separated and defined the two terms in their book *Ordinances and Sacraments of the Church.*[2] Other publications used both terms, most often referring to marriage and the Lord's Supper as sacraments and other ministries as ordinances.[3] In 1978, however, Peter Judd published the book *The Sacraments* and exclusively used the term "sacraments," probably because of the increasing focus on God's grace in Community of Christ theology. Today, Community of Christ uses only the term "sacraments" in all written and verbal communications.

Community of Christ defines sacraments as "special ministries given to the church to convey the grace of Jesus Christ to his followers and all those he yearns to touch with his compassion."[4] When celebrating sacraments, we use common items in symbolic ways. That means tangible elements like water, bread, and our hands are used to convey sacred actions and meaning. We also use words (for instance, the words for a baptism or a blessing) and perform specific, defined actions.[5]

The eight sacraments celebrated by the church are baptism, confirmation, the Lord's Supper (or Communion), marriage, blessing of children, laying on of hands for the sick, ordination to the priesthood, and the evangelist blessing (formerly known as the patriarchal blessing, but after the ordination of women to the priesthood, that term no longer seemed appropriate). All eight sacraments can be traced back to scripture references from the Bible, mostly the New Testament. This is a very important point for Community of Christ. Though we no longer claim to have reestablished the organizational pattern of the New Testament church, we do try to live according to our understanding of the gospel and of missional and sacramental activities as seen in the New Testament.

All sacraments except for the evangelist blessing and the laying on of hands for the sick are practiced primarily in the community, either in congregational settings or at campgrounds, sometimes on beaches or in private homes, or, as in the case I described above, in public pools rented for the occasion. Sacraments in Community of Christ are communal experiences, which ensure both the support of the community (for a newly blessed child, for instance, or for a baptismal candidate) and the common experience of a sacred act. This allows all participants to reconnect with God and their own faith journey. On the other hand, sacraments reach far wider than just the one worshipful experience as the church practices the idea of "sacramental living" in our daily lives. We see sacraments in connection with continuing revelation on a personal basis. Sacraments allow us to have fairly frequent experiences with God and help us shape our testimony of God's grace and mercy. Suzanne McLaughlin says, "Does not our participation in the sacraments open us up to new understandings, open us to new experiences of the Divine, of God's relationship with us, and our relationship with God and each other?"[6]

In the past half century, Community of Christ has developed from a very exclusive church ("We are the one true church" was a common statement up to the 1970s or so) to a very inclusive church, affirming the worth of all persons more thoroughly through its theology and Enduring Principles.[7] This changed self-image can also be seen in a transformation of some of the sacraments. In the 1980s, Community of Christ felt called to ordain not just men but also women to the priesthood and has gained valuable ministry because of this change. Vital to this new understanding was Doctrine and Covenants section 156, received in 1984, which gave guidance to the church on the calling of women to priesthood.[8]

Another sacrament that underwent changes is Communion (or the Lord's Supper). The 1994 World Conference asked the First Presidency to develop new guidelines for the administration of Communion. Whereas it used to be a sacrament open only to members of Community of Christ, it now can be served to "all who believe in Christ, which usually is expressed in water baptism, whether members of Community of Christ or not."[9] Only ten years later, and in accordance with World Conference Resolution 1282,[10] the wording of the Communion prayers was expanded, giving ministers the option to use either the traditional wording or a more modern and gender-neutral version of the prayers, as well as a version in which bread and wine (really grape juice since 1913) were blessed within the same prayer. In alignment with several of Community of Christ's Enduring Principles and by action of national or field conferences, the sacrament of marriage can now be offered in many nations to people of a same-sex orientation, allowing the blessing of the sacred vow to be present in marriage relationships that were not possible until a short time ago. Additionally, in many places members of the LGBTQ+ community living in committed marriage relationships can now be called to the priesthood.

Some might say that Community of Christ takes it upon itself to change ancient sacraments to fit a modern world. That may be so in some ways. The church, however, describes the sacraments as having some universals and some particulars in their procedures and executions. A universal can be described as "the broad principle that is being brought to life by the sacrament, and the particulars are the rituals or practices that enact this broad principle."[11] In developing the sacraments to meet the needs of today's world and especially to be inclusive and value the worth of all persons, some particulars of some sacraments have been changed. The universals, the original sense and meaning of a given sacrament, have remained the same.

Similarly, Community of Christ recently gave guidelines on administrating most of the sacraments in online settings.[12] The need arose out of the growing number of online groups with members who lived far away from each other yet met regularly for worship and fellowship. They are not able to celebrate such sacraments as the Lord's Supper or ordinations in person, but they now can do so online. Again, particulars to the sacraments were adjusted, but the universals remain.

As much as I enjoy fellowship and worship on a regular basis, as much as I grow in my relationship with God through church life, sacraments are probably where I can experience God's Spirit most vividly. Be it in an online setting, at a baptism during family camp, or maybe during a much more private sacrament of laying on of hands for healing, the sacraments are a very important part of church life as well as communal and personal sacramental living. As such, they enrich our common life as disciples and ministers in Christ.

ORDINANCES IN THE CHURCH OF JESUS CHRIST OF LATTER-DAY SAINTS

CASEY PAUL GRIFFITHS

Casey Paul Griffiths is an associate teaching professor of church history and doctrine at Brigham Young University in Provo, Utah.

A revelation given in September 1832 to Joseph Smith declares that "in the ordinances thereof the power of Godliness is manifest and without the ordinances thereof, and the authority of the Priesthood, the power of Godliness is not manifest."[13] Ordinances, usually called "sacraments" by our friends in Community of Christ, are central to our connection with each other as church members and essential in forming our relationship with God and seeing his grace made manifest in our lives. From the first time a baby receives a name to the time a person's final resting place is dedicated, ordinances are one of the most important blessings that members of The Church of Jesus Christ of Latter-day Saints receive as part of their discipleship. Ordinances provide church members with opportunities to serve and bless one another and are one of the primary ways members seek to worship and emulate the Savior. When members engage in these ordinances, they are following Christ's acts and are thus "put[ting] on Christ" (Galatians 3:27).

Latter-day Saints generally divide the ordinances of the church into two categories. First, ordinances of salvation and exaltation, wherein members make sacred covenants with God that facilitate deliverance from sin and death during and after this life. Other ordinances offered by the church are not essential for salvation but offer ways to receive renewal, comfort, guidance, and healing.[14] Ordinances of salvation and exaltation are generally available only to church members, beginning with baptism and confirmation, which signal entrance into the church. The other ordinances are offered to all people who ask for them. It is not uncommon for a priesthood holder in the church to use his authority to provide a blessing of healing or comfort to a person of another faith. Ordinances of salvation and exaltation are offered to any person who qualifies through righteous living and commitment to live the commandments. There is no worthiness condition or gospel commitment required for a person to receive the ordinances that offer comfort, guidance, or healing.

Latter-day Saints and members of Community of Christ share several of the ordinances of salvation and exaltation, such as baptism, confirmation, and the gift of the Holy Ghost. Other ordinances of salvation reflect the doctrinal and historical divergences of both traditions. Ordinances such as the temple endowment, eternal marriage, and the sealings of families find their origins in the later teachings of Joseph Smith. These ceremonies were further developed by such leaders as Brigham Young, John Taylor, and Wilford Woodruff after the church relocated its headquarters to the Intermountain West. During this period, we began to develop separately from the members who would eventually form Community of Christ. Ordinances performed in temples represent one of the most significant differences in worship between the members of the two churches.

We honor the elegant temple that was built in Independence, Missouri, by Community of Christ and was dedicated as a monument to peace. We are deeply grateful for the love and care the members and leadership of Community of Christ have shown to the house of the Lord built by the Saints in Kirtland, Ohio. But temples built by The Church of Jesus Christ of Latter-day Saints serve a profoundly different role in our faith than the Independence and Kirtland temples do for members of Community of Christ. Temples, large and small, have been built throughout the world in diverse locations. One of our most important proclamations declares that "sacred ordinances and covenants available in holy temples make it possible for individuals to return to the presence of God and for families to be united eternally."[15]

In our dialogue with our sisters and brothers in Community of Christ, the largest gaps between our worldviews and cosmologies generally stem from misunderstandings over the nature of temple ordinances. This is due in part to the sacredness of these ordinances and some of the hesitancy that members of our church feel in discussing these ceremonies outside the hallowed walls of the temple itself. Over time, the church has led members to be more open about the ordinances of the temple, offering open houses before temples are dedicated that anyone can attend and producing videos explaining the clothing and ordinances of the temple.[16] But a large gulf in understanding these ordinances still remains between members of the two faiths.

In temples, men and women participate in and administer ordinances that provide instructions and allow them to make covenants that bring them closer to God. These ordinances culminate in promises given "to their exaltation and glory in all things, as hath been sealed upon their heads, which glory shall be a fulness and a continuation" (LDS Doctrine and Covenants 132:19). While members can receive ordinances such as baptism and confirmation as early as when they are eight years old, temple ordinances are reserved for church members when they are older. In many ways, the ceremonies of the temple represent the entrance into adulthood for church members. Temple ordinances can be broken down into several basic ceremonies: first, the initiatory ceremony; second, the endowment ceremony; and finally, the temple sealing. Within temples, Latter-day Saints also perform baptisms, confirmations, and all the ordinances of salvation and exaltation on behalf of the deceased. Because much of the confusion between our two faiths results in a lack of understanding about these ordinances, a moment to explain each is useful.

First, the initiatory ordinance consists of symbolic washings and anointings pronouncing blessings upon the receiver. These anointings are similar to those shared in the Old Testament when God directed that "Aaron and his sons thou shalt bring unto the door of the tabernacle of the congregation, and shalt wash them with water. . . . Then shalt thou take the anointing oil, and pour it upon his head, and anoint him" (Exodus 29:4, 7). These washings and anointings, once offered only to the sons of Aaron, are offered in temples to all worthy men and women. Women perform this ordinance for other women, while men perform this ordinance for other men. As part of this ceremony, men and women are given a sacred temple garment that they wear under their clothes inside and outside the temple. These garments perform a function similar to cassocks worn by Catholic priests, yarmulkes worn by some members of the Jewish faith, or headscarves worn by Muslim women.

Though technically the initiatory ceremonies are part of the endowment ordinance, they are treated separately. After a person has experienced the washings and anointings of the initiatory ordinance, he or she experiences the next ceremony, commonly called the endowment. The word *endowment* means "a gift," and Latter-day Saints believe they are given several gifts from God through this ordinance. The endowment provides its recipients with greater knowledge of God's purposes and teachings, increased power to carry out God's will, comfort and peace, and promised blessings in this life and in the eternities.[17] Many Latter-day Saints count their participation in the endowment as one of the most sacred experiences of their lives.

Temple sealings are often associated with eternal marriage. Many couples in the Church of Jesus Christ are married "for time and eternity," while others who previously entered civil marriages come to the temple to have their marriages solemnized for eternity. The phrase "till death do us part" is not uttered in temple sealings, because Latter-day Saints believe that their family relationships will last beyond this life. This includes not only marriage relationships but the relationships of parents and children. One of the most moving ceremonies I have witnessed in the temple happened when I saw a couple who had received an earlier civil marriage come to the temple to have an eternal sealing performed. After that ceremony, the door to the room was opened and their two-year-old son ambled into the room. All three were then sealed together as a family for eternity.

While members of other faiths often express concern over the mystery and exclusivity surrounding temple ordinances, Latter-day Saints see these ceremonies as sacred rather than mysterious and as inclusive rather than exclusive. All ordinances of salvation and exaltation can be performed on behalf of the living or by proxy for the dead. We believe that all people will have the opportunity to embrace or reject these covenants of their own volition in this life or the next. One of the presidents of our church, Joseph F. Smith (a cousin of the venerable Joseph Smith III, who was a president of Community of Christ), saw in a 1918 vision that people after this life are "taught faith in God, repentance from sin, *vicarious* baptism for the remission of sins, the gift of the Holy Ghost by the laying on of hands, and all other principles of the gospel" (LDS Doctrine and Covenants 138:33–34; emphasis added).

While I have confined most of my discussion to temple ordinances, a very meaningful part of my experiences has also come from ordinances that are not linked with salvation or exaltation. As the New Testament directs, "Is there any sick among you? let him call for the elders of the church; and let them pray over him, anointing him with oil in the name of the Lord" (James 5:14). On one occasion, I was given an opportunity to participate in this sacred ordinance. My next-door neighbors, a young couple in their twenties, asked me to come to their home to assist in giving a blessing of healing. Their first child was born only a few days before, and she was experiencing a mild case of jaundice. The mother held her baby while the young father and I carried out the blessing. I performed the first part of the ordinance by anointing the infant, placing a small drop of pure olive oil on her head. Then the father, his hands trembling and his voice nervously shaking, gently laid his hands on the baby's head and pronounced a blessing. His voice became more calm as a spirit of peace pervaded the room. All of us joined in a sincere "amen" when the blessing was finished. Afterward we visited with one another for a time, and they shared the details of the birth while I shared stories about my own family and children.

It is perhaps in settings like these that the "power of godliness" is most evident in the ordinances of our faith. It can be felt in magisterial settings such as the temple or in simple settings within the home. In each place I have witnessed the influence of God "moving in his majesty and power" (LDS Doctrine and Covenants 88:47; CofChrist Doctrine and Covenants 85:12c). While I am profoundly grateful for the covenants that bring salvation, I am also thankful for the little moments of grace found in the ordinances of the gospel of Jesus Christ.

RESPONSE TO CASEY PAUL GRIFFITHS

Casey, I would like to start out by saying that I deeply appreciate this form of exchange. I find it fascinating to learn about the different understandings and interpretations of my sisters and brothers in the Restoration movement and how they arrived at their views. In reading your essay, it became immediately clear to me that the two churches base their interpretations on different sources and faith foundations. We differ in our understanding of the purpose of sacraments, the place where sacraments are to be served, and who may offer sacraments and who may receive them. But there also are similarities, which I find very reassuring.

From reading the description of the ordinances celebrated in The Church of Jesus Christ of Latter-day Saints, it appears that much of the basis of today's ceremonies and sacraments stems from Joseph Smith Jr., particularly in his later years, as well as from his successors in the church. On the other hand, Community of Christ appears to rarely reference the church's beginnings, relying much more on references to the New Testament. Interesting as well is the development of the ordinances and sacraments. Casey, you describe some of the ordinances that were further developed by church leaders like Brigham Young and Joseph F. Smith. These leaders were prophets in the 1800s, making it seem that the ordinances and sacraments have not changed significantly in more than a century. As described in my chapter, however, Community of Christ has authorized some changes and developed some sacraments in more recent years to meet the needs of today's recipients and participants.

A large section of your essay describes ordinances performed in temples. I did not mention temples in my chapter, because there is no sacrament in Community of Christ that can be performed only in a temple, thus making temples not relevant to my essay. Also, temples are described and explained in detail in another chapter of this book. But it is apparent that the two churches place a different emphasis on the location where a sacrament can or should be performed. In Community of Christ, it does not matter where the sacrament is performed as long as the setting allows the participants to enter a worshipful atmosphere and be open for God's Spirit to interact with them through the sacrament. In the Church of Jesus Christ, on the other hand, several of the ordinances can be performed only at a set location (that is, a temple).

Together with the difference in requirements for the location where ordinances/sacraments are performed also comes a different understanding of who can perform and receive them. Whereas in Community of Christ ordained men and women can perform sacraments with equal rights, in the Church of Jesus Christ, women can perform ritualistic washings only on one another in the temple. Otherwise, it is only men who can perform ordinances. In Community of Christ, anybody can receive a sacrament, be it a church member or not, a prisoner or a bank employee, a member who regularly pays tithing or an immigrant worker who has no penny to spare for tithing. The only exception is the sacrament of ordination, which requires the candidate to be a church member in good standing. The requirement of who can perform or receive ordinances is one of the differences that I find hardest to understand. I wonder who has the right to determine if I am worthy of ordinances of salvation and exaltation. In the Community of Christ mindset of the "Worth of All Persons" (one of the church's Enduring Principles),[18] it would be hard to determine whether a person is "worthy" to receive a sacrament (or ordinance). Having said that, I do believe that Community of Christ has come to its current attitude over time. In the past, more emphasis was placed on the "worthiness" of a person when receiving sacraments. And even now, worthiness might be more of an issue in some parts of the world than in others.

Another major difference is that Community of Christ does not perform or allow any ceremonies on behalf of the dead. Initially, the Reorganization under Joseph Smith III took a passive stand. The early Community of Christ did not deny that the doctrine was taught and practiced under Joseph Smith Jr., but officially they did not adopt this practice for themselves. Eventually the doctrine was rejected, and in the 1960s the sections of the Doctrine and Covenants pertaining to this issue were removed.[19] I would question, "Who is to say that my deceased relatives actually want to have these ceremonies performed for them?" I wonder why such decisions are made pertaining to faith issues for people who are deceased and unable to let us know their preferences. Having said that, I also do not believe that only the faith, traditions, and sacraments of a specific church are able to make me a true believer and grant me salvation. I chose Community of Christ as the church where I want to live out my faith, but in my eyes, this is by no means the only church, nor do I believe that any church is actually necessary for my salvation.

In summary, I find it fascinating to read about the ordinances in The Church of Jesus Christ of Latter-day Saints. I do not understand all the reasoning, and I could not believe all the teachings, but everybody has a right to his or her own faith. By trying to learn about the faith of others, I can ponder my own beliefs and strengthen my faith. Thank you, Casey, for going on this journey of faith with me and helping me understand some aspects of your church better!

Response to Eva M. Erickson

Eva, I wasn't surprised to find that both of us were able to immediately call to mind experiences in which we had witnessed a sacred ordinance or sacrament. It seems that in both of our faiths, the ordinances and sacraments are one of the most vital ways to create experiences that allow all of us to feel close to God and see the divine presence in our lives. Religion is never more joyful than when we feel the grace of Jesus Christ in our experience, and these sacred ceremonies excel at creating moments when we can all connect over something larger than ourselves.

There is so much to admire about these ceremonies in both of our faiths, and I have no doubt that God is pleased whenever anyone in any faith tradition sincerely reaches out for divine power.

At the same time, since this is a comparison between the two faiths and the way we do things, let's compare! I offer first a few questions and then some holy envy for what I see among my friends in Community of Christ. My first question: Community of Christ has a wonderful tradition of focusing on connection to God in the here and now, but what about the hereafter? The ordinances Eva described allow a person to connect with God, but are they linked to an individual's eternal salvation? What is the difference after this life if a person never receives these sacraments or makes covenants with God? Jesus taught, "He that believeth and is baptized shall be saved; but he that believeth not shall be damned" (Mark 16:16; LDS Ether 4:18; see also CofChrist Ether 1:115; LDS Doctrine and Covenants 68:9; CofChrist Doctrine and Covenants 68:1g). While I admire the focus on this life, what effect do ordinances have in the next life? In our faith tradition, ordinances are divided into those necessary for salvation (meaning after this life) and those that bless us in this life. Do ordinances and sacraments in Community of Christ affect someone only in this life, or do they also impact the life a person experiences after death?

It is clear that many of our differences center on two concepts. First, as Eva mentioned, Community of Christ does not claim to be "the only true and living Church upon the face of the whole earth" (LDS Doctrine and Covenants 1:30; CofChrist Doctrine and Covenants 1:5e). We believe that for ordinances to be efficacious, they must be performed by the proper priesthood authority. Second, in The Church of Jesus Christ of Latter-day Saints there is an extensive theology of the afterlife, including proxy ordinances for the deceased.

It is strange that we spring from the same source, since there is such a striking difference in the way we see the impact of how ordinances and sacraments affect an individual's eternal salvation. Please do not interpret these inquiries as hostile. I am genuinely curious to know how members of your faith see the next life and its relationship to the covenants we make here. In our faith, the ordinances play a major role both in our mortal experience here on earth and in our experience in the eternities. It is so vital to us that in our temples we devote a considerable amount of our time and resources to ensure that every person, living or dead, has a chance to engage in them. Is there a common ground where the two faiths can meet on this point?

Now that I have raised my questions, let me express some holy envy. There is so much to admire about the way the members of Community of Christ work to make these sacred ordinances available to all of the church's membership. One of the most meaningful experiences I have had with Community of Christ was in a meeting when church leaders discussed whether ordinances could be administered over distance using technology. In all my dealings with Community of Christ, there is a wonderful spirit of inclusiveness. When it comes to your ordinances and sacraments, the leadership and members genuinely do all in their power to make sure that all people, no matter where they are from or what their backgrounds are, have a chance to receive of the grace of Christ through these sacred ordinances and sacraments.

In all my dealings with members of Community of Christ, I have witnessed a wonderful openness and have always felt welcome to join in experiencing the divine. In all religions there is a tension between being a chosen people and "a peculiar people" (Deuteronomy 14:2), set aside from the rest of the world, and in "creating sacred community" (CofChrist Doctrine and Covenants 161:3c). In ordinances the "community" in Community of Christ is most evident. I feel genuine holy envy for the openness the members show toward these sacred ceremonies that connect them to God. I have felt that connection alongside my sisters and brothers in Community of Christ.

CONCLUSION

Very few discussions result in absolute agreement, but discussions that promote respect, understanding, and harmony are always welcome. They give us insights and help our own faith to grow. There is no doubt that the beliefs of members of Community of Christ and The Church of Jesus Christ of Latter-day Saints toward ordinances and sacraments have widely different approaches to the questions of priesthood author-ity, the role of the church and the individual, and the question of sal-vation in the next life. But we can both agree wholeheartedly about the importance of ordinances and sacraments in the spiritual lives of individuals. Many of the moments when we feel closest to God come when we participate in these sacred acts. The beauty of ceremonies such as baptisms, marriages, and blessings helps members of both churches make the hand of God a reality in their lives and experience the grace of Jesus Christ. So, while our teachings and practices have developed and been followed in widely different ways, we can both agree that "in the ordinances thereof, the power of godliness is manifest" (LDS Doctrine and Covenants 84:20; CofChrist Doctrine and Covenants 83:3c).

Notes

1. Peter A. Judd, *The Sacraments: An Exploration into Their Meaning and Practice in the Saints Church* (Independence, MO: Herald Publishing House, 1978), 22.

2. See Charles E. Brockway and Alfred H. Yale, *Ordinances and Sacraments of the Church* (Independence, MO: Herald Publishing House, 1962), 9, 14. In this book, ordinances are defined as "a decree or commandment of God" and are seen as one of the elements of each sacrament.

3. See F. Henry Edwards, *Fundamentals: Enduring Convictions of the Restoration* (Independence, MO: Herald Publishing House, 1936); and Alan D. Tyree, ed., *Exploring the Faith* (Independence, MO: Herald Publishing House, 1987).

4. Community of Christ, *Sharing in Community of Christ: Exploring Identity, Mission, Message, and Beliefs*, 4th ed. (Independence, MO: Herald Publishing House, 2018), 37.

5. See Andrew Bolton and Jane Gardner, eds., *The Sacraments: Symbol, Meaning and Discipleship* (Independence, MO: Herald Publishing House, 2005), 24.

6. Suzanne McLaughlin, "The Sacraments: Funding Our Image," in *Theology*, ed. Donald J. Breckon and William T. Higdon, vol. 2, *Authority, Membership, and Baptism* (Independence, MO: Graceland/Park Press, 1994), 47.

7. See "Enduring Principles," Community of Christ, https://www.CofChrist.org/enduring-principles. Community of Christ describes the Enduring Principles as follows: "Our Enduring Principles define the essence, heart, and soul of our faith community. They describe the personality of our church as expressed throughout the world."

8. CofChrist Doctrine and Covenants 156:9c says, "Therefore, do not wonder that some women of the church are being called to priesthood responsibilities. This is in harmony with my will and where these calls are made known to my

servants, they may be processed according to administrative procedures and provisions of the law."

9. Community of Christ, *Sharing in Community of Christ*, 46.

10. World Conference Resolution (WCR) 1282 was adopted in April 2004.

11. Bolton and Gardner, *Sacraments*, 40.

12. See "Sharing the Sacraments of Community of Christ When In-Person Contact Is Not Possible," October 7, 2020, https://www.CofChrist.org/Common /Cms/Sharing-Sacraments-110220.pdf.

13. "Revelation, 22–23 September 1832 [Doctrine and Covenants 84]," p. 1, The Joseph Smith Papers, https://www.josephsmithpapers.org/paper-summary /revelation-22-23-september-1832-dc-84/1; see also LDS Doctrine and Covenants 84:20–21; CofChrist Doctrine and Covenants 83:3c.

14. See *General Handbook: Serving in The Church of Jesus Christ of Latter-day Saints*, 18.1–18.2, ChurchofJesusChrist.org.

15. "The Family: A Proclamation to the World," ChurchofJesusChrist.org.

16. See the church's videos "Temples through Time," 5:58, https://youtu.be /Y6a1OhpWeZA; "Two Apostles Lead a Virtual Tour of the Rome Italy Temple," 11:31, https://youtu.be/dhWgPwEQQ98; and "What Are Temple Garments?," 1:10, https://youtu.be/5vvN4qJRBMO.

17. See "About the Temple Endowment," https://www.ChurchofJesusChrist.org /study/manual/about-the-temple-endowment/about-about-the-temple -endowment.

18. See "Enduring Principles."

19. For further reading about baptism for the dead in Community of Christ, see the author's unpublished seminary paper titled "Baptism for the Dead." The paper can be requested by emailing emerickson@cofchrist.eu.

PROPHETS AND POLITY

Taunalyn Ford and Matthew J. Frizzell

PROPHETS AND POLITY IN THE CHURCH OF JESUS CHRIST OF LATTER-DAY SAINTS

TAUNALYN FORD

Taunalyn Ford received her PhD from Claremont Graduate University. She is currently a postdoctoral research fellow at the BYU Neal A. Maxwell Institute for Religious Scholarship.

The congregation stood on March 22, 1980, as President Spencer W. Kimball entered the Salt Lake Tabernacle with his wife, Camilla, for a special Young Women fireside. I was a member of the choir that evening, and according to my journal, watching the prophet enter "brought tears to my eyes and to most everyone else's." After the meeting, I was able to walk down from the choir seats and shake the hand of President Kimball. I wrote in my journal, "I've never felt the spirit that strong. I was shaking all over and I couldn't stop. I knew he was a prophet of God."[1] This young teenage recollection of meeting the prophet reflects the high esteem that members of The Church of Jesus Christ of Latter-day Saints hold for those they sustain as "prophets, seers, and revelators." Dialogue with Community of Christ colleagues has opened my mind to how the dynamic of prophets and polity for both "mountain" and "prairie" Saints has evolved over time.

This essay will briefly chart the origins and evolution of a few themes from a metaphorical prophet-polity DNA that I believe we share with our Restoration cousins. While not exhaustive, the themes I will address include the paradox in the relationship of prophets and polity; the concepts of conferences, councils, and common consent; the role of priesthood; and finally, prophets and polity in globalization.

PROPHET-POLITY PARADOX

Restoration scholars have identified a paradox in the history and structure of the Latter Day Saint movement, describing it as "both democratic and authoritarian."[2] The paradox boils down to the "polarity of authoritarianism and individualism."[3] Joseph and early Latter Day Saints struggled with the contradictory nature of an organization that centered on a prophet who spoke authoritatively as a mouthpiece for God to the church and the world while also relying on the freedom and even responsibility of members to receive their own personal revelation.

At the organization of the church in 1830, Joseph Smith "was seen as one prophet among potentially many."[4] Competing claims of prophetic authority were addressed in September of 1830 when Joseph received a revelation that has become central to the polity of the Church of Jesus Christ.[5] An 1831 revelation declared that "no one shall be appointed to receive commandments and revelations in this church excepting my servant Joseph Smith, Jun., for he receiveth them even as Moses." Oliver Cowdery, to whom the revelation was addressed, was compared to Aaron and called to "speak or teach by the way of commandment unto the church," but he was not to "write by way of commandment" (LDS Doctrine and Covenants 28:2, 4–6; see also CofChrist Doctrine and Covenants 27:2a, c–d). A subsequent revelation to several elders promised, "If thou shalt ask, thou shalt receive revelation upon revelation, knowledge upon knowledge," with no limitations but the precondition of asking (LDS Doctrine and Covenants 42:61; CofChrist Doctrine and Covenants 42:17a). This "inexplicable contradiction" was the conundrum "at the heart of Joseph Smith's Mormonism." Joseph Smith was "designated as the Lord's prophet, and yet every man was to voice scripture, everyone to see God."[6]

Although biographers often emphasize his authoritarian style of leadership, Brigham Young also worked under this paradoxical balance of power.[7] According to John Turner, Brigham Young "often stressed that he wanted church members to receive revelations for themselves, but such divine promptings would confirm, not contradict or question, his doctrine and direction."[8] Like Turner, observers may sometimes view the balance in the prophet-polity paradox from Brigham Young forward to the current president of the church as leaning in favor of "conformity and obedience" to prophetic authority, and there is some truth in that. I suggest, however, that while prophetic authority has been privileged and cherished among mountain Saints, and even regrettably sometimes at the expense of a "hospitable environment for those members more inclined to question,"[9] we should nuance the idea that all Latter-day Saints have surrendered their right to question and seek their own revelation.

President Dallin H. Oaks has articulated an interdependency between prophets and polity in the church today: "Our Heavenly Father has given His children two lines of communication with Him—what we may call the personal line and the priesthood line."[10] President Oaks compared the personal line to the Protestant emphasis on "the priesthood of all believers," and the priesthood line to Catholic or Orthodox insistence "that authoritative ordinances (sacraments) are essential and must be performed by one authorized and empowered by Jesus Christ."[11] Oaks emphasizes balance as he cautions against relying too much on individualism that can erase the importance of divine authority or relying too much on priesthood authority at the expense of personal growth. In his first general conference address as prophet, President Russell M. Nelson admonished, "I urge you to stretch beyond your current spiritual ability to receive personal revelation."[12]

CONFERENCES, COUNCILS, AND COMMON CONSENT

Conferences, councils, and common consent are foundational in the prophet-polity paradox. Community of Christ and The Church of Jesus Christ of Latter-day Saints share this organizational DNA from what was initially a "Methodist pattern of quarterly conferences of elders."[13] Joseph Smith built on this pattern of holding quarterly general church conferences, but he also organized ad hoc conferences or councils (initially synonymous terms) when needed. Although Joseph sometimes received revelations during the conferences of the early church,[14] conferences were originally more administrative.

Church polity under Joseph Smith has been compared to "an archeological site, containing layers of organizational forms, each layer created for a purpose at one time and then overlaid by other forms established for other purposes later."[15] A division in the DNA distinguishing conferences and councils is an example of one of these geological layers. The minutes from the organization of the first high council in 1834 were canonized and elevated to the level of other revelations. The pattern continued when the Council of the Twelve was organized in 1835.[16] According to Richard Bushman, "At a moment when Joseph's own revelatory powers were at their peak, he divested himself of sole responsibility for revealing the will of God and invested that gift in the councils of the Church, making it a charismatic bureaucracy."[17]

Brigham Young led the Utah church as president of the Quorum of the Twelve until the First Presidency was organized in December of 1847.[18] Since that time the church has continued to be led by "prophets, seers, and revelators" who fill the councils of the First Presidency and Quorum of the Twelve. These general church councils are supported by the councils of Seventy and councils at the stake and ward levels. President Stephen L. Richards proclaimed, "The genius of our Church government is government through *councils.*"[19] Quorums and presidencies, including those of auxiliaries—Relief Society, Young Women, Primary, and Sunday School—have also functioned as councils. Auxiliary presidencies serve as members of general, stake, and ward councils. In this way, women have served in important leadership positions in general and local church government.[20]

The overarching principle of all these layers of leadership was that "all things shall be done by common consent in the church" (LDS Doctrine and Covenants 26:2; CofChrist Doctrine and Covenants 25:1b; see also LDS Doctrine and Covenants 28:13–14; CofChrist Doctrine and Covenants 27:4c–5a). The use of parliamentary procedure was another common cultural practice for church polity in the early nineteenth century. Today, common consent, also referred to as "sustaining," is a fundamental practice in The Church of Jesus Christ of Latter-day Saints. The "business" of the ward, stake, or entire church takes place briefly at the beginning of sacrament meetings or stake or general conferences. Members raise their right arms to the square to support or oppose leaders, policies, and doctrine. Most of the work of discussion and decision-making is performed behind the scenes by councils. In the rare case of hands uplifted in opposition, members are asked to meet with their local leaders later to discuss their concerns. A vote in favor assumes that one sustains the motion with his or her "actions, faith, and prayers."[21]

PRIESTHOOD AND POLITY

Priesthood is at the heart of the prophet-polity dichotomy.[22] For Latter-day Saints, priesthood connotes the entirety of God's power as well as that portion of God's power that is conferred on men who are ordained to priesthood office.[23] Priesthood is organized and hierarchical[24] yet subject to principles of righteousness[25] and delegated through conferral of keys or authority by the laying on of hands by a priesthood officer.[26] According to the *General Handbook*, "Jesus Christ holds all the keys of the priesthood," which are conferred upon his apostles.[27] Only the prophet or president of the church, "who is the senior Apostle, is authorized to exercise all these keys."[28]

During my lifetime, I have witnessed changes to policies concerning the blessings of the priesthood (see next section) and increasing emphasis on the priesthood power that is delegated to women.[29] Although I have not been ordained to priesthood offices, I have always felt priesthood power and authority in my callings and covenants—particularly temple covenants. Hearing this truth affirmed of late is a source of strength and a confirmation of my own spiritual impressions.[30] Along with other Latter-day Saints, I believe that God determines who in the polity receives priesthood ordination and reveals this through the prophet.

POLITY AND GLOBALIZATION

The tension in the prophet-polity paradox is most pronounced in the process of globalization. Latter-day Saint missionaries began a process of globalization in reverse as converts were commanded to gather to a centralized Zion as early as September 1830 (see LDS Doctrine and Covenants 28, 29:8; CofChrist Doctrine and Covenants 27, 28:2c). Conceptions of Zion have evolved in the ongoing Restoration, encompassing places like Independence, Missouri; various city-stakes like Kirtland or Nauvoo; and regions like Deseret. The westward pull for mountain Saints began to lose momentum in the early 1950s. Out-migration and nascent globalization began under the prophetic leadership of David O. McKay, who instigated the building of stakes and temples outside the Intermountain West and encouraged members to build Zion in their own countries.[31] Internationalization was facilitated through an effort to correlate a "patchwork quilt of curriculum" into a unified message that could be exported outside North America.[32] What became known as priesthood correlation brought budgets, periodicals, and other programs under the centralized control of committees headed by members of the Quorum of the Twelve. Correlation efforts differed from those of other Christian denominations that prioritized indigenization in the postcolonial era.

Jehu Hanciles, professor of world Christianity, has argued, "Successful globalization requires at least two defining attributes: localization and multidirectional (reciprocal) transformation."[33] Mormon studies scholars emphasize the "Americanness" of the global church because of this centralized priority of conformity under correlation. However, Latter-day localization has been mapped in many parts of the world despite the centralized culture of the church.[34]

Perhaps "the clearest example, to date, of multidirectional transformation" in Latter-day Saint globalization "is the lifting of the priesthood ban in 1978."[35] The unidirectional top-down nature of the prophetic revelation had a counterbalance in the polity of the church in Africa and Brazil. Administering the church in areas where new members could not hold the priesthood or enjoy temple blessings presented complexities that the apostolic leadership of the church had been aware of since the 1940s. The commission to take the restored gospel to all nations "seemed increasingly incompatible with the priesthood and temple restrictions."[36] Reciprocity was evident because "non-Western realities contributed to a historic policy change"; however, the change "in turn had a profound effect on the growth of Mormonism in non-Western contexts."[37] Such tensions in the prophet-polity paradox may be more evident in globalization,[38] yet the strength of church polity remains entwined in the individual convictions of Latter-day Saints who sustain prophets, seers, and revelators and thank God for a prophet.[39]

PROPHETS AND POLITY IN COMMUNITY OF CHRIST

MATTHEW J. FRIZZELL

Matthew J. Frizzell, PhD, is adjunct faculty and former dean of Community of Christ Seminary at Graceland University. He currently serves as director of human resource ministries for Community of Christ International Headquarters in Independence, Missouri.

I was ten years old in the spring of 1984 when my father brought me to my first Community of Christ World Conference at the Auditorium in Independence, Missouri. My family is several generations Community of Christ, and attending World Conference was a pilgrimage. I didn't know it would be the historic conference at which Doctrine and Covenants section 156 would be presented and passed.

Section 156 brought about two historic changes that continue to shape Community of Christ today. First, the church was called to build the Temple in Independence, Missouri. This long-awaited Temple would be "dedicated to the pursuit of peace. It [would] be for reconciliation and for healing of the spirit."[40] Second, women were called to priesthood ordination.[41] The words of section 156 resonated with the clarity of both reason and revelation: "*All* are called according to the gifts which have been given them. This applies to priesthood as well as to any other aspects of the work" (CofChrist Doctrine and Covenants 156:9b; emphasis added).[42] Women would be ordained to hold, express, and fulfill priesthood ministry.

Some church members expressed strong dissent to section 156 in the days and years following its approval. Some resolved to repeal or overturn the divine counsel in legislative sessions. I remember the flurry of strong emotions and parliamentary motions objecting to women's ordination. Members debated and questioned the revelation, the prophet-president's discernment and authority, and change itself. Even as a young boy, I felt (what I now know is) the Holy Spirit present and working amid the strong feelings and dissent. God's liberation, the Spirit's comfort, and compassionate tolerance for honest debate and mixed emotions in the body sustained the conference. It could be felt as we sang hymns, prayed, and worshipped. This was my first real experience with theocratic democracy, and the experience remains with me.

Polity is a term that properly belongs to politics. By politics, I mean the science and study of governance and rule. For churches, polity refers to how the church is organized and governed. Joseph Smith III defined the Restoration as a "theocratic democracy."[43] My testimony of the 1984 World Conference depicts theocratic democracy in motion. Theocracy refers to the divine origin and structure of prophetic leadership and priesthood. Priesthood members are called to office, and priesthood orders meet in quorums. Democracy governs through the membership's shared authority, which rules by common consent. Common consent defines how a quorum, conference, and church as a whole act as a body. A member of the priesthood may share in both theocracy and democracy within the church. In their roles and ministry offices, priesthood members act as priesthood. In quorums and conferences, these same members have voice and vote to discern, debate, and consent or dissent within the church. Theocracy and democracy, therefore, comingle and coexist. Both principles are manifested through leadership, governance, and the church's response to the Spirit and to God's direction in relation to the world in which we live and serve.

Common consent holds Community of Christ polity together. God's call to act by faith in common consent is drawn from Community of Christ Doctrine and Covenants 27:4c, which counsels that "all things must be done in order and by common consent in the church."[44] Common consent does not mean blind obedience to church authorities. Nor does it mean an implicit expectation that we agree on every issue, or that agreement is a sign confirming God's authority in the church or an individual's righteousness.[45] Community of Christ honors faithful disagreement.[46] Common consent is dynamic; it ebbs, flows, and evolves. Living under the principle of common consent is a process, sometimes felt as a struggle or tension that dwells within theocratic democracy. Our scriptures depict wrestling and struggling with God as a faithful response to and the nature of a covenant life with God.[47] The Holy Spirit dwells, speaks, and works through prophetic voices and within the hearts of people in this process and its tensions. We worship, sing, debate, listen, discern, and reason together in prayer, study, and faith. In a living covenant, the search for common consent liberates and binds us to God and each other.

PRIESTHOOD

Within our polity, theocracy concerns the church's prophetic leadership and its priesthood structure. Before ordination, would-be priesthood members in Community of Christ are called by other priesthood members and approved administratively.[48] Then the individual and priesthood call are sustained by common consent through democratic action of the congregation or appropriate conference. A call to priesthood office is for life unless another priesthood call is initiated and accepted. A priesthood member may also be released from the priesthood voluntarily, involuntarily, or by suspension or superannuation. No one in Community of Christ holds priesthood office by divine right (like age or family lineage) or progression of membership or other office. Since Jesus's call to follow asks us for a whole-life response, priesthood roles are defined by spiritual and administrative functions of church polity.

Ordination to priesthood liberates and binds some priesthood members to administer the sacraments.[49] Priesthood calls mean that some members carry out specific ministerial responsibilities, such as peacemaking, teaching and family ministry, missionary work, spiritual leadership, and administration.[50] In Community of Christ, Aaronic Priesthood members are ministers of presence. Melchisedec Priesthood members provide sacramental ministry[51] and serve in a variety of administrative roles and functions within the church. All are called by God according to their giftedness, but not all serve in priesthood.

The priesthood is led by the First Presidency, a quorum consisting of two counselors and one prophet-president. The name *prophet-president* reveals the combined governance structures of theocracy and democracy. The prophet's role is theocratic. It is to spiritually discern God's will and lead the church according to God's spiritual direction. The prophet is the only priesthood member responsible for discerning God's will and presenting letters of divine counsel to the whole church, which may be presented for consideration and inclusion in the Doctrine and Covenants.[52] In the prophet's role as president, the prophet-president, along with two counselors, presides over World Conference. Currently held every three years, World Conference is the church's highest democratic legislative body.[53]

CONFERENCES

Globally, Community of Christ is organized primarily into geographical fields, mission centers, and congregations. Mission centers are usually geographical organizations of congregations[54] led by a mission center president appointed by the First Presidency and democratically sustained by the mission center at a conference.[55] Like World Conference, mission centers hold conferences and can legislate. Individual congregations also confer in what are sometimes called "business meetings." Any baptized member of the congregation has voice and vote. Congregations are led by a democratically annually elected pastor or presiding elder.[56]

National and field conferences of multiple mission centers meet and legislate for special purposes in Community of Christ. Examples include conferring about diverse ethical and cultural matters, such as same-sex loving relationships. Section 164 of the Doctrine and Covenants identifies national and field conferences, which I discuss at the end of this essay.

GLOBALIZATION, DIVERSE CULTURES, AND CHALLENGES TO POLITY AND COMMON CONSENT

In the 1960s, Community of Christ more than doubled its international presence.[57] As the church expanded into diverse cultures, the Community of Christ identity, mission, and organization faced new and old challenges. Church missionaries' encounter with polygamy in East India and Nigeria in the 1960s is emblematic of these challenges. Cultural and religious diversity remain challenges for church governance and common consent in Community of Christ as a world communion today. Such diversity shapes our understanding of scripture and religious authority, morality and ethics, and our doctrine and identity.

In 1967, an apostle on mission in India stood in the waters of baptism. A man in a polygamous marriage waded into the water, pleading to be baptized.[58] The apostle refused to baptize him. Community of Christ history, identity, and teaching were founded on a rejection of polygamy in the early Restoration movement.[59] This wasn't the first time missionaries had encountered polygamy in cultures abroad,[60] but this reencounter with polygamy required informal and formal consideration as the church began to expand. The First Presidency, Council of Twelve, and members and priesthood held discussions about evangelism and polygamy in other cultures, but little was initially published about these dialogues. These dialogues weighed how to understand indigenous cultures and non-Christian peoples, the real consequences to families and plural wives if men abandoned them, and the redemptive purposes of the gospel.[61] Consideration of these issues eventually grounded the church's position on polygamy. The search for common consent led leaders to accept baptizing persons in polygamous marriages, but with conditions. Previous marriages would be tolerated, but members engaging in new polygamous relationships after baptism risked loss of membership.

Community of Christ Doctrine and Covenants section 150 addressed this situation,[62] shaping how common consent in discerning gospel and cultural issues occurs today. Specifically, section 150 affirms that Christian marriage is monogamous. Section 150 also affirms global evangelism, naming apostles as "the chief witnesses of the gospel" called to interpret and administer the gospel in the circumstances in which people are found (see CofChrist Doctrine and Covenants 150:10a–11b).[63] Section 162 affirms the church's democratic polity and the body's role as a "prophetic people" (see CofChrist Doctrine and Covenants 162:1a, 2c).[64] Under the direction of their spiritual authorities, a prophetic people discern God's will for the "time and in the places where [they] serve."[65] Adopted in 2010, section 164 urges Community of Christ to further "develop cultural awareness and sensitivity" (7a) and clarifies the role of World Conference to address "fundamental principles of ethical behavior and relationships within the church" (7b). Further, national or field conferences are for "broader dialogue, understanding, and consent" on pressing issues in nations for the "restoring work of the gospel to move forward with all of its potential" (7d).

Response to Matthew J. Frizzell

Matt's reminiscence of the 1984 RLDS World Conference reminds me of my own experience attending some of the sessions of Community of Christ World Conference in 2019. The gathering lasted nine days and brought together elected delegates from congregations all over the world. It was lovely to be among friends from Community of Christ at this important gathering, but what I most admired was the emphasis on listening. The general church leaders listened to the individual delegates, who spoke from microphones set up in stations around the Auditorium in Independence. Delegates and leaders were encouraged to listen to the voice of the Spirit and "the body of Christ" and then vote accordingly. Official minutes of the conference noted, "World Conference is necessary for conducting church business and discerning divine direction as a prophetic people."[66] I saw this in action, and it put into relief the purpose of conferences early in Restoration DNA.

The most obvious difference between Community of Christ World Conference and The Church of Jesus Christ of Latter-day Saints general conference is that World Conference is a "democratic legislative body," and Latter-day Saint general conferences are semiannual "worldwide gatherings" in which "Church leaders from around the world share messages or sermons focused on the living Christ and His gospel."[67] Interfaith dialogue reveals elements present in our own tradition that we may have taken for granted. Observing the equivalent of general conference for Community of Christ as a legislative body and not simply a series of meetings caused me to think about how we as Latter-day Saints sometimes take for granted the significance of our sustaining vote as well as the hours of work that are done behind the scenes in councils. President Nelson's description of this revelatory process is illustrious: "In our meetings, the majority never rules! We listen prayerfully to one another and talk with each other until we are united. Then when we have reached complete accord, the unifying influence of the Holy Ghost is spine-tingling!"[68]

Elder Jeffrey R. Holland once began a televised general conference address by sharing a picture of a baby named Sammy. He noted that the baby's hands were busy holding his bottle when it was time to sustain the prophet, but in the next picture, Sammy's chubby little leg was in the air. Elder Holland said, "Sammy gives entirely new meaning to the concept of voting with your feet."[69] In all seriousness, however, this method of voting has been practiced in the Restoration from its earliest days. The choice of members to walk away in both Restoration churches has most often been the democratic rejection of theocratic authority. Likewise, the power that holds the Restoration polity together is the vote of the uplifted hand by individual members.

What I found to be particularly unique at Community of Christ World Conference was the welcoming of dissenting voices and debate.

Matt's description of "the Holy Spirit present and working amid the strong feelings and dissent" may seem foreign to Latter-day Saints, who are encouraged to express opposition privately with local leaders. Matt quoted an official statement from his church leaders in 2013: "Community of Christ honors faithful disagreement." Matt charts the dispersion of prophetic and priesthood power in the ordination of women, the authorization of members to act as a "prophetic people" in discerning cultural adaptations, and finally the allowance of making differing decisions in "national or field conferences."

In Latter-day Saint doctrine, high value is placed on maintaining unity, avoiding contention, and sustaining leaders. Matt noted in our conversations that Community of Christ was initially a collection of dissenters and that the "Brighamites" were a collection of followers. These different approaches to navigating conflict in the polity have roots in the prophetic innovations of Nauvoo. I have been fascinated and slightly disoriented when hearing a Community of Christ colleague refer to the "dark days of Nauvoo" or express discomfort with the hymn "Praise to the Man." Likewise, I admire the respectful curiosity these same colleagues extend when seeking to understand Latter-day Saint temple theology and other post-Kirtland doctrines that we value in The Church of Jesus Christ of Latter-day Saints. Regardless of our differing views of Joseph the Prophet, I believe the fruit of our dialogue has been to envision Restoration polity less as two sects of a religious movement and more as parts of the body of Christ.[70]

Response to Taunalyn Ford

In my experience, ecumenical dialogue is always enlightening. It has a way of confirming some assumptions and shattering other prejudices. Discussing polity is particularly interesting in ecumenical dialogue because polity is unique to each faith community. Polity shapes how we experience our religious beliefs and practices by the way they are structured into a shared communal life.

For The Church of Jesus Christ of Latter-day Saints and Community of Christ, polity is even more interesting because we share so much of it. As Joseph Smith Restoration traditions, we share formative history, scriptures, language, and polity itself. Both churches are led by prophet-presidents and lay claim to common consent. Our priesthood offices and structures parallel one another but are lived out differently.[71] The Church of Jesus Christ of Latter-day Saints and Community of Christ governance structures of councils and conferences are similar, but their representation and character are not the same. Compare a general conference in Salt Lake City with a World Conference in Independence, Missouri—they feel different. Taunalyn's and my opening stories shed light on those differences. Her general conference story affirms her spiritual experience meeting a divine prophet. My story affirms my experience of God's presence amid open conflict and dissent. These stories indicate cultural differences between our churches. Recognizing differences in culture is significant because church culture and church polity interact in a way that is like how skin and soft tissues hang on and give shape to skeletal structure. As organizational polity and culture interact, they influence and shape the body, as well as one another. The two work together dynamically over time to make a whole.

In dialogue with Church of Jesus Christ friends and scholars, the similarities and differences between our faith movements are always obvious and felt. In my response, therefore, I want to focus on two themes that intersect in Taunalyn's and my essays: the representation and role of authority and the challenges of globalization. One marks a contrast between our churches, and the other a commonality.

The representation and role of authority in our faith traditions mark a difference. Both churches have a hierarchical priesthood with prophet-presidents at the top. Both churches are governed by layers of organization utilizing councils and conferences. But the role and representation of authority in these structures differ.

In addition to women's roles in temple ordinances, Taunalyn lists women's auxiliaries—Relief Society, Young Women, Primary, and Sunday School—among the organizations that function as councils within the Utah-based church. Under Community of Christ's definition of polity, I agree with Taunalyn. As I dialogue with Latter-day Saint colleagues, it's clear that women and women's organizations are vital to their church's organization and function.

In contrast, women's organizations in Community of Christ have declined significantly in light of evolving gender roles in the church. When women began to be ordained to priesthood office in the 1980s, they initiated a process of integrating into priesthood and the leading quorums, councils, and sacramental life of the church. I think many church members recognize that the inclusion of women in these quorums and councils parallels a change in the representation and role of authority in Community of Christ.[72] I believe it's fair to generalize that the nature of authority in Community of Christ has evolved to become less hierarchical and more relational. In a few generations, the nature of calling and authority has become less focused on calling to office and more focused on priesthood function and calling as they relate to the person's individual giftedness.

How does this compare to The Church of Jesus Christ of Latter-day Saints? That deserves longer discussion. Within the tradition of the mountain Saints, the role and authority of women are a rich and expanding discussion. But there's no doubt that the role and representation of women in priesthood marks a difference between our churches' polities and cultures.

Despite differences, both churches enter the twenty-first century facing the challenges of globalization and expansion into new cultures. Taunalyn is an expert in this area. She helpfully explains that in The Church of Jesus Christ of Latter-day Saints, the concepts of Zion have evolved over time. The pull inward to gather has evolved with a call outward to global expansion and mission. A similar evolution in Zionic mission has taken place in Community of Christ. As both churches enter the twenty-first century, they face difficulties bringing Restoration faith to new cultures in a way that maintains each church's unique identity. In The Church of Jesus Christ of Latter-day Saints, this challenge has been managed through priesthood correlation. Taunalyn also explained how globalization shaped the change to her church's priesthood ban in 1978. Globalization has meant Community of Christ has also faced its own US-centrism, racial biases, and justice issues as it has listened to and learned from new cultures. This trend continues today. Community of Christ's approach to the challenges of cultural diversity has also led to increased discernment in the church's leading quorums and has been handled through its open canon. The questions of how to maintain Community of Christ culture and identity in nations and cultures the church has expanded into, and has been in for decades, also continue.

CONCLUSION

Joseph Smith III defined Community of Christ polity as theocratic democracy. In 1844, Joseph Smith declared, "I go emphatically, virtuously, and humanely for THEODEMOCRACY."[73] The DNA is shared regardless of modern genetic characteristics. A major conclusion from our dialogue is that globalization creates challenges for both churches in navigating the prophet-polity dynamic. If polity and culture interact and evolve, introducing Restoration faith to new cultures will continue to put pressure on church polity and its authorities to maintain Restoration faith's unique identity, tradition, and practice. That means our Restoration churches will have to grapple with our roles in colonialization, indigenization, and decentralization of church authority for the sake of the gospel in the earth's far-flung places. To mediate these challenges, theocratic democracy will be put to the test. In the end, the globalization of Restorationism depends on its polity—theocratic democracy—to bring divine will together with democratic authority in both harmony and dissent.

NOTES

1.   Taunalyn Ford, journal, in author's possession.
2.   See Terryl Givens, *People of Paradox* (New York: Oxford University Press, 2007). See also Richard Bushman, *Joseph Smith: Rough Stone Rolling* (New York: Alfred A. Knopf, 2005), 153; Nathan Hatch, *The Democratization of American Christianity* (New Haven, CT: Yale University Press, 1991); Michael Hubbard MacKay, *Prophetic Authority: Democratic Hierarchy and the Mormon*

Priesthood (Urbana: University of Illinois Press, 2020); and Thomas O'Dea, *The Mormons* (Chicago: University of Chicago Press, 1957).

3. Givens, *People of Paradox*, 14.

4. D. Michael Quinn, *The Mormon Hierarchy: Origins of Power* (Salt Lake City: Signature Books, 1994), 7–8. See also Bushman, *Rough Stone Rolling*, 118–22.

5. See LDS Doctrine and Covenants 28, CofChrist Doctrine and Covenants 27, and *The Joseph Smith Papers*. Hiram Page's revelations through his seer stone had convinced the members in Fayette, including Oliver Cowdery and members of the Whitmer family. "Oliver Cowdery and the Whitmer family began to conceive of themselves as independent authorities with the right to correct Joseph and receive revelation." See Bushman, *Rough Stone Rolling*, 120.

6. Bushman, *Rough Stone Rolling*, 175.

7. See John G. Turner, *Brigham Young: Pioneer Prophet* (Cambridge: Harvard University Press, 2012); Givens, *People of Paradox*, 17; Leonard J. Arrington, *Brigham Young: American Moses* (New York: Alfred A. Knopf, 1985).

8. Turner, *Brigham Young*, 414

9. Turner, *Brigham Young*, 412.

10. Dallin H. Oaks, "Two Lines of Communication," *Ensign*, November 2010, 83.

11. Oaks, "Two Lines," 84.

12. Russell M. Nelson, "Revelations for the Church, Revelation for Our Lives," *Ensign*, May 2018, 95. President Nelson concluded this admonition by quoting the promise of the Lord in LDS Doctrine and Covenants 42:61: "If thou shalt [seek], thou shalt receive revelation upon revelation, knowledge upon knowledge."

13. Bushman, *Rough Stone Rolling*, 251.

14. Revelations given in general or "special" conferences: LDS Doctrine and Covenants 1, 21, 38, 42, 52, 67, 70, 75, 82, 84, 88, and 96. Other revelations that were received just prior to or just after a conference include LDS Doctrine and Covenants 20, 28, 29, 30, and 31.

15. Bushman, *Rough Stone Rolling*, 253.

16. See section heading for LDS Doctrine and Covenants 102.

17. Bushman, *Rough Stone Rolling*, 257–58.

18. Church History Topics, "First Presidency," https://abn.ChurchofJesusChrist .org/study/history/topics/first-presidency.

19. Quoted in Ezra Taft Benson, "Church Government through Councils," *Ensign*, May 1979, 87. See also Michael Magleby, "To Sit in Council," 50–53.

20. The precedent for women serving in presidencies began with the establishment of the Female Relief Society of Nauvoo in 1842. In August of 2015, women began to sit on three executive councils at the general level; see Sarah Jane Weaver, "Women to Take Part of General Church Councils," *Church News*, August 19, 2015.

21. See also Church History Topics, "Common Consent," https://www.Churchof JesusChrist.org/study/history/topics/common-consent.

22. "Priesthood would grow into one of the defining principles of Mormonism. Despite Protestant aversion to the term, Joseph continued to expand

priesthood down to his final days in Nauvoo." Bushman, *Rough Stone Rolling*, 159. See also LDS Doctrine and Covenants 107.

23. See also Dale G. Renlund and Ruth Lybbert Renlund, *The Melchizedek Priesthood: Understanding the Doctrine, Living the Principles* (Salt Lake City: Deseret Book, 2018), 147. Richard Bushman emphasizes that "though kindred in spirit, priesthood government went far beyond classical republicanism or idealized monarchy in bringing people to God. Priesthood government sought to redeem people, not just serve their interests. Priests were godly teachers rather than protectors of the people's rights. Priesthood government was redemptive." Bushman, *Rough Stone Rolling*, 268.

24. See LDS Doctrine and Covenants 107.

25. See LDS Doctrine and Covenants 121:36.

26. See LDS Doctrine and Covenants 107. See Joseph Smith Papers glossary, "Keys," https://www.josephsmithpapers.org/topic/keys.

27. These include the keys of the Aaronic and Melchizedek Priesthoods, the keys of the gathering of Israel, the keys of the Abrahamic covenant, and the sealing keys restored by Elijah; see LDS Doctrine and Covenants 110. See *General Handbook: Serving in The Church of Jesus Christ of Latter-day Saints*, 3.0, ChurchofJesusChrist.org; LDS Doctrine and Covenants 13; 27:12–13; 110; 128:9–10.

28. See *General Handbook*, 3.0.

29. See *General Handbook*, 3.2 and 3.4.3.

30. See Russell M. Nelson, "Spiritual Treasures," *Ensign*, November 2019, 76–79; Dallin H. Oaks, "The Keys and Authority of the Priesthood," *Ensign*, May 2014, 49–52. See also Barbara Morgan Gardner, *The Priesthood Power of Women: In the Temple, Church, and Family* (Salt Lake City: Deseret Book, 2019).

31. See Taunalyn F. Rutherford, "'Her Borders Must Be Enlarged': Evolving Conceptions of Zion," in *Raising the Standard of Truth: Exploring the History and the Teachings of the Early Restoration* (Provo, UT: Religious Studies Center, Brigham Young University; Salt Lake City: Deseret Book, 2020), 181.

32. See Matthew Bowman, *The Mormon People: The Making of an American Faith* (New York: Random House, 2012), 194.

33. Jehu Hanciles, "'Would That All God's People Were Prophets': Mormonism and the New Shape of Global Christianity," *Journal of Mormon History* 41, no. 2 (April 2015): 35–68, 43.

34. For instance, I argue for localization and hybridity among Latter-day Saints in India. See Taunalyn Ford Rutherford, "Conceptualizing Global Religions: An Investigation of Mormonism in India" (PhD diss., Claremont Graduate University, 2018). See also Marjorie Newton and others on Māori/Mormon hybridity; Marie Vinnarasi Chintaram, "The Challenge of Hybridity: Mormonism in Mauritius, 1980–2020" (master's thesis, Utah State University, 2021); Melissa Wei-Tsing Inouye, "A Tale of Three Primaries: The Gravity of Mormonism's Informal Institutions," in *Decolonizing Mormonism: Approaching a Postcolonial Zion*, ed. Gina Colvin and Joanna Brooks (Salt Lake City: University of Utah Press, 2018), 229–62.

35. Hanciles, "'Would That All God's People Were Prophets,'" 59.

36. See Church History Topics, "Priesthood and Temple Restriction," https://abn.ChurchofJesusChrist.org/study/history/topics/priesthood-and-temple-restriction.

37. Hanciles, "'Would That All God's People Were Prophets,'" 61.

38. Hanciles, "'Would That All God's People Were Prophets,'" 61.

39. See Wallace F. Bennett, "We Thank Thee O God for a Prophet," in *Hymns* (Salt Lake City: The Church of Jesus Christ of Latter-day Saints, 1985), no. 19.

40. Community of Christ Doctrine and Covenants 156:5a. The Temple was completed and dedicated April 17, 1994.

41. It is noteworthy that 1984 was also a pivotal year for women in ministry for Southern Baptists. Responding to second-wave feminism and the women's equality movement, America's churches became polarized over the role and authority of women in ministry. The affirmation of women's ordination in the RLDS Church stands in sharp contrast to the action of the Southern Baptist Convention meeting in Kansas City, Missouri, June 12–14, 1984, at which the "Resolution on Ordination and the Role of Women in Ministry" was passed. This resolution affirmed that "man [is] the head of woman," that the "New Testament does not mandate that all who are divinely called to ministry be ordained," and that women are encouraged to serve in all aspects of church life "other than pastoral functions and leadership roles entailing ordination." See the "Resolution on Ordination and the Role of Women in Ministry," https://www.sbc.net/resource-library/resolutions/resolution-on-ordination-and-the-role-of-women-in-ministry/. For a brief history of women's ordination, see Nancy Ross, David Howlett, and Zoe Kruse, "The Women's Ordination Movement in the RLDS Church: Historical and Sociological Perspectives," *Mormon Studies Review* 9 (2022): 15–26.

42. Community of Christ Doctrine and Covenants 9c addresses women in priesthood specifically: "Therefore, do not wonder that some women of the church are being called to priesthood responsibilities."

43. Clarifying theocratic democracy, Community of Christ governance documents state that the church "was brought into being by divine initiative, is guided and administered by divine authority, is sustained by the light of the Holy Spirit, and exists for divine purposes. In response to divine initiative, members share responsibility for governing the church." "All things must be done in order and by common consent in the church, by the prayer of faith" (Community of Christ Doctrine and Covenants 27:4c; LDS Doctrine and Covenants 26:2). See *Church Administrators' Handbook* (Independence, MO: Herald Publishing House, 2005), 5. For commentary on the meaning of theocratic democracy as Restoration church governance, see Maurice L. Draper, "Theocratic Democracy-Restoration Church Government," *Saints' Herald*, December 1, 1968, 800–801, 814; December 15, 1968, 842–44.

44. LDS Doctrine and Covenants 26:2.

45. "Common consent is a goal that all decision-making processes in the church seek to achieve. It is not confined to one specific process. In common consent,

there is general agreement that a decision has been made by the appropriate person or body, that all relevant perspectives have been considered, and that the process used to arrive at the decision fosters the spirit of community within the church. Common consent is a central element in the polity of the Community of Christ, but its definition has always been somewhat elusive. On one hand, it means something more than majority rule, but it means something less than full unanimity on the course of action to be taken. Perhaps the definition of common consent is elusive because common consent is, above all, a goal to be achieved. Depending on the prevailing culture and the operational context, a number of methods might be used to achieve this end." See *Church Administrators' Handbook*, 6.

46. See World Church Leadership Council, "Faithful Disagreement Definition and Principles," Community of Christ, March 2013. Available at http://www .latter-dayseekers.org/uploads/7/9/3/8/79384866/faithful-disagreement -definition-and-principles.pdf.

47. The archetype of wrestling with God and God's blessing is depicted in the stories of Israel's origins, especially Jacob's wrestling with God, represented as a man or angel, until daybreak in Genesis 32:22–32. This pattern of wrestling and struggling with God as the nature of Israel's relationship with God into and through covenant is depicted in the wilderness, Israel's challenges under royal rule, and Israel's relationship to the prophets.

48. In practice, details on the process of calling members to the Aaronic, Melchisedec, and High Priesthood vary in Community of Christ. The following is not an exhaustive explanation of priesthood calling but provides insight on select aspects of priesthood calling. Generally, elders of the Melchisedec Priesthood call other elders and members to the Aaronic Priesthood. Aaronic and elder calls are approved by mission center presidents and sustained by the appropriate body. Members of the Council of the Presidents of Seventy call elders to the office of Seventy. As a general principle, members of the High Priesthood call members to the High Priesthood. Callings to specific offices of the High Priesthood vary. Apostles call evangelists. The First Presidency calls bishops. The prophet-president calls apostles, counselors to the First Presidency, and members of the Presiding Bishopric.

49. Deacons and teachers in the Aaronic Priesthood cannot administer sacraments. Priests are also of the Aaronic Priesthood and may baptize and serve Communion, or the Lord's Supper. The Melchisedec Priesthood offices of elders, quorums of seventy, and the High Priesthood (high priests, evangelists, order of bishops, Council of Twelve, and First Presidency) may administer all sacraments of the church except evangelist blessings. The evangelist blessing is a sacrament only evangelists may administer. The sacrament of evangelist blessings was known as "patriarchal blessing" until the ordination of women in 1984.

50. For an overview of priesthood offices, orders, and quorums of Community of Christ, see *Church Administrators' Handbook*, "Quorums and Orders," 21–26, "Priesthood and Ordination," 27–33.

51. Supported by priests who can baptize, lead Communion, marry, and ordain other priests, teachers, and deacons.

52. The Doctrine and Covenants is considered modern-day scripture for Community of Christ. For inclusion in the Doctrine and Covenants, a letter of counsel from the prophet-president must be presented for consideration at a World Conference and then approved. In Community of Christ, sections of the Doctrine and Covenants have been both added and removed over the life of the church. Removal or relegation of a section of the Doctrine and Covenants by conference action is very rare. However, the addition and removal of scripture from canon is an example of the shared authority and function of theocratic democracy within the Reorganized Church.

53. As presider over World Conference, the First Presidency executes the will of the conference as passed through its legislation. The First Presidency, like all priesthood quorums, may bring legislation to the World Conference for consideration. Lower conferences, committees, and caucuses (such as the Youth Caucus or Mass Meeting of Elders) may also introduce legislation at World Conference. Lower conferences are described below.

54. Community of Christ is a global communion present in over sixty nations but numerically small. As a result, in places with a high concentration of church members, mission centers may consist primarily of congregations in one metropolitan area. In areas where members are widespread, a mission center may consist of an entire country or part of a continent. A mission center may have ten Community of Christ congregations or over one hundred.

55. Most often, the mission center president is an elder or member of the High Priesthood.

56. Note that pastors or presiding elders are democratically elected. This differs from mission center presidents, who are appointed and sustained, and the general officers, who are called and sustained by the World Conference.

57. Prior to 1960, the church's international presence was primarily in Canada, Europe, Australia, and Tahiti. Like many other American churches and institutions, the RLDS Church was transformed by the wave of US globalization in the latter twentieth century. The effects of globalization on the Restoration gospel continue to be felt and have had both transformative and schismatic consequences. Much has been written about the transformation of the RLDS movement. See Roger D. Launius, "Coming of Age? The Reorganized Church of Jesus Christ of Latter Day Saints in the 1960s," *Dialogue* 28, no. 2 (Summer 1995): 31–57; and W. Grant McMurray, "History and Mission in Tension: A View from Both Sides," *John Whitmer Historical Association Journal* 20 (2000): 34–47. On the international expansion of the RLDS Church, see Maurice L. Draper, *Isles and Continents* (Independence, MO: Herald Publishing House, 1982). For more recent research on RLDS international expansion, see Dima Hurlbut, "Gobert Edet and the Entry of the RLDS Church into Southeastern Nigeria, 1962–1966," *Journal of Mormon History* 45, no. 4 (2019): 81–104; David Howlett, "Why Denominations Can Climb Hills: RLDS Conversions in

Highland Tribal India and Midwestern America, 1964–2000," *Church History* 89, no. 3 (September 2020): 633–58; and David Howlett, "The Community of Christ (RLDS Church): Structuring Common Differences in the Philippines," in *Palgrave Handbook of Global Mormonism*, ed. R. Gordon Shepherd, A. Gary Shepherd, and Ryan Cragun (New York: Palgrave/Macmillan, 2020), 655–76.

58. For an account of this encounter with polygamy in Nigeria and India during international expansion, see Maurice L. Draper, "Polygamy among Converts in East India," *Courage* 1 (December 1970): 85–88.

59. For an excellent account of RLDS apologetics regarding Joseph Smith Jr.'s involvement with polygamy and its importance in RLDS identity, see David J. Howlett, "Remembering Polygamy: The RLDS Church and American Spiritual Transformations in the Late Twentieth Century," *John Whitmer Historical Association Journal* 24 (2004): 149–72.

60. Draper notes that his discussions concerning polygamy prior to the incident in East India in 1967 focused on the polygamous practices previously known in Nigeria. See Draper, "Polygamy among Converts," 87.

61. See Alma R. Blair, "RLDS Views of Polygamy: Some Historiographical Notes," *John Whitmer Historical Association Journal* 5 (1985): 18. See also the considerations of Verne Deskin's opposition to the official statement on baptism of polygamous persons in "You Are Involved with Polygamy," *Courage* 1 (December 1970): 89–92.

62. Section 150 of Community of Christ Doctrine and Covenants was presented and approved at World Conference in 1972.

63. The commission to interpret and administer the gospel in the circumstances and conditions in which people are found is stated in theological language: "The church must be willing to bear the burden of their sin, nurturing them in the faith, accepting that degree of repentance which it is possible for them to achieve, looking forward to the day when through patience and love they can be free as a people from the sins of the years of their ignorance. To this end and for this purpose, continue your ministry to those nations of people yet unaware of the joy freedom from sin can bring into their lives. In this way they will be brought to a knowledge of the teachings of my gospel and be made ready and willing to help spread the message of reconciliation and restoration to other worthy souls" (para. 10b–11a).

64. Section 162 was presented in 2004.

65. Community of Christ Doctrine and Covenants 162:1c states, "As a prophetic people you are called, under the direction of the spiritual authorities and with the common consent of the people, to discern the divine will for your own time and in the places where you serve." Adopted in 2010, Community of Christ Doctrine and Covenants 164 gives further direction concerning the role of ethical principles and national or field conferences to "provide opportunities for broader dialogue, understanding, and consent."

66. Official Minutes of Business Meeting, April 13, 2019, https://www.CofChrist .org/common/cms/resources/Documents/2019WCMinutes-April13.pdf. Accessed February 1, 2022.

67. General Conference, https://www.ChurchofJesusChrist.org/learn/general-conference.

68. Nelson, "Revelations for the Church," 95.

69. Jeffrey R. Holland, "The Message, the Meaning, and the Multitude," *Ensign*, November 2019, 6.

70. For example, I experienced some difficult life changes while working on this chapter with Matt. I was blessed by Matt's patience, compassion, and discipleship in addition to his brilliant scholarship. He was both colleague and a ministering brother to me.

71. For example, in The Church of Jesus Christ of Latter-day Saints, men in good standing enter the priesthood as part of their personal and spiritual development. In Community of Christ, individuals enter the priesthood only when a call is initiated by other priesthood members. Community of Christ also ordains women to offices traditionally held only by men in the Church of Jesus Christ.

72. It is important to note, however, that my reflections regarding women's ordination and evolving gender roles do not apply equally across cultures and congregations of Community of Christ. Our discussion of the challenges of globalization and polity must include how gender and authority are expressed differently throughout a global church. They vary by culture as well as social convention. Likewise, ordination of women and women's authority in ministry vary across congregations and cultures in Community of Christ.

73. Joseph Smith, "The Globe," *Times and Seasons*, April 15, 1844, 510; emphasis in original.

PERSONHOOD

Barbara Morgan Gardner and Christie Skoorsmith

PERSONHOOD IN THE CHURCH OF JESUS CHRIST OF LATTER-DAY SAINTS

BARBARA MORGAN GARDNER

Barbara Morgan Gardner is an associate professor of church history and doctrine at Brigham Young University.

"I'm not Moana; I'm Elsa!" my dark-brown-curly-haired, brown-eyed, Polynesian four-year-old daughter declared. "You don't want to be Elsa," my dark-brown-straight-haired, brown-eyed, six-year-old daughter responded. "She's selfish and mean and shoots ice out of her fingers. She even tries to freeze her sister's heart." "But she's beautiful," my four-year-old retorted. "Mom, can you straighten my hair, make it blonde, and make my skin white?" I went to my home office and brought downstairs a few items I've kept since I was a child and had,

Barbara, Alli, Jane, and Dustin on the day the girls were adopted in July 2020. Photo by Celeste Olsen.

although never intentionally, made a collection of. These items were among my most prized possessions: my brown-skinned, dark-brown-haired (some curly and some straight), brown-eyed dolls.

As a child, I hated dolls. In fact, I teased my sister relentlessly for playing with hers. I wanted nothing to do with them. "Who would waste time playing with dolls when you could play football?" I thought. "For that matter, why would anyone choose to wear a dress, braid their hair, or kiss a boy?" Things my sister and the girls in my neighborhood and school did simply did not interest me. Yet the dolls remained, and the collection grew.

These treasures didn't seem to fit with who I was. As far as I was concerned, considering the things I liked to do, the way I dressed, and how I cut my hair, I was more like a boy than a girl. In my child-hood and youth, I believed I was clearly more like my five brothers than my seven sisters. At times I even wondered if somehow someone had made a mistake, or perhaps I was even in the wrong body. Being asked whether I was a boy or a girl was a question I became accustomed to. I don't ever remember discussing the subject with my parents. They just loved me for being me. Unlike my daughter, I never asked to be some-one else, I believe simply because I knew deep down who I really was. Intrinsically, I knew that although I didn't fit the stereotypical cultural definition of a girl, I was still a daughter of God. Somehow, I knew that it was my relationship with God, not cultural norms or other people's opinions about my gender, that determined who I was.

Fundamental to a Latter-day Saint understanding of personhood is a basic understanding of what Book of Mormon prophets titled "the great plan of happiness" (Alma 42:8). This plan contains the doctrine of where we came from, who we now are, and what we have the potential to become. Personhood, according to Latter-day Saints, is not understood in terms of cultural shifts, temporary status, scientific data, popular opinion, politics, individual choice, or traditional phenomenon but rather in the eternal doctrine of one's relationship to heavenly parents: a father (God) and mother (Goddess) in heaven.

At the beginning of an official document of The Church of Jesus Christ of Latter-day Saints known as "The Family: A Proclamation to the World," the Church's highest two quorums unitedly declared, "All human beings—male and female—are created in the image of God. Each is a beloved spirit son or daughter of heavenly parents, and, as such, each has a divine nature and destiny. Gender is an essential characteristic of individual premortal, mortal, and eternal identity and purpose."[1] Although this paragraph encompasses many fundamental truths, for the purposes of this essay, we will look more closely at the Latter-day Saint doctrine and its associated history regarding the divine nature and destiny of each individual, or, in other words, the Latter-day Saint perspective on personhood.

DIVINE NATURE

For members of The Church of Jesus Christ of Latter-day Saints, the relationship between heavenly parents and spiritual offspring is literal. Just as mortal children are the offspring of earthly parents, so are all humans—whether black, brown, or white; female or male; asexual, bisexual, gay, straight, or transgender—spiritual offspring of our heavenly parents. Every individual is therefore divine, meaning each person literally has divine spiritual DNA in him or her. This reality transcends time, space, and human understanding. As C. S. Lewis boldly declared,

"There are no ordinary people. You have never talked to a mere mortal. Nations, cultures, arts, civilizations—these are mortal, and their life is to ours as the life of a gnat. But it is immortals whom we joke with, work with, marry, snub, and exploit."[2] Hopefully, regardless of our personal stance regarding personhood, we learn to love each of God's children as he does.

In their heavenly parents, these spirits, or divine offspring, saw true joy and happiness and desired to become like them. Becoming like our heavenly parents required a mortal experience. This mortal experience, provided by our heavenly parents, became a probationary period in which individuals could use their agency to exercise faith, make and keep sacred covenants, experience God's love, and obey or disobey God's laws. Included in these laws is the first commandment God gave to Adam and Eve: to multiply and replenish the earth.[3] To Joseph Smith, in this dispensation, the Lord also declared, "In the celestial glory, there are three heavens or degrees; and in order to obtain the highest, a man must enter into this order of the priesthood [meaning the new and everlasting covenant of marriage]" (LDS Doctrine and Covenants 131:1–2).

Through a line-upon-line process and through the grace of Christ, each individual is on a mortal path to perfection, a process of becoming like our heavenly parents. Knowing that no individual would become perfect on his or her own and that, because of the Fall of Adam and Eve all people would physically die, God prepared a plan that included a Savior, who would redeem every individual from death and, for those who desire, from sin. "The worth of souls is great in the sight of God," the Lord declared to Joseph Smith, Oliver Cowdery, and David Whitmer as they were called upon to organize the Quorum of the Twelve in the final dispensation. And what makes these souls worth so much? God explained, "For, behold, the Lord your Redeemer suffered death in the flesh; wherefore he suffered the pain of all men, that all men might repent and come unto him" (LDS Doctrine and Covenants 18:10, 11; CofChrist Doctrine and Covenants 16:3c).

The worth of a soul, therefore, is not determined by culture, color, sexual orientation, human laws, church policies, socioeconomic status, roles, propensities, righteousness, or wickedness but rather by his or her connection with our heavenly parents and the Atonement of the Savior. This reality was clearly taught by the Prophet Joseph Smith. Joseph was far advanced in his respect for humanity regardless of cultural norms related to God's laws. He taught and believed that all women and men, regardless of race, ordination, or any other mortal distinction, had divine nature and were of equal value to the Lord. It was the Lord himself who, against religious tradition, referred to the first woman as "glorious Mother Eve" (LDS Doctrine and Covenants 138:39). "All are alike unto God," the Lord declared (LDS 2 Nephi 26:33; CofChrist II Nephi 11:115).

Perhaps basing human worth on legitimate mortal experiences or temporary policies, some believe that Latter-day Saint women are somehow demeaned by not being ordained to priesthood office. It is critical to understand, however, that the Church's organizational structure is a temporary framework, not an eternal doctrine. Latter-day Saint women understand that in the temple, a most sacred place in mortality and a shadow of eternity, women are endowed with priesthood power, perform priesthood ordinances, are clothed in the garment of the holy priesthood, enter the highest order of the priesthood, are equal partners with their husbands in mortality, and are promised the ability to rule and reign as equal partners with their husbands in eternity as goddesses and gods. Although it is difficult at times to separate experiences in mortality that could be perceived as demeaning, in the most sacred places on earth and in eternity, the doctrine of divine nature puts all our heavenly parents' children at a value much higher than a mere mortal could perceive.

God's value and definition of humankind are not affected by mortals' moral relativism, politics, policies, or popular opinion but instead are founded on God's truths, which never change. Although God has not revealed all truth, the truth regarding the eternal nature of gender is among the most important of God's eternal truths. To the Prophet Joseph, God himself declared, "Truth is knowledge of things as they are, and as they were, and as they are to come" (LDS Doctrine and Covenants 93:24; CofChrist Doctrine and Covenants 90:4b). Truth—God's eternal doctrine—does not change. Thus, although we do not have all truth regarding ethnicity, socioeconomic status, timing for mortality, gender dysphoria, and so on, we do know that all people are divine sons and daughters of God, and, as such, all mortals are eternal brothers and sisters. Perhaps this could answer the question asked of me by a navy chaplain at a conference I attended: "Why do Latter-day Saint chaplains treat all people, both enemies and friends, Black and White, atheist and Mormon, as if they were their own brothers and sisters?" My simple response was "Because they are."[4]

DIVINE DESTINY

This first eternal truth—the divine worth of all individuals—leads us to the second eternal truth, that every individual has a divine destiny. As the proclamation states, "Each is a beloved spirit son or daughter of heavenly parents, and, as such, each has a divine nature and destiny."[5] Humankind is not merely a creation of heavenly parents but is their offspring and thus has an inherent ability to become like them. Latter-day Saints agree with the words penned by C. S. Lewis: "It is a serious thing to live in a society of possible gods and goddesses, to remember that the dullest and most uninteresting person you talk to may one day be a creature which, if you saw it now, you would be strongly tempted to worship."[6]

Speaking at the funeral of his friend only two months before his own martyrdom, the Prophet Joseph Smith instructed the Saints, "You have got to learn how to be Gods yourselves; to be kings and priests to God, the same as all Gods have done; by going from a small degree to another, from grace to grace, from exaltation to exaltation, until you are able to sit in glory as doth those who sit enthroned in everlasting power."[7]

As members of The Church of Jesus Christ of Latter-day Saints, we see all people, regardless of nationality, race, sexual orientation, socioeconomic status, gender, and so forth, as potential gods and goddesses. No individual has more divine potential than another. Realizing this divine potential depends not on what one is in mortality but rather on one's choices, or use of agency. To become as God, we must do as God would have us do, and in fact, as God once did. As Lorenzo Snow wrote, "As man now is, God once was: As God now is, man may be."[8]

While all people have equal divine potential, and equal opportunity in regard to that potential, perhaps not all have equal desire. As is taught by the Lord through the Prophet Joseph, all humankind will receive "that which they are willing to receive," based on obedience to God's "laws" (LDS Doctrine and Covenants 88:32–38; CofChrist Doctrine and Covenants 85:6g). Thus, the main purpose of the Restoration of the gospel of Jesus Christ, under the direction of the young Prophet Joseph, was to help God's children to return to and live with and become like him. As President Spencer W. Kimball taught, "The whole intent of the gospel plan is to provide an opportunity for each of you to reach your fullest potential, which is eternal progression and the possibility of godhood."[9] Not allowing for that possibility for their children would position our heavenly parents as stewards rather than parents. As author Henry Ward Beecher once declared, "Whatever is only almost true is quite false, and among the most dangerous of errors, because being so near truth, it is the more likely to lead astray."[10]

My now six-year-old daughter, who would still rather be Elsa than Moana, may not understand social norms and the biology of race and gender, but she does understand her relationship to her heavenly parents. She is their daughter. And although I had no interest in dolls, it seems that my heavenly parents knew who I was better than society, politics, or popular culture did—even better than I did. They knew that someday, in spite of my childhood propensities and what society would teach, I would be grateful to be a mother of a beautiful Moana who thinks she's Elsa. Whether my daughter is Moana, Elsa, or even Kristoff, her worth and my love for her do not change. In fact, regardless of her decisions, my love for her will increase as I draw closer to the Savior. My hope is that my daughter and I will both use our agency in such a way that it will bring us happiness now and in the eternities and that we will be instruments in God's hands to help others have the same according to their righteous desires.

PERSONHOOD IN COMMUNITY OF CHRIST

CHRISTIE SKOORSMITH

Christie Skoorsmith is the quality manager and international business manager for SPIO Inc., which manufactures medical devices for children with special needs.

What is a person? Personal attributes like race, gender, sexual orientation, religious beliefs, socioeconomic status, birth order, or physical characteristics can be used to define us as individuals and as different from one another. But do these attributes define our personhood? Or are certain attributes just the circumstances that arose from our particular birth, into a particular family, in a particular geographical location, at a particular time? We can call these attributes circumstantial characteristics.

Alternatively, we can think of the eternal characteristics of personhood that are universal to all people. These eternal characteristics could be defined as the divine part of us that is not tied to our circumstances of birth but that simply makes each of us a child of God. This includes the capacity to relate, reason, feel empathy for another, know joy, and more. These attributes are the eternal "person-ness" of each human that has ever, or will ever, live, regardless of the circumstances of his or her birth.

When Community of Christ members talk about the worth of persons, it is this eternal characteristic that we refer to in defining personhood. First and foremost, we are human. No matter what the circumstances of our births happen to be, all of us are simply children of God, capable of relationships with the Divine and with one another.

HOWEVER . . .

Discussing one's circumstantial and eternal traits is all well and good when we are theorizing, but real life is so much more complicated than this academic exercise. So how do those terms measure up to our lived experience?

Christie with her family—Christian, Eva, Adrien, and Leo Skoorsmith. Photo by Nate Gawdy.

I remember the moment my daughter told me she was a boy. Time slowed down, and I felt I was in an alternate reality. Even though I knew intellectually that gender was not fixed, emotionally I felt that my child was a girl. The confusion I experienced in that moment was real. But I chose to focus not on the physical, circumstantial aspects of my child—the fact that my child was born with female parts instead of male parts—but on the "eternalness" of who I knew my child to be—a beautiful, wonderful child of God. My child's physical body had no bearing on who he knew himself to be.

That was four years ago now, and when I look into the happy, shining eyes of my son, I know that I focused on the right thing. Because Community of Christ does not have different church roles based on gender, I am secure in knowing that whatever gender my children know themselves to be, they are equally accepted and able to participate in all aspects of church life and ministry.

COMMUNITY OF CHRIST THROUGH THE YEARS

From the beginning of the Restoration movement, the idea of the worth of persons has been central to the teachings of Community of Christ. In June 1829, before the Restoration church was even organized, came these words: "Remember the worth of souls is great in the sight of God" (LDS Doctrine and Covenants 18:10; CofChrist Doctrine and Covenants 16:3c) and "The one being is as precious in his sight as the other" (LDS Jacob 2:21; CofChrist Jacob 2:27).

However, the church's way of expressing the worth of all persons has, at times, been complicated and less than ideal.[11] Joseph Smith III, the first prophet of the Reorganization, struggled with the balance between expressing his own beliefs and trying to preserve the peace in a church with members that were grappling with women's right to vote and postslavery racial tensions.

Joseph Smith III authorized the ordination of Blacks in 1865 yet was cautious about interracial marriage and felt there was too much resistance from church members to ordain women to the priesthood (see CofChrist Doctrine and Covenants 116). So, in many ways, Joseph Smith III's actions simply reflected the cultural views of the time and his desire to act as a bridge between the more radical and the more conservative members of the church. For these and other reasons, some have called Joseph Smith III a "pragmatic prophet."

It wasn't until the 1930s, when Frederick Madison Smith was the president of the church, that the conversation about women's ordination to the priesthood began to change. Frederick Madison stated that he believed that at some time in the future women would be ordained to the priesthood. Fifty years later he was proven right.

In 1984 the church received revelation through Wallace B. Smith, a great-grandson of Joseph Smith III, that women could be ordained to the priesthood because "all are called according to the gifts of God" to serve (CofChrist Doctrine and Covenants 156:9b). I was nine years old when this policy was changed. I remember the day my mother was ordained a teacher in my congregation. I remember feeling so happy and proud of her. She eventually became a priest, an elder, a high priest, and then an apostle. Now, in retirement, she currently holds the office of evangelist. My mother has been a role model for me in my own path with the church. I am not sure I would be the elder I am today without her influence in my life.

Over time, other policies have changed, such as recognizing the right of our LGBTQ+ members to hold the priesthood and be married, as well as recognizing that baptism in other denominations can serve as a path to membership in our church.[12]

The equal worth of all persons has been an increasing focus in Community of Christ over the last fifty years, both theologically and in practice (see CofChrist Doctrine and Covenants 151:9; 161; 163). First and foremost, we focus on people as individuals of great worth in the sight of God. Then we practice the full inclusion of all persons—no matter their race, sexual orientation, gender, physical ability, or religious background. And we ground this belief in how we see Jesus include all people, including the marginalized, and in the continuing guidance of the Holy Spirit in the church today.

The Worth of Persons

Today I continue to be grateful that I am the parent of two transgender children. They have brought such understanding and insight into my life just by being authentically and fully themselves. They have taught me so much about recognizing and listening to that eternal child of God that is in each of us, regardless of what our circumstances of birth happen to be. That divine spark is the essence of what personhood is for members of Community of Christ, no matter an individual's race, gender, sexual orientation, religious beliefs, or physical characteristics and abilities. We all matter. We all are loved. We all are accepted as children of God. We are grateful for the apostle Paul's argument that through baptism into Christ there is no slave or free, Jew or Gentile, male or female (see Galatians 3:28). We extend Paul's argument to say that not only is gender abolished as a defining characteristic of what it means to be a person but so also are race and sexual orientation.

For Community of Christ, the thread of the inestimable worth of persons in the sight of God is strong, revealed in Christ, grounded in scripture, enhanced through modern-day revelation, enacted in our policies, and expressed in our lived experiences. In recent years that thread has intensified and become the heartbeat of our movement. As the Book of Mormon so robustly and wonderfully states, "The Lord inviteth them all to come unto him, and partake of his goodness; and he denieth none that come unto him, black and white, bond and free, male and female; and he remembereth the heathen, and all are alike to God, both Jew and Gentile" (LDS 2 Nephi 26:33; CofChrist II Nephi 11:113–15). We all come from God; we all are alike in God. In God we are all persons of worth.

RESPONSE TO CHRISTIE SKOORSMITH

Christie, I felt, through our phone conversation, dialogue, and your essay, a connection not only with our children and others that we love but also with each other. You have sons that you love regardless of their choices, and I have daughters that I love regardless of theirs. We both share a basic belief that we, and all people, are children of God and on that basis alone are worthy recipients of God's love.

It seems that there is no question that we both, as individuals and as representatives of our faiths, have a deep love of people and a deep sense of their worth. It seems, as you state, that it is in the expression of that love or worth that we have philosophical differences. I appreciate how you explained that the expression of worth has been complicated in Community of Christ and then acknowledge that worth in your faith is demonstrated by authorizing priesthood ordination for both Blacks and women and in recognizing and giving rights to LGBTQ+ members. If I am understanding correctly, worth is demonstrated in Community of Christ, or at least expressed, by ordination, opportunity, and full inclusion.

In your article, you explained that you "focus on people as individuals of great worth in the sight of God. Then we practice the full inclusion of all persons—no matter their race, sexual orientation, gender, physical ability, or religious background. And we ground this belief in how we see Jesus include all people, including the marginalized." It is in this demonstration of worth that perhaps we differ. I do believe, as I believe you do, that Christ loved all people and valued them as having great worth, even infinite worth. I do not, however, believe that Christ therefore was fully inclusive.

When Christ was on the earth, he did not ordain gentiles to priesthood offices. Does this mean that Christ valued the gentiles less than he did others? Was not ordaining the gentiles to priesthood offices, and therefore a lack of inclusion of all races, a demonstration that they were less worthy of Christ's love? Does Christ's calling of only men as his apostles, and therefore a lack of inclusion of all genders, demonstrate that he valued men over women? Was Christ's command for the woman caught in adultery to "sin no more" (John 8:11) a demonstration that he valued or loved her less based on her actions? To all these questions, I would give a resounding "No!" It seems that Christ clearly loved all people, but his love did not equal complete inclusion or lack of law.

Is it possible for us, as a people, to love and value individuals as Christ did without agreeing with popular or cultural shifts and demands? I believe there is a dangerous and false dichotomy in the world today that teaches that if you don't give me what I want, or what popular culture says is right, then you don't love or value me. Christ didn't say, "If you love me, do whatever you want." He said, "If ye love me, keep my commandments" (John 14:15). Many today are asking for a God of comfort rather than a God of love. It seems that the world does not want to love as Christ loved but rather to have Christ love as we love. As was prayed in one of W. H. Auden's plays, "O God, put away justice and truth for we cannot understand them and do not want them. . . . Leave Thy heavens and come down to our earth. Become our uncle. Look after Baby, amuse Grandfather, escort Madam to the Opera, help Willy with his homework, introduce Muriel to a handsome naval officer. Be interesting and weak like us, and [then] we will love you as we love ourselves."[13]

The scriptures teach us that "God is love" (1 John 4:8). If God truly is love, then perhaps we need to know more about God to understand love. As we understand God better and try to become more like him, we will learn to love and perceive worth the way he does. "For God so loved the world, that he gave his only begotten Son" (John 3:16). God's love required perfect obedience to law and the fulfillment of eternal suffering on the part of his Only Begotten Son. What kind of loving God would demand this kind of obedience and allow this kind of suffering? Our God! The God of love! Thus, one's worth is tied to the Atonement of Jesus Christ and is understood only when one's eye is single to his glory. God is a God of both love and law. Perhaps it is better said this way: God's love includes, by his nature, his law.

Let me see if I can explain this idea in personal terms. I remember, shortly after adopting our oldest daughter, Alli, experiencing a difficult situation that others have likely experienced. I woke Alli up early in the morning for swim lessons, had her take a shower, and helped her wash her hair and get dressed. We had eggs and toast for breakfast, practiced her letters and numbers, and walked together to her school. After Alli arrived home from school that afternoon, I helped her learn to ride her bike, and she practiced the piano. Then we attended a playdate with other mothers and kids from her school so we could get to know one another and provide friendship for our kids. After an enjoyable time for everyone, we went home and made and ate dinner. Alli even helped make and serve brownies, which she loved! After dinner, we cleaned up the dishes as a family and played a game of Spot It! And then we sent Alli upstairs to change into her pajamas and brush her teeth.

It was at this point that Alli completely lost it. With tears in her eyes, she vehemently cried, "My birth mom would never do this to me!" She went on, "My birth mom loved me more than you. She let me watch TV all day, never made me learn how to ride a bike. I could eat whatever I wanted, sleep all day, and never go to school. I didn't have to play the piano, I didn't have to brush my teeth, there was no bedtime." She then began sobbing uncontrollably. "My birth mom let me do anything and gave me everything." It became clear to me that in Alli's little six-year-old mind, her worth and our love for her as parents were tied to letting her do whatever she wanted to do—and not making her do the things she didn't want to do. Her understanding of love and worth was skewed by her experience with her birth mom.

I do not need to go into detail about how Alli was raised the first five years of her life for a mature reader to understand that even though I felt deeply for Alli, I wasn't going to express my love to her and help her understand her worth by doing what she perceived was love, as demonstrated by her birth mother who abandoned her. No! I loved her too much for that. I saw in Alli a divine daughter of God, with the potential to become not only an incredible woman but a force for good now and throughout eternity. As a mother, I wanted and still want to give her what is best for her, and part of this means that Alli must follow family rules and meet expectations she does not yet understand. Do I value or love Alli less because I do not give her what she thinks is best at this time in her life?

When asked how he governed his people so effectively, Joseph Smith taught, "I teach them correct principles and they govern themselves."[14] He also taught that "God himself finds himself in the midst of spirits and glory, because he was greater, and because he saw proper to institute laws, whereby the rest could have a privilege to advance like himself."[15] The purpose of God's laws is to help us become like him: happy, joyful, loving, kind, gentle, wise, omniscient. By following God's laws, we become as he is. I believe that understanding and living correct principles brings the greatest amount of joy and happiness possible. Alli will be given agency to govern herself dependent on her grasping correct principles. I believe anything less would be hurtful, if not cruel. Perhaps my greatest expression of love for Alli is in helping her choose to use her God-given agency to show God how much she values and loves him; in so doing, I am helping her reach her divine potential. Will my love for Alli weaken or her worth diminish in my eyes or God's eyes if she decides to choose otherwise? Of course not!

C. S. Lewis invited, "Imagine yourself as a living house." He continued,

> God comes in to rebuild that house. At first, perhaps, you can understand what He is doing. He is getting the drains right and stopping the leaks in the roof and so on; you knew that those jobs needed doing and so you are not surprised. But presently He starts knocking the house about in a way that hurts abominably and does not seem to make any sense. What on earth is He up to? The explanation is that He is building quite a

different house from the one you thought of—throwing out a new wing here, putting on an extra floor there, running up towers, making court-yards. You thought you were being made into a decent little cottage: but He is building a palace. He intends to come and live in it Himself.[16]

The way God has loved for centuries may not always make sense and may even, against mortal desires, "hurt abominably." Christ himself understands that kind of suffering. In fact, I believe God's suffering is inextricably tied to his love.

One of the ways God demonstrates his love for his children is by sending divinely called messengers to provide guidance. Both The Church of Jesus Christ of Latter-day Saints and Community of Christ believe in prophets and divine revelation. Members in both faiths believe that their prophet has received revelation on many topics, including that of personhood. To me, the topic of personhood is an absolute, unchang-ing truth. The prophet simply will not receive revelation that changes God's eternal truths. Policies and procedures change, but doctrines, including God and his children and their divine nature and potential, will not. Thus, any man may now receive the priesthood as a matter of policy and procedure, but that man's nature as a son of God will not change. My daughter may dress up as Elsa or even as Kristoff all she wants, but her eternal marriage to a man is still required for exaltation.

It seems, perhaps, that in Community of Christ there is no eternal or absolute doctrine of this nature. I am unsure. Can doctrine change? Are there eternal truths? Is there an eternal nature to God, or is he fluid? What is your personhood relationship to God? Is God changing? If so, does your relationship with him change as he changes? How does cul-ture influence prophetic revelation? Would you stay in the church if the prophet taught against your current belief in personhood?

I have no question that both of us, Christie, are living the best we can according to what we know. This dialogue has helped me not only understand better what you believe and why you do what you do but also what I believe and why I do what I do, and the significance of both. My holy envy for you as a member of Community of Christ is your ability to seemingly not judge but just love. Too often, members of the Church of Jesus Christ believe it is up to us to uphold God's law, and we forget that we are neither the judge nor the gatekeeper. We focus so much on doctrine that we forget to be disciples! This caution by President James E. Faust in the October 1987 general conference is worth considering: "Let us not become so intense in our zeal to do good by winning arguments or by our pure intention in disputing doctrine that we go beyond good sense and manners, thereby promoting contention, or say and do imprudent things, invoke cynicism, or ridicule with flippancy." He continued, "In this manner, our good motives become so misdirected that we lose friends and, even more serious, we come under the influence of the devil. I recently heard in a special place, 'Your criticism may be worse than the conduct you are trying to correct.'"[17]

I appreciate your example of being a true Christian and a true disciple.

Response to Barbara Morgan Gardner

Barbara, reading your essay was very enjoyable and interesting. One of the things I enjoyed the most about our dialogue was connecting mother to mother. Raising a family in a secular world while holding on to your core values can be tricky for women of faith, as we are. I felt that tension in your piece, and I could really relate to the experience you shared of your daughter relating more to Elsa, a white girl, than to Moana, a Polynesian girl, as you hoped she would. I often find myself wishing my children could relate to the role models I choose for them instead of the ones they choose for themselves.

In your essay, you state that you feel Community of Christ's beliefs and teachings have changed over the years to reflect changes in culture, that we do not stay fixed to absolute "truths" but that our "truth" changes as culture influences us. I can see how that critique makes sense coming from the perspective of a member of The Church of Jesus Christ of Latter-day Saints, but I see it a bit differently.

Another way to think of this concept is to see that the expression of our ancient core values of love, acceptance, and the worth of persons, which we trace back to the teachings of Jesus in the New Testament, adapt as we gain new knowledge of how people live in our modern world. A central value that Community of Christ holds dear is that any modern-day revelation and teaching must be measured against the ultimate love of Jesus. Does the teaching uphold the worth of persons and create a better, more loving world? If it passes that test, then it is more likely to be accepted as revelatory. An inclusive and accepting lens of gender seems to be more closely aligned with a loving, accepting God who wants to share that love with all people. Just because it took us a while to accept that idea does not mean we were swayed by modern culture. Indeed, it is the opposite. We are always learning to understand, embrace, and apply the truth, which sometimes our predecessors lived and practiced better than we have done. Some of these "new" insights are new to us, but they are not new to God. Indeed, some of these insights may have their roots in ancient cultures and religious traditions that predate the modern world. Since you mentioned Moana and Polynesian culture, I will take an example from that part of the world.

In 2007 I accompanied my mother on one of her trips to French Polynesia, where she was assigned as an apostle. When we were there, we learned that Polynesian culture recognizes people called *mahu* (which we might translate as "transgender") and has for centuries, long before colonists came to the area. *Mahu* were not just tolerated but were regarded as legitimate and contributing members of ancient Polynesian communities. While we were in French Polynesia, we met two *mahu* from two different families that were important and successful members of Community of Christ and French Polynesian culture. One was a famous singer whose show we attended in a large stadium full of thousands of people. This is just one example of how Community of Christ is not just reacting to modern Western culture but is creating loving community and embracing the value of ancient beliefs in cultures around the world that uphold the worth of persons. We may be late in learning about these issues, but when we do, and when they correspond with Jesus's teachings, we choose to embrace them and not fear them.

There are many examples, all over the world, of ancient and modern cultures upholding and valuing people that span the gender and sexual spectrum. One example, closer to home, is the "two spirit" people that many First Nations communities in the Americas have historically recognized and continue to recognize. These two-spirit individuals embody both feminine and masculine qualities. We might call them "nonbinary folx." Because two-spirit persons express both the feminine and masculine, they are seen as being closer to the Great Spirit (which is a common way to speak of the Divine in many First Nations cultures and is understood to reflect all genders). As such, some First Nations communities have traditionally given two-spirit persons places of honor, elevating them to seers and wise counselors with important and sacred roles. Community members would often come to them for advice, guidance, blessings, and teachings. They acted in ways and roles that we give to our ministers today. The origins of both of our churches involved a profound appreciation of America's First Nations people. Perhaps we should explore further how they treat and have treated, with great respect, those called "two spirit."

In Community of Christ, we see God as embodying both the Divine Feminine and the Divine Masculine, a position attested in Genesis 1:26–27. We don't see the Godhead as two separate people, Divine Mother and Divine Father, as the Church of Jesus Christ does, but as one loving, non-gender-specific being. This perspective helps us see that gender is a spectrum, not two fixed points, that is evidenced in our world, both modern and ancient.

Likewise, for members of Community of Christ, this spectrum view of gender is carried into the afterlife. We believe we are not bound by our physical reproductive anatomy in either the physical, mortal world or the spiritual, postmortal world, unlike what members of the Church of Jesus Christ believe. This belief allows us to listen to that still, small voice inside each of us that knows who we are, regardless of the physical anatomy we were born with. I wonder, has the Church of Jesus Christ set into rigid doctrine nineteenth-century American ideas of gender and patriarchy that were such a large part of Joseph Smith Jr.'s culture in his day? Does creating a strongly gendered theology of existence from Heavenly Father and Heavenly Mother, through premortal, mortal, and postmortal life, make it difficult for leaders of The Church of Jesus Christ of Latter-day Saints to hear with compassion the voices of the LGBTQ+ community asking for equal respect and full inclusion?

I was interested in your reference to the "new and everlasting covenant of marriage" and the idea that a man must enter into it to achieve the highest degree of celestial glory (LDS Doctrine and Covenants 131:1–2). Then in the Latter-day Saint Doctrine and Covenants 132 I read that the "new and everlasting covenant of marriage" includes polygamy. I'm surprised that this polygamy section is still part of the Church of Jesus Christ's canon of scripture. Is polygamy abolished or only suspended by Wilford Woodruff's official declaration of 1890? With polygamy, how can men and women be equal and full persons in the "new and everlasting covenant of marriage"? I also found the words directed to Emma Smith, coercing her to accept other women as Joseph's wives, to be abusive and threatening (LDS Doctrine and Covenants 132:51–56).

As this relates to my family, my two transgender sons would not consider living in a female body for eternity—assigned to female roles and practicing polygamy (due solely to the body parts they were born with)—heaven or celestial glory. For them it would be the opposite, just as, one can imagine, it would be for a cisgender man in the Church of Jesus Christ if he were assigned the role of female for eternity.

From Genesis we know that God created the heavens and the earth, and it was good. If God created everything and it was good, Community of Christ members believe that God must have created gender diversity and nonbinary folx as well. If we believe that God created us in God's image, then God's image must include the six-year-old trans kid, the gender-exploring sixty-six-year-old, and the gay schoolteacher. If God created all people with loving intention, as Community of Christ members believe, then that means God created all people, and they are good, full stop. For Community of Christ members, this is a divine and eternal truth—that all are worthy, just as they are, no exceptions.

Therefore, it may be that expressing this diversity is one of the greatest, most religious, and sacred things we can do—to fully express who God created us to be, in all our qualities, creativity, and iterations. And it is good.

CONCLUSION

It's incredible how quickly a friendship and bond can form between two individuals, regardless of their differences, if they are willing to listen and speak heart to heart. Prior to this dialogue about "personhood," we did not know each other. As we spoke about our own children, families, and concerns, we quickly realized we were both speaking from a place of love and concern and were clearly trying to do what was best for those we loved with what we knew. Although on paper our religions may vary in their expressions of personhood, both Community of Christ and The Church of Jesus Christ of Latter-day Saints are approaching this topic from a position of deeply grounded love for people.

During this dialogue, we recognized how important it is to stretch beyond our comfort levels and even force ourselves into the realms of others with whom we do not always see eye to eye. Loving others, letting them practice their faith, and supporting them in their faith, even when it differs from our own, is crucial in this divided world. For us, supporting each other in our own faith traditions became more important than trying to help the other person believe in ours. It was with true joy and excitement that we got to be neighbors for a while during this dialogue. If anything will change the world, it will be that people will sit down with their neighbor and, with open hearts, listen to each other and work to understand.

NOTES

1. "The Family: A Proclamation to the World," ChurchofJesusChrist.org.
2. C. S. Lewis, *The Weight of Glory* (San Francisco: HarperCollins, 2001), 45–46.
3. Recognizing that there are some exceptions for people to be able to do that, Latter-day Saint leaders have taught that no one will be kept from eternal life because of decisions out of their control in mortality.
4. Notes from conversation kept by Barbara Gardner.
5. "Family: A Proclamation," paragraph 2.
6. C. S. Lewis, *Weight of Glory*, 45–46.
7. "Discourse, 7 April 1844, as Reported by *Times and Seasons*," p. 614, The Joseph Smith Papers, https://www.josephsmithpapers.org/paper-summary/discourse-7-april-1844-as-reported-by-times-and-seasons/2.

8. Eliza R. Snow, *Biography and Family Record of Lorenzo Snow* (Salt Lake City: Deseret News Press, 1884), 46. The couplet, which has never been canonized, has been formulated in slightly different ways. See also *The Teachings of Lorenzo Snow*, ed. Clyde J. Williams (Salt Lake City: Bookcraft, 1984), 1–2.

9. Spencer W. Kimball, "Privileges and Responsibilities of Sisters" (women's fireside address, September 16, 1978), https://www.ChurchofJesusChrist.org /study/general-conference/1978/10privileges-and-responsibilities-of-sisters.

10. Quoted in Harold E. Will, *Will's Commentary on the New Testament*, vol. 5, *Acts* (Grafton, WV: Missionary Publications, 1976), 345.

11. I am grateful for conversations with Community of Christ Church historians Barbara Walden, Lachlan Mackay, David Howlett, and Ron Romig.

12. "Baptism, Confirmation, and Church Membership," Policy 10.01, 2011.

13. W. H. Auden, *For the Time Being* (London: Faber and Faber, 1945).

14. James R. Clark, comp., *Messages of the First Presidency* (Salt Lake City: Bookcraft, 1966), 3:54.

15. "Minutes and Discourses, 6–7 April 1844, as Published by *Times and Seasons*," p. 615, The Joseph Smith Papers, https://www.josephsmithpapers.org/paper -summary/minutes-and-discourses-6-7-april-1844-as-published-by-times-and -seasons/13.

16. C. S. Lewis, *Mere Christianity* (New York: Touchstone, 1996), 175–76.

17. James E. Faust, "The Great Imitator," *Ensign*, November 1987, 35.

THE FIRST VISION AND CONTINUING REVELATION

Lachlan Mackay and Keith J. Wilson

THE FIRST VISION AND CONTINUING REVELATION IN COMMUNITY OF CHRIST

LACHLAN MACKAY

Lachlan Mackay serves in Community of Christ's Council of Twelve Apostles and oversees the Northeast USA Mission Field and coordinates the church's historic sites.

"There he had an experience with the divine."[1] This description of Joseph Smith's First Vision, as his conversion experience is often known today, comes from the orientation movie at Community of Christ's Joseph Smith Historic Site in Nauvoo, Illinois. By the 1950s, the First Vision would become the foundational event of the faith for many members, although it did not start out that way.

When asked by Nauvoo visitors about the vague language in the movie's description of Joseph Smith's First Vision, I attempt to explain (in a way that's not overwhelming) that Joseph left multiple accounts of the grove experience, that his accounts vary significantly in detail, and that although it is clear to me that Joseph had an experience in the grove, the specifics of that experience are not so clear. I share that in the past, many people joined the faith based on Joseph's conversion experience as described in his 1838 account, rather than on any experience of their own. Anti-Mormons have wielded other versions of the First Vision as a weapon to discredit the faith of these believers and "save" them from so-called deceptions. For these reasons, Community of Christ used more encompassing language for the Nauvoo orientation movie, language that is uncomfortable for some who want a more detailed account of the First Vision. I make every effort to minimize the potential discomfort caused by discussing First Vision accounts while still sharing openly and honestly.

The newer Kirtland Temple orientation movie treats the First Vision differently. It is informed by Joseph's 1832 account, the only one written in his hand, and shares that "Joseph . . . found a secluded grove near his home and poured out his heart in prayer. There he had a vision of Jesus Christ. This personal conversion experience set him on a path that led to the publication of the Book of Mormon, an additional scriptural witness to the Bible, and the founding of the Church of Christ in 1830."[2]

Community of Christ chose to focus on the 1832 version of the First Vision because it is Joseph's earliest-known account and is perhaps more accurate but also because we realized that the more expansive language used in the Nauvoo-site movie ("an experience with the divine") was generating discomfort among visitors and too often becoming an unintended point of contention.

It seems that through at least 1840, most members of the church knew little or nothing of the First Vision. The *Saints' Herald* (our denomination's primary periodical) was first published in 1860, and references to the First Vision are scattered in its pages across the decades, particularly from 1865 to 1958. The centennial of the vision was the dominant focus of our 1920 general conference.[3] The First Vision's role in the life of the church, though, was as *part* of the story rather than *the* story. Likely in response to Fawn Brodie's 1945 publication of *No Man Knows My History*, Israel A. Smith (church president from 1946 to 1958, and grandson and staunch defender of Joseph Smith Jr.) elevated the role of the First Vision through the 1949 publication of a Community of Christ edition of *Joseph Smith Tells His Own Story*.[4] In 1951, this title was chosen as the first Community of Christ tract to be published in Spanish, a clear sign of the elevated status of the vision during Israel's tenure.[5]

Also in the 1950s, Community of Christ began to tentatively engage in missionary outreach in Asia, and leaders became increasingly convinced that a message focused on Joseph Smith and the restoration of the one true Christian church would not serve the church well in cultures that were not traditionally Christian.[6] In a greatly oversimplified version of what happened next, church leaders took a step back, reexamined the faith's core principles, and reformulated the message. In the following decades, the church shifted its focus to center more on Jesus and less on Joseph Smith. This process also resulted in reconnecting the First Vision with its earliest meaning—the story of Joseph's conversion rather than the foundational event for Joseph's call to restore the church.

In his 1980 article "Joseph Smith's First Vision: An Analysis of Six Contemporary Accounts," World Church historian Richard Howard describes the evolving role of the First Vision this way:

> Joseph's First Vision could not have been the central reason for the decision of many to unite with the Latter Day Saint movement in the first decade of its existence. After all, it seems clear that that event, which from 1840 to the present has gradually become so important to so many Latter Day Saints, simply was not generally known to the membership during the first decade of the church's life. Whatever the church's reasons for being from 1830 to 1840, the First Vision was not among them as a conscious reality of vital significance to the members. By actions of the church and its leaders from 1842 on, that event has come to have a position of central importance in the literature, imagination, and theology of the various Latter Day Saint communities that have emerged from the original church.[7]

Howard's article was presented at the 1977 John Whitmer Historical Association Conference before it was published in the first volume of *Restoration Studies* by the church's Herald Publishing House, and it played a critical role in increasing awareness among RLDS members that there were multiple accounts of the vision with some significant variations in detail.

The 1832 account of the vision with the appearance of Jesus and passages like "I was crucifyed [*sic*] for the world" and "clothed in the glory of my Father" are particularly helpful as Community of Christ increasingly focuses on Christ.[8] This earliest account is gradually becoming a reminder that from the first stirrings of what would eventually grow into the church, Christ has been at our center. The First Vision is taking on other contemporary meanings as well.

In years past, Community of Christ had a program that brought members from around the world to historic church sites. The goals of this program were to introduce members to our history and strengthen their language skills. Previous conventional wisdom was that our mostly white, male, nineteenth-century, North American story would not speak to international members. My time working with this program challenged and even overturned that understanding. In many cases, our international members today are living our nineteenth-century story of poverty, oppression, and persecution, so they understand and connect even more quickly to our history than North American members do.

In 2004, I visited what is now known as the Sacred Grove with two program participants, both from nations in Africa. Andrew Bolton, later a Community of Christ apostle, was with us as well. It was raining, but we had umbrellas, and we slowly walked together through the trees without saying much. We stopped, several of us offered prayers, and when we made it back to the car, we talked about the meaning of the Sacred Grove. One of the two women made a comment that has stayed with me: "If God cared about a poor, uneducated farm boy, maybe God even cares about me, a poor African grandmother."

At some level, I was troubled by the statement. The woman's words suggested that she doubted her worth in the eyes of God. But they also illustrated ways that the First Vision is meaningful to contemporary

Community of Christ members. The vision draws together three of our Enduring Principles: Continuing Revelation, the Worth of All Persons, and All Are Called (to be disciples of Christ). If God can work through an impoverished and uneducated teenager, then God can work through anyone. God still speaks. All are of worth. All are called. That is the message of the First Vision today.

CONTINUING REVELATION

Visions are one form of revelation, but Community of Christ members today more often encounter God through other revelatory forms, including the addition of sections to the Doctrine and Covenants. The understanding that God reveals God's divine will today, as God did in the past, is an essential element of Community of Christ. God still speaks. This concept is expressed in our Enduring Principle of Continuing Revelation, and it is also a basic belief of the church: "We affirm the Living God is ever self-revealing. God is revealed to the world in the testimony of Israel, and above all in Jesus Christ. By the Holy Spirit we continue to hear God speaking today. The church is called to listen together for what the Spirit is saying and then faithfully respond."[9] Formally, this means adding new sections to the Doctrine and Covenants. The "testing" of a new section of the Doctrine and Covenants involves the discernment of different priesthood orders and quorums as well as meetings of nonpriesthood and youth. A final decision is made by the World Conference delegates. However, God's self-revealing is much bigger than this and touches members and friends as they grow in following Jesus, the Peaceful One.

God's revelation is ongoing, and we believe the revelatory process is conceptual (the thoughts are inspired, but the word choice is not) rather than plenary (each word is inspired and without error). As a result, we do not ascribe to a dictation theory of revelation—that the writer's only role is to apply God's words to paper. The humanity of the prophetic figure conveying revelation cannot be separated from the process. Joseph Smith Jr.'s willingness to edit his revelatory texts suggests he was comfortable, at least on some level, with the idea that revelation was conceptual. When reflecting on the Doctrine and Covenants, Apostle Dale Luffman summarized our perspective on revelation this way: "Community of Christ does not believe revelation is verbal, literal, or inerrant. Scripture is rather viewed as the written testimony of God's interaction with creation, inspired by the Holy Spirit. It is not the words of a written text that we follow but the God who inspires those words."[10]

Building on the church's 1830s emphasis on common consent, Community of Christ members in recent decades have been invited to participate in the prophetic task of receiving revelation. In a World Conference address to the church given soon after his 1996 ordination as prophet-president, W. Grant McMurray said, "We need to talk, my friends, about the way we have begun to move from our identity as a people with a prophet to our calling as a prophetic people."[11] The conversation continued in 2004: "As a prophetic people you are called, under the direction of the spiritual authorities and with the common consent of the people, to discern the divine will for your own time and in the places where you serve. You live in a world with new challenges, and that world will require new forms of ministry" (CofChrist Doctrine and Covenants 162:2c). President Stephen M. Veazey picked up the theme in 2007: "God is calling for a prophetic community to emerge, drawn from the nations of the world, that is characterized by uncommon devotion to the compassion and peace of God revealed in Jesus Christ" (CofChrist Doctrine and Covenants 163:11a). In an increasingly complex and challenging world, Community of Christ strives to be not only a people with a prophet but also a prophetic people.

In summary, Joseph Smith Jr.'s conversion experience, now known as the First Vision, was relatively unknown in the earliest years of Community of Christ. Awareness of and emphasis on this theophany grew slowly in the second half of the nineteenth century, and the 1920 RLDS general conference used the vision as its central theme. By the 1950s, the First Vision had become the founding event of the church. The church's movement toward international expansion, which started in the 1950s, generated a growing emphasis on Jesus over Joseph, and the First Vision began to transition back to its original role in the life of the church as the story of Joseph's conversion. Today the First Vision is also meaningful to Community of Christ members as a reminder of the worth of all persons, that all are called to be disciples of Christ and that revelation continues. Visions are one kind of revelation, and continuing revelation is both a core value and a basic belief in Community of Christ. Revelation is understood to be conceptual rather than plenary, and in recent decades the church has increased its emphasis on transitioning from a people with a prophet to a prophetic people.

The First Vision in The Church of Jesus Christ of Latter-day Saints

KEITH J. WILSON

Keith J. Wilson is an associate professor of ancient scripture at Brigham Young University.

As a fifteen-year-old member of The Church of Jesus Christ of Latter-day Saints, I can vividly remember my earliest formal encounter with the First Vision. My scoutmaster and I were teaching my best friend about the Restoration of the gospel. After outlining the foundational events of the beginning of the church, my leader turned to me and invited me to share my personal feelings about these happenings. I began by sharing my thoughts on Joseph Smith and the First Vision. For the first time in my young life, I deeply believed and felt the truthfulness of that event. This experience commenced my lifelong devotion to this seminal Restoration vision.

The gospel of Jesus Christ has always embraced visions as a form of God's communication with humankind. This assertion is more than evident in the scriptures. During Old Testament times, the Lord set the standard for visions when he declared, "If there be a prophet among you, I the Lord will make myself known unto him in a vision" (Numbers 12:6). Accordingly, the scriptures confirm that most prophets received visions in their leadership roles. Moses, Isaiah, Elijah, and Jeremiah all received significant visions. This pattern continued in the New Testament with such notables as Stephen and John the Revelator. The Book of Mormon begins with Lehi's vision and ends with Moroni's visions of the latter days. In addition, the latter-day Restoration began with Joseph Smith's seminal First Vision, and the period was then punctuated with multiple visionary events, such as the vision of the three degrees of glory and the vision of the spirit world (LDS Doctrine and Covenants 76 and 138, respectively).

All in all, visions are a central doctrine of The Church of Jesus Christ of Latter-day Saints. In 1842, Joseph Smith penned the Wentworth Letter to a Chicago newspaper editor. In a creedal-like manner, Joseph declared in the seventh doctrinal stanza of that letter, "We believe in the gift of tongues, prophesy [sic], revelations, *visions*, healing, interpretation of tongues and so forth" (emphasis added; see LDS Articles of Faith 1:7). Thus, in a modern setting, the founding Prophet of the Restoration formalized the significance of visions in our faith. But what exactly is a "vision"? And what distinguishes it from other forms of revelation? The *Encyclopedia of Mormonism* describes a vision as "a visual mode of divine communication in contrast with hearing words spoken or receiving impressions to the mind."[12] Ever since the formative days of the Church of Jesus Christ, visions have played a prominent role in the church's beliefs.

While the early history of our faith is replete with visionary accounts, no vision stands larger for us than the quintessential First Vision, which Joseph received around the year 1820. The history and provenance of the First Vision merit closer introspection. Perhaps the First Vision can be used as a template for our perceptions of the doctrine of latter-day visions.

When the teenage Joseph first experienced the vision, he was shocked by the brusque reception he received from outsiders. Joseph Smith recalled his surprise when he first related this vision to a Methodist minister. In Joseph's words, the preacher responded that "[the vision] was all of the devil, that there were no such things as visions or revelations in [those] days; that all such things had ceased with the apostles" (LDS Joseph Smith—History 1:21). This experience so unnerved the young boy prophet that he seemed to retract his epiphany from public view and thereafter focused solely on tangible Restoration evidences like the Book of Mormon. In the decade that followed, Joseph published the Book of Mormon and organized the church. With the foundational elements in place in 1832, Joseph broke his silence and recorded his earliest written account of the First Vision. Three more directly dictated accounts followed in 1835, 1838, and 1842. Other secondary tellings of the vision surfaced, but these four accounts constitute the personally dictated memoirs of the First Vision.

So how did the historical development of the First Vision proceed? And what elevated the 1838 account in The Church of Jesus Christ of Latter-day Saints? As mentioned previously, Joseph withdrew his experience from public scrutiny after the minister openly berated him. For more than a decade, Joseph maintained his self-imposed silence. Then some twelve years later, in 1832, Joseph quietly penned his initial remembrance of the First Vision. This account was relatively short; it projected the basic outline of the vision, focusing primarily on his standing before God. Joseph did not release this text to the public, and it was obscured in a private record book until 1965, when it was first published.[13] Three years after this initial 1832 account was drafted, in 1835, Joseph recorded a very similar iteration of the First Vision. This account was also short and light on details. Like the 1832 rendition, it was also filed away in private archival holdings and was unknown until the 1960s.

After the Saints departed from Kirtland and relocated to frontier Missouri, they faced continued resistance and persecutions. In 1838, some eighteen years following the First Vision, Joseph felt compelled to openly set the record straight. His introduction to the notable 1838 account began with "Owing to the many reports which have been put into circulation by evil-disposed and designing persons, in relation to the rise and the progress of the Church, . . . I have been induced to write this history, to put all inquiries after truth in possession of the facts" (LDS Joseph Smith—History 1:1). Joseph then proceeded to chronicle a rather detailed account beginning with the First Vision and continuing through to the restoration of the Aaronic Priesthood in 1829. This is the account of the First Vision that appears today in scripture used by The Church of Jesus Christ of Latter-day Saints.

The last of the four accounts was dictated in 1842, when Joseph Smith responded to a newspaper editor, John Wentworth. Wentworth never put the account in print, but Joseph published this version in the *Times and Seasons* on March 1, 1844. This was the first published account of the vision in the United States, and while it was fairly brief, it would have been the description that most Nauvoo members would have known at the time. Of these four extant accounts, only two were published in the early church. Since the 1842 account was published first, how did the 1838 account supplant the 1842 account and become the official First Vision version of the Latter-day Saints?

Joseph dictated the 1838 account to his secretary, George Robinson, beginning in April 1838. After five days of transcribing and editing, they had completed eight manuscript pages of text, which included the description of the First Vision.[14] Their work was suspended shortly after they began, due to the 1838 Missouri hostilities and Joseph's imprisonment. The following June, in 1839, with the help of James Mulholland, Joseph was able to finish the account. In comparison with the other three dictated versions, the 1838 recitation was couched in more institutional terms. In previous accounts, Joseph had focused more on his personal standing before God, but in this telling, he concentrated on his struggles of knowing which church to join and dealing with all the opposition that had suddenly surfaced. Also, the 1838 account was written with the intent to publish it as the first part of an intended multi-volume *History of the Church*. Thus, it was edited and presented in the context of the larger restoration of all things.

Consequently, Joseph was inclined to share this account more openly with others. One such person was a trusted friend, Orson Pratt. In December 1839, while Joseph was en route to Washington to plead the cause of the Saints, he met with Orson in Philadelphia, where they remained for eight days. Later, when Orson described his understanding of the First Vision, he emphatically stated that he had heard it "as it came from [Joseph's] own mouth."[15]

Later that same year, while proselyting in Scotland, Orson published his first missionary tract, titled *A[n] Interesting Account of Several Remarkable Visions*. Included in that thirty-one-page pamphlet was the first printed version of the 1838 First Vision account. Orson was so enamored with his missionary tract that, when he returned from

Scotland in 1841, he had it printed in New York and distributed in Nauvoo. The demand for *Interesting Account* prompted Orson to print two more editions in New York as well as subsequent editions in England (1848), Germany (1852), France (1850), Australia (1851), Denmark (1851), and Holland (1865).[16] Orson was so relentless in his preaching and promoting of the First Vision that one historian referred to him as the "Defender of the First Vision."[17] Also noteworthy is that Orson was the first person to refer to this seminal event as "the First Vision."[18]

Later, at the 1880 church general conference, a sixty-nine-year-old Pratt watched as the 1838 account of the First Vision was canonized in church scripture as part of the Pearl of Great Price. Orson must have felt great pride that October day knowing that his love for and emphasis on the First Vision had largely sparked the church's endorsement of the miracle's account.

The First Vision after Canonization

Shortly before the First Vision was canonized, two Latter-day Saint artists incorporated the event into their trades. C. C. A. Christensen produced a traveling art show of vignettes from early church history in which the First Vision was prominently depicted, and George Manwaring, perhaps building on Christensen's art display, composed the well-known hymn "Oh, How Lovely Was the Morning." These expressions combined with the canonization to significantly raise the collective consciousness of the First Vision in the church. After the death of Orson Pratt, President George Q. Cannon of the First Presidency took up the First Vision cause and repeatedly made it the center point of his sermons. He was subsequently joined in this effort by church historian B. H. Roberts, who in 1893 systematized the vision by citing five reasons for its importance. Thus, the stage was set doctrinally for a major reshaping of church identity.

At the turn of the century, the church was locked in a struggle for survival with the federal government over the doctrine of polygamy. Joseph F. Smith, a lineal descendant of Joseph Smith's brother Hyrum, had been called before Congress in 1904 to pledge his word that the Latter-day Saints would no longer practice polygamy. When Joseph F. returned to Utah, he realized that the Saints would need to focus on the Prophet's first revelation instead of his last[19] and commenced a multifaceted program to embed the vision more prominently into the minds and beliefs of the members. First, he encouraged the church to purchase the traditional Palmyra site of the vision. Additionally, the church produced a new missionary pamphlet, *Joseph Smith Tells His Own Story*. And finally, he preached repeatedly on the "the most important event in the history of the world excepting only the revelation of Godhood in the person of our Lord Jesus Christ."[20] As a fitting tribute to Joseph F. Smith's emphasis, two years after his death, in 1920, the church celebrated the centennial of the First Vision. General conference, a commemorative cantata, a special edition of the *Improvement Era*, and numerous pageants all expressed the church's deep convictions of the First Vision. This seminal event was no longer just a doctrinal mainstay but a cultural keystone as well.

Meanwhile, in the larger Christian milieu, Charles Darwin, higher biblical criticism, and the Scopes Trial had all served notice that prevailing Christianity was passé. This enlightened tidal wave also affected the church through its flagship academy, Brigham Young University. A group of academics openly promulgated that the First Vision should not be treated as historical fact but instead should be viewed as a mental suggestion without an objective reality.[21] The church responded a few years later, in 1938, when J. Reuben Clark Jr., a member of the First Presidency, announced that all teachers in the church's educational system had to affirm two cardinal truths: "First—that Jesus Christ is the Son of God," and second that "the Father and the Son actually and in truth and very deed appeared to the Prophet Joseph in a vision in the woods."[22] With this address, the church positioned this fundamental tenet of the Restoration as a lightning rod for the faithful.

Seven years later, this lightning rod received its first major strike when Fawn Brodie published her highly critical book, *No Man Knows My History*. In her diatribe, she psychoanalyzed Joseph Smith with statements like "Dream images came easily to this youth, whose imagination was as untrammeled as the whole West."[23] Church president David O. McKay, Brodie's uncle, did not take her assault on Joseph's First Vision lightly. He subsequently challenged the church membership to "proclaim . . . that the Church is divinely established by the appearance of God the Father and his Son Jesus Christ to the Prophet Joseph Smith."[24]

The church accepted President McKay's challenge and included the First Vision in the first missionary discussions, in general conference talks, and in other church materials. In the decade that followed (1950–60), the church saw large increases in its membership. When the church celebrated its sesquicentennial in 1980, a special children's program was performed in every local congregation. The script for the presentation featured a family asking their children what they learned from the First Vision. It was a fitting celebration of the one-hundred-year rise in the prominence of the First Vision. As one historian summarized the First Vision's trajectory, "It was indeed not just Joseph Smith's theophany, but [had become] the great Mormon theophany."[25]

In more recent times, the church has steadfastly anchored itself to the First Vision. President Gordon B. Hinckley declared emphatically, "We declare without equivocation that God the Father and His Son, the Lord Jesus Christ, appeared in person to the boy Joseph Smith." He continued, "Our whole strength rests on the validity of that vision. It either occurred or it did not occur. If it did not, then this work is a fraud. If it did, then it is the most important and wonderful work under the heavens."[26] This statement aptly describes today how members of The Church of Jesus Christ of Latter-day Saints countenance the importance of the First Vision.

RESPONSE TO KEITH J. WILSON

Keith's devotion to the Prophet Joseph Smith and the First Vision is evident in the spirit in which he writes. I found his overview of the rise of the First Vision in The Church of Jesus Christ of Latter-day Saints to be both fascinating and helpful. His chapter has solved for me an enduring mystery: How could the First Vision play such very different roles in two communities that have in common the fourteen years from the organization of the church to Joseph's death? Although the vision clearly did not play a central role in the church by 1844, there were several published and widely available accounts of the vision before the assassination of Joseph and Hyrum Smith.

What happened in the years that followed? The significance of the First Vision rose and fell in Community of Christ. That does not seem to have been the case for The Church of Jesus Christ of Latter-day Saints, with President Hinckley eventually tying the truth or falsehood of the church to the validity of the First Vision.

Keith touched on several points that clarify both churches' journeys with the First Vision. The first point relates to the context of the 1838 account. While earlier accounts focused on God forgiving Joseph's sins and on Joseph's conversion experience, the 1838 account focuses on how wrong existing churches were, with their abominable creeds and corrupt professors (see LDS Joseph Smith—History 1:19). What was different by the late 1830s? By this time, the church's conflict with its "Christian" neighbors was growing and would eventually result in the extermination of the Latter-day Saints from Missouri. The 1838 account of the vision reflects Joseph's response to this conflict.

Perhaps the most critical points in understanding the different role the First Vision would come to play in The Church of Jesus Christ of Latter-day Saints in comparison with Community of Christ are, first, Orson Pratt's passion for sharing the vision and, second, the related 1880 canonization of the 1838 account. This shift from history to scripture is very difficult to undo and significantly elevated the trajectory of the vision in the life of The Church of Jesus Christ of Latter-day Saints.

I appreciate Keith's candor in linking Joseph F. Smith's early twentieth-century emphasis on the First Vision to the need to establish a new pillar of identity to replace the discarded focus on plural marriage. Perhaps the most surprising revelation from this joint writing project is Fawn Brodie's likely role in causing both churches to further emphasize the vision in the mid-twentieth century.

I am concerned that The Church of Jesus Christ of Latter-day Saints' continued emphasis on the 1838 account of the First Vision is setting up members for a faith crisis, because I can't forget my discussion with angry or distraught historic site visitors and friends who are members of the Church of Jesus Christ. Information about earlier accounts of the vision with significantly different details is simply too widely available to ignore, and attempting to do so leads to the sense among some believers that their church leaders have deceived them. The Gospel Topics essay "First Vision Accounts" could be an important corrective, but it is not easily found online by those who are not already aware of its existence.

Although the topic in question was different at the time (Joseph Smith and polygamy versus First Vision accounts), well-meaning Community of Christ leaders have found themselves in similar positions in generations past with similar results. Please learn from our mistake.

RESPONSE TO LACHLAN MACKAY

To be sure, Community of Christ and The Church of Jesus Christ of Latter-day Saints have much more in common through our Restoration roots than we have differences. Both faiths were birthed through the Prophet Joseph Smith's inquisitiveness, both are devoutly Christ centered, both accept an open canon with ongoing revelation, and both value the concept of Zion or a Christ-centered community. Openly acknowledging our many commonalities, however, does not mean that we no longer have any points of divergence in our faith traditions. In the last 175 years, we have differed over polygamy, prophetic succession, and original church properties—to name a few.

The doctrine of the First Vision, however, presents a unique case study in the history of our two faiths. This seminal event was fully embraced by both churches for one hundred years. Then in about 1960, Community of Christ gradually adopted a more cautious interpretation of the First Vision, which eventuated in its current position that the event really should not be considered a "first vision" as much as a young man's personal, spiritual experience. In Lachlan's words, it is no longer *plenary* as much as it is simply *personalized*. Meanwhile, for The Church of Jesus Christ of Latter-day Saints, the First Vision has become more and more the epicenter of the Restoration. In 1998, church president Gordon B. Hinckley declared, "Our entire case as members of The Church of Jesus Christ of Latter-day Saints rests on the validity of this glorious First Vision. . . . Nothing on which we base our doctrine, nothing we teach, nothing we live by is of greater importance than this [vision]."[27] So what caused this stark divergence between our two Restoration faiths? As cited by Lachlan, the First Vision was vibrant in the RLDS Church up until 1952. President Israel Smith took great ownership of his grandfather's vision. But from the 1960s onward, new progressive leaders such as Maurice Draper, Clifford Cole, and Charles Neff were placed in the First Presidency and the Council of the Twelve Apostles. These leaders had doubts about the validity of Joseph's experiences.[28] Coinciding with societal pressures of the times, they began to redirect the church away from the distinctives of the Restoration and back toward a more traditional Christian orientation. Then in 1965 a titanic doctrinal shift occurred when RLDS scholar Robert Flanders published the book *Kingdom on the Mississippi*, which, among other things, demonstrated that Joseph practiced polygamy. From this point forward, the RLDS leadership increasingly adopted the mantra "We worship Jesus, not Joseph."

In 1980, the RLDS Church made an additional shift in emphasis and interpretation of Joseph Smith's First Vision when church historian Richard Howard published an article in which he examined the multiple accounts of Smith's theophany. Howard opined that the First Vision was not the foundational event of the Restoration and that it had been manufactured or "imagined" by subsequent leaders.[29] Thus, the First Vision for the church has become just a religious experience for a young boy who was concerned about his standing before God.

For The Church of Jesus Christ of Latter-day Saints, the upward trajectory of the First Vision since 1950 has only become more pronounced. In the early sixties, the First Vision became the centerpiece of missionary materials. When multiple accounts of the First Vision began to receive attention in the 1960s, apologetic scholars belonging to the church jumped to its defense. Scores of books and articles in both scholarly and church venues have been published over the past fifty years defending the credibility of the First Vision.[30] The apex of this defense perhaps occurred in 2016 when the church published an online defense of the First Vision under the title "First Vision Accounts."[31] Some four years later, as the church commemorated the two hundredth anniversary of the First Vision, President Russell M. Nelson announced a new church proclamation, just the sixth in the organization's two-hundred-year history. This official proclamation centered on the church's restored nature and the faith's beginnings with the First Vision. The document reads in part, "In humility, we declare that in answer to his prayer, God the Father and His Son, Jesus Christ, appeared to Joseph and inaugurated the 'restitution of all things' (Acts 3:21) as foretold in the Bible. In this vision, he learned that following the death of the original apostles, Christ's New Testament Church was lost from the earth. Joseph would be instrumental in its return."[32]

For The Church of Jesus Christ of Latter-day Saints, the First Vision is a virtual treasure trove of doctrinal truths. Most significant of these is the firsthand witness that Jesus is the Christ and the Savior of the world. Not far behind is the reality of a Heavenly Father who works in tandem with his Son. Add to these the fact that God has restored the fulness of his gospel and has organized a church here upon this earth. Central to this church is the doctrine that God leads his work directly through a prophet.

In addition to many institutional truths, the First Vision circumscribes many personal truths as well. Preeminent among these is that the Savior truly saves each individual. In addition, the fact that God hears and answers personal prayers is verified. Add to this the truth that Satan is real and that he seeks to thwart righteousness. And the list goes on and on. In short, the First Vision has become the church's doctrinal doorway to finding Christ both institutionally and personally.

When viewed simultaneously, Community of Christ's and The Church of Jesus Christ of Latter-day Saints' views of the foundational doctrine of the First Vision have grown further apart. We do have much in common. But a common view of the First Vision is no longer one of those areas.

CONCLUSION

The role of the First Vision in the life of both The Church of Jesus Christ of Latter-day Saints and Community of Christ has evolved through the years. Relatively unknown in the earliest years of the church, the First Vision became foundational for both faiths up until the 1950s. Over the last fifty years, Community of Christ has gravitated to the 1832 account of the vision, and the vision is now primarily viewed as an account of Joseph Smith Jr.'s personal conversion experience. Additionally, the vision is also meaningful to Community of Christ members as a reminder of the worth of all persons, that all are called to be disciples of Christ, and that revelation continues. Continuing revelation is a Community of Christ core value. Revelation is understood to be conceptual, and there is a growing emphasis on becoming a prophetic people.

In contrast, for The Church of Jesus Christ of Latter-day Saints, the most detailed First Vision account of 1838 has become a central tenet of the Restoration. This account, which was first canonized in 1880, has grown more and more prominent in the church since then. In recent years, the Church of Jesus Christ has acknowledged, published, and blended all four First Vision accounts; nevertheless, the 1838 account has remained the backbone of the church's message.

The unvarnished issue between our two Restoration faiths is much larger than just a divergence concerning the First Vision over the last seventy years. The issue is really centered in whether Joseph Smith's revelations are accepted as if dictated by God to him or if they are understood to be filtered through the humanity or frailties of the boy prophet. On the day that Joseph Smith organized the latter-day church, he recorded the Lord as declaring, "Wherefore, meaning the church, thou shalt give heed unto all [Joseph Smith's] words and commandments which he shall give unto you as he receiveth them" (LDS Doctrine and Covenants 21:4; CofChrist Doctrine and Covenants 19:2a). Later Joseph also revealed that the latter-day revelations were given unto the Lord's servants in their language and weakness (see LDS Doctrine and Covenants 1:24; CofChrist Doctrine and Covenants 1:5a). The Church of Jesus Christ believes they have embraced the path back to Jesus Christ that

Joseph Smith revealed in the restoration of all things, while Community of Christ believes they are called to be both a people with a prophet and a prophetic people as they strive to continue moving toward Jesus, the Peaceful One. Both of our faiths are centered on Jesus Christ, but as reflected in our understandings of the First Vision, our doctrines have diverged rather decisively.

Notes

1. *Journey of the Saints: Nauvoo* (Independence, MO: Herald Publishing House, 2009), DVD.
2. *Journey of the Saints.*
3. "1820–1920 Centennial Program," *Saints' Herald*, March 24, 1920, 265.
4. "Joseph Smith Tells His Own Story," *Saints' Herald*, July 18, 1949, 691.
5. "José Smith relata su propia historia," *Saints' Herald*, October 15, 1951, 1008.
6. For more details, see Matthew Bolton, *Apostle of the Poor: The Life and Work of Missionary and Humanitarian Charles D. Neff* (Independence, MO: John Whitmer Books, 2005).
7. Richard P. Howard, "Joseph Smith's First Vision: An Analysis of Six Contemporary Accounts," *Restoration Studies* 1 (Independence, MO: Herald Publishing House, 1980), 96.
8. "History, circa Summer 1832," p. 3, The Joseph Smith Papers, https://www .josephsmithpapers.org/paper-summary/history-circa-summer-1832/3.
9. Anthony J. Chvala-Smith, ed., *Exploring Community of Christ Basic Beliefs: A Commentary* (Independence, MO: Herald Publishing House, 2020), 127.
10. Dale Luffman, *Commentary on the Community of Christ Doctrine and Covenants* (Independence, MO: Herald Publishing House, 2019), 1:10.
11. W. Grant McMurray, "A Prophetic People," *Saints' Herald*, June 1996, 226.
12. Allen E. Bergin, "Vision," *Encyclopedia of Mormonism*, ed. Daniel H. Ludlow (New York: Macmillan, 1991), 4:1511.
13. Paul R. Cheesman, "An Analysis of the Accounts Relating Joseph Smith's Early Visions" (master's thesis, Brigham Young University, 1965), 126.
14. "History, 1838–1856, volume A-1 [23 December 1805–30 August 1834]," pp. 1–3, The Joseph Smith Papers, https://www.josephsmithpapers.org/paper-summary /history-1838-1856-volume-a-1-23-december-1805-30-august-1834/1; see also Dean C. Jessee, *Personal Writings of Joseph Smith*, 2nd ed. (Salt Lake City: Deseret Book, 2002), 226.
15. Orson Pratt, in *Journal of Discourses* (London: Latter-day Saints' Book Depot, 1860), 7:220.
16. Milton Backman Jr., "Defender of the First Vision," in *Regional Studies in Latter-day Saint Church History: New York* (Provo, UT: Brigham Young

University, 1992), 38; see also Stephen Harper, *First Vision: Memory and Origins* (New York: Oxford University Press, 2019), 61.

17. Backman, "Defender of the First Vision," 33.

18. Stephen Harper, "Raising the Stakes," *BYU Studies Quarterly* 59, no. 2 (2020): 27.

19. Kathleen Flake, *The Politics of the American Religious Identity: The Seating of Senator Reed Smoot* (Chapel Hill: University of North Carolina, 2004), 109–37.

20. John Henry Evans, *One Hundred Years of Mormonism* (Salt Lake City: Deseret News Press, 1905), 18.

21. "Report of Horace Cummings to General Church Board," quoted in *Brigham Young University: The First One Hundred Years* (Provo, UT: Brigham Young University Press, 1975), 1:423.

22. J. Reuben Clark Jr., "The Charted Course of the Church in Education" (Salt Lake City: The Church of Jesus Christ of Latter-day Saints, 1992), 2, https://www.ChurchofJesusChrist.org/bc/content/shared/content/english/pdf/language-materials/32709_eng.pdf.

23. Fawn McKay Brodie, *No Man Knows My History* (New York: Alfred A. Knopf, 1945), 25.

24. David O. McKay, in Conference Report, April 1954, 25.

25. James B. Allen, "Emergence of a Fundamental: The Expanding Role of Joseph Smith's First Vision," in *Exploring the First Vision* (Provo, UT: Religious Studies Center, Brigham Young University; Salt Lake City: Deseret Book, 2012), 251.

26. Gordon B. Hinckley, "The Marvelous Foundation of Our Faith," *Ensign*, November 2002, 80.

27. Gordon B. Hinckley, "What Are People Asking about Us?," *Ensign*, November 1998, 71.

28. Clifford A. Cole, "An Oral History Memoir" (unpublished manuscript, 1985), Community of Christ Archives, 4–5; see also Bolton, *Charles D. Neff,* 23.

29. Howard, "Joseph Smith's First Vision: An Analysis," 96.

30. See James B. Allen, "Eight Contemporary Accounts of the First Vision—What Do We Learn from Them?," *Improvement Era* 73 (1970): 4–13; Richard L. Anderson, "Joseph Smith's Testimony of the First Vision," *Ensign*, April 1996, 10–21; Milton V. Backman, *Joseph Smith's First Vision: The First Vision in Its Historical Context*, 2nd ed. (Salt Lake City: Bookcraft, 1971); Steven C. Harper, *Joseph Smith's First Vision: A Guide to the Historical Accounts* (Salt Lake City: Deseret Book, 2012).

31. Gospel Topics Essays, "First Vision Accounts," https://www.ChurchofJesusChrist.org/study/manual/gospel-topics-essays/first-vision-accounts.

32. "The Restoration of the Fulness of the Gospel of Jesus Christ: A Bicentennial Proclamation to the World," ChurchofJesusChrist.org.

Apostasy and Restoration

Gina Colvin (Ngā Puhi, Ngāti Porou)
and Jordan T. Watkins

Apostasy and Restoration:
A Community of Christ Commentary

Gina Colvin (Ngā Puhi, Ngāti Porou)

Gina Colvin is a New Zealand Māori who grew up a Latter-day Saint. She currently worships locally with the Anglican Church and internationally with Community of Christ.

M y mountain is Hikurangi.
My river is Waiapu.
My people are descendants of Porourangi.
I preface this essay with my mihi, *my statement of identity. I do this because, above all else, I am the granddaughter of a long line of grandmothers whose bones have been laid down in the belly of the mother,* Papatuānuku, *in this land,* Aotearoa *(New Zealand). It is through them that I have come to be, and their presences are inextricably spiritually entwined with me. I say this because* Pākehā *(white) Western religious institutions, while powerful*

in the way that they have captivated and organized my religious attention,
are seldom potent enough to steal away the self that resides in the deep inner
ancestral realms that precede me and have formed me.

My Māori family has been a part of the Latter Day Saint[1] Restoration
since its earliest days in *Aotearoa* (New Zealand). Like most *Ngāti Porou*
who became Latter Day Saints, my family members joined the church
because they felt the Anglican Church (*Te Hāhi Mihinare*)[2] had failed
to support Māori interests. As the settler population grew, so did the
demands of its political organizations associated with the Anglican
Church. A slew of legal violations followed that led to the confiscation
and alienation of Native land. The mainstream churches hardly pro-
tested.[3] In truth, the early Latter Day Saints didn't object to land confis-
cations either, but they didn't have as much dirt on their hands as the
European churches who'd had decades of troubled history with Māori.
Consequently, while the message of the Latter-day Saint missionaries
was terribly unpopular with the settlers, the church's mission to Māori
quickly picked up momentum.[4]

I was raised by my settler-descended Anglican mother, who joined
the Utah-based Brigham Young expression of the Latter Day Saint
Restoration just five days before my birth. She came to the Latter-day
Saints via my Māori father's family. From my father, Hemi Ruwhiu, I
am a third-generation Latter-day Saint.

Yet my longing and love for ecumenism and belonging in the larger
body of Christ subsequently led to charges of apostasy. In 2019 I was
called into a Latter-day Saint ward membership council to answer those
charges. Church leaders thought I was apostate; I thought the Latter-day
Saint Church was in a state of apostasy. It was an impossible scenario.
Though those charges were suspended, the chill of church discipline
lingered, and I consequently formally disaffiliated the following year.[5]

Yet my lingering love of the Restoration saw me becoming increasingly interested in and involved with Community of Christ. I began to
see my Christian ministry playing out through this small, progressive
worldwide faith full of Restoration radicals who were having conversations that resonated with me as a newly minted contextual and pastoral
theologian. I was confirmed in Community of Christ in 2019 in the

temple in Missouri. The seduction of a faith that made more of restoration than apostasy was irresistable.

Religiously socialized in The Church of Jesus Christ of Latter-day Saints, I believed, as I was growing up, that the apostasy and restoration narrative was straighforward. Jesus established a church. The church had fallen into a state of unfaithfulness to the teachings of Jesus. This was apostasy. Joseph Smith's call and vocation was to restore what was lost. This was restoration. I appreciated the simplicity of it. Institutions break, are denatured, and stray from their original values. But there is yet hope.

I believed this of every institution, including my own, that there were no guarantees of faithfulness and that without a hermeneutics of institutional suspicion and the spiritual practice of ongoing revision, repentance, and reform, one's own tradition could become corrupted. I was optimistic that given the emphasis on repentance in the Latter-day Saint tradition, the same expectations for human transformation and freedom from sin would be held at an institutional level. As Community of Christ Graceland Seminary teacher and theologian Tony Chvala-Smith has pointed out, "All great rebirths and revivals in the history of the Christian church have occurred not when Christians in crisis decided to abandon their past and look elsewhere for illumination, but when they boldly but humbly re-embraced their past in the firm faith that God, who had spoken there before, would speak there again."[6]

When I publicly pointed out the failings of the Latter-day Saint Church around issues of social justice and inclusion, I was put on notice as a troublemaker and asked to rein in my objections. My calls for institutional reform were greeted with frosty indifference by church leaders, who were more concerned with my "airing of the church's dirty laundry in public." I had stepped over a line. In the sociology of religion, disaffiliation is given the name *apostasy*.[7] However, before I had disaffiliated from the Latter-day Saint Church, I was considered apostate.

As a result of my alleged apostasy, I came to see that the idea of apostasy is given much more weight in the Brighamite tradition than is the idea of restoration. But the apostasy spoken of by the Utah church is invariably personal. Apostasy is considered in light of one's opposition to the church and its leaders.[8] Yet in Community of Christ, the idea of *restoration* occupies much of its unique theological terrain, while apostasy is hardly anywhere seen.

It wasn't always so. Like the mountain Saints, the prairie Saints[9] were similarly concerned with boundary maintenance that held some of its founding ideas inviolate. The central teaching was that the Latter Day Saint Restoration was the locus of Jesus Christ's spiritual activity and the hope of humanity's salvation. In consequence, both the Latter-day Saint and Community of Christ faiths held a shared claim that theirs was the "one true church."[10] Former Community of Christ president Grant McMurray reflected on growing up in Community of Christ: "I needed to deal with the fact that we understood ourselves to be the One True Church—not just vis-à-vis the Mormons, but vis-à-vis all other expressions of Christianity."[11]

The one-true-church doctrine and apostasy, in the Latter-day Saint and Community of Christ traditions, were at one stage important identity makers that differentiated both traditions purposefully from the mainstream. However, members of Community of Christ were growing weary of claims of exclusivism. As Matthew Frizzell pointed out, the transformations (among other contextual pressures) set in motion by the baby boomers were significant: "Eventually, the 'scripts' that told of the church's divine origins, the 'fullness' of its scriptural canon, its sole priesthood authority, and special eschatological purpose were confronted by the forces of a generation dismantling the worldview that corresponded with this version of [Community of Christ]. For a large contingency of the Baby Boom, their changing world needed a religion that would change."[12]

Community of Christ responded to the need for change in consequence of the increasing ghettoization of its faith, which had become mired somewhat by the unsustainable literalisms of the nineteenth-century church. Community of Christ began to throw open the windows to the fresh winds of the Spirit, engaging with the question of reform cautiously but emphatically.[13]

Two major forces propelled Community of Christ out of Latter-day Saint sectarianism (including a departure from the myth of restoration and apostasy) into a new expression of the Restoration. In the first instance, Community of Christ's international expansion meant that by the 1960s missionaries were returning from their overseas (non-US) missions with questions as to the relevance of an apostasy and restoration narrative for non-Christians.[14] The apostasy and restoration narrative might have been germane in the Christian West, but it seemed a spiritually unnecessary ontological leap for the non-Christian East to form their faith around a uniquely North American theological claim of Christian difference. Additionally, Community of Christ missionary experiences in the developing world caused the church to think about the relevance of the social gospel[15] more than mythologized nineteenth-century North American claims of supernatural visions and revival charisms.

Historical criticism and the cultural turn in the arts and social sciences also played a part in the reformation of Community of Christ. Historical criticism led to the development of methodologies that examine ancient texts to discover the world behind those words. The cultural turn at the same time forced an emphasis on how meaning is culturally made, thus lurching social inquiry away from epistemological positivism.[16] In this changing intellectual environment, the professionalization of Community of Christ and its leaders brought critically trained and informed historians (as well as theologians) into church leadership. With the support of the First Presidency, church historian Richard Howard published a paper that exposed the multiple versions of Joseph Smith Jr.'s First Vision.[17] Howard's study of the Book of Mormon manuscript demonstrated that Joseph Smith Jr. had changed his mind on wording over time, which undermined the membership's belief in a plenary revelation through the Prophet. Similar studies of early Doctrine and Covenants sections and the "Inspired Version" of the Bible demonstrated that human elements were indeed shaping our scriptures. If Community of Christ had the fulness of the gospel, it wasn't as pure as many had mythologized it to be.

The end of the 1960s was a pivotal time for Community of Christ. At that time, the membership of the Utah-based church had increased substantially, making it so it could afford to be exclusive from mainstream

Christianity, while the Missouri-based Saints could not. Because of this, Community of Christ became increasingly influenced by and interested in creating a shared theological dialogue with Protestants in an age of increasing ecumenism. In 1959, the Saint Paul School of Theology (a Methodist seminary) opened near the Community of Christ Auditorium in Kansas City, Missouri. Community of Christ leaders were soon in dialogue with Protestant theologians at Saint Paul. When some Community of Christ leaders began to study theology at Saint Paul, it became apparent that the broader Christian conversation entailed an intelligence, integrity, and depth that church leaders had missed while holding too tightly to ideas of Christian apostasy.[18] The early Latter Day Saint Restoration notion that every other Christian around you is in error, while church members belong to the one and only true church, did not serve Community of Christ well. It didn't foster relationships; it forced separation, underscored practices of boundary maintenance, and created an insufferable community arrogance. Confronting the institutional sins and apostasy of Community of Christ meant that the concept of restoration took on new gravitas and meaning. Members of Community of Christ began to see themselves as culturally bound and hemmed in by mythology and historical narratives that didn't serve their collective spiritual growth well.

This led to a significant shift in Community of Christ's self-understanding, commissioned by the First Presidency, that spread out across the church. In 1966, the First Presidency commissioned a set of study papers for a new curriculum. These papers, which came to be known as the "Position Papers," were intended to be internal documents but were leaked to Community of Christ membership ahead of the 1970 World Conference. These leaked documents circulated among conservative Community of Christ members and created a staunch opposition to the changes that nevertheless seemed inevitable. The Position Papers and the "New Curriculum" cemented the conservative movement within the church. Those who sided with the conservative movement would later break off and call themselves "Restorationists."[19]

Following up on these developments, Community of Christ's Basic Beliefs Committee produced an important book, *Exploring the Faith*,[20] that signaled a sea of change in Community of Christ thought that would bring the church more in line with traditional Christianity than with traditional Restoration movements. It became apparent that the discourse of exclusivity that had historically drawn lines between the Restoration tradition and the larger Christian conversation was neither spiritually nor relationally helpful in light of Community of Christ's new direction. Community of Christ opted to open up a dialogue with mainstream Christianity, which meant dropping some of its truth claims, including the doctrine of apostasy.[21]

Beyond the United States, Community of Christ was growing, forcing the question "How well served is the world church by our America-centric narratives?" An era of historical query, institutional and theological reform, and new identity formation was born. The apostasy question was quietly dropped because it was incommensurate in this new period of self-awareness and growth. Looking for and pointing fingers at others' wrongs no longer served the spiritual interests of the church, whose leaders, in recognition of the church's rebirth as first and foremost a faith of Christian discipleship, chose to change the name from the Reorganized Church of Jesus Christ of Latter Day Saints to Community of Christ.[22]

Why The Church of Jesus Christ of Latter-day Saints didn't respond to the new intellectual currents of the postwar period and instead integrated its religious identity with the Christian Right when Community of Christ reformed as a progressive faith is probably a question for American politics.[23] Needless to say, the 1970s saw the polarization of the two Restoration traditions and the instantiation of the churches' fundamentally different political orientations, particularly in North America. With the radical progressive changes, Community of Christ now saw the apostasy discourse as redundant. However, the idea of the Restoration was maintained because it invoked the hope intrinsic to the movement: restoration, reconciliation, renewal, and a refreshed theological spirit.

A beloved hymn of Community of Christ is "For Everyone Born," by fellow Kiwi Shirley Erena Murray.[24] The lyrics invite us to be creators of justice, joy, compassion, and peace. For Community of Christ, this mission is accomplished through its unique restoration theology, which enjoins all Saints to live in restorative, reconciling, and gracious relationship with one another, with the Divine, and with the earth. While leaving behind claims of apostasy, Community of Christ has made restoration a spiritual practice rather than a matter of historical conjecture.

Thus, as someone for whom the accusation of personal apostasy has weighed heavily, being in a faith community that has made a purposeful departure from an emphasis on universal apostasy into a more generous understanding of the Restoration as paramount has been a wonderful spiritual relief.

Apostasy and Restoration in The Church of Jesus Christ of Latter-day Saints

JORDAN T. WATKINS

Jordan T. Watkins is an assistant professor of church history and doctrine at Brigham Young University.

Members of The Church of Jesus Christ of Latter-day Saints believe in a robust restorationism that encompasses the Old and New Testaments and radically stretches backward into a premortal existence while also making abundant space for new sacred texts, truths, and practices. Early members came to believe that the Restoration involved a return of divine communication; a recovery of hidden scriptures and lost gifts, priesthood authority and powers, and practices; the redemption of a people; the resurrection of bodies; and eternal reunions. As this restorationism evolved, it yielded different conceptions of apostasy. Narratives of restoration and apostasy emerged through a dialectic and in relation to internal developments and outside forces.

The earliest understanding of restoration developed from Joseph Smith's revelations. His followers believed an angel had appeared to him with instructions to uncover and translate an ancient record. The

Book of Mormon indicated that "the great and abominable church" had removed "plain and precious things" from the Bible (CofChrist I Nephi 3:141, 171; LDS 1 Nephi 13:6, 29). This new book of scripture spoke of restoring truths and a people—Israel—a favorite theme among early believers.[25] The Book of Mormon shaped the early believers' restorationism in various ways, but most of all, their acceptance of the book's canonical status reinforced the idea that God had called Joseph Smith as a living prophet. Smith's other scriptural productions bolstered those understandings.

The emphasis on the return of prophetic revelation was soon tied to another claim: God restored authority to administer saving ordinances. At the organization of the Church of Christ in 1830, a question arose about whether converts from other Christian denominations needed rebaptism. The Lord answered, "It is because of your dead works that I have caused this last covenant and this church to be built up."[26] In 1831, the Lord added that the Christian world had "strayed from [the Lord's] ordinances & [had] broken [his] everlasting Covenant." Thus, the Lord "spake unto [Smith]" that his "everlasting Covenant might be established" and that Smith might have "power to lay the foundation of this Church," which the Lord described as "the only true & living Church."[27] While understandings of priesthood restoration developed gradually, this language of life and death conveyed the idea that divine power had been lost and restored.[28]

Although early converts embraced the idea that divine authority existed in the Church of Christ, many of them understood their prior religious experiences as preparatory to their conversion. For example, some former Methodists described their earlier enjoyment of spiritual gifts as a valuable staging ground on their religious journey.[29] Furthermore, some of Smith's revelations suggested that the religious experiences of figures such as Sidney Rigdon, a former Campbellite, had readied them for the new Restoration message, even as the revelations also explained that these converts had been called to a "greater work" with greater power.[30]

This emphasis shaped apostasy narratives that asserted the loss of revelation and authority between the postapostolic era and Smith's call.

During the 1830s and 1840s, figures such as Rigdon, Oliver Cowdery, Parley P. Pratt, Orson Pratt, and Benjamin Winchester insisted that Protestants—including Christian primitivists who assumed Protestant corruption—could not just set aside Catholic decline and recover apostolic purity without revelation and authority. While they allowed that some historical figures, including the proto-Reformation Waldensians and the post-Reformation John Wesley, had shone as best they could in the darkness, these writers generally found little redeemable in the past, including in the Reformation.[31] In an 1840 pamphlet, Orson Pratt registered the belief in "a general and awful apostasy from the religion of the New Testament." He thought of apostasy in terms of the absence of "a priesthood authorized of God to administer ordinances" and a loss of "ancient gifts, and powers, and blessings." He found restoration in the Book of Mormon, which he believed contained the same gospel "as that in the New Testament," and in the "many revelations and prophecies" Smith had received.[32]

Smith's revelations linked priesthood and priesthood ordinances to the biblical past.[33] During the 1830s, as his followers built a temple in Kirtland, Smith revealed washings, which he connected to the New Testament, and anointings, which he tied to the Old Testament.[34] Latter-day Saint restorationism uniquely embraced both testaments and cultivated interaction with ancient prophets.[35] Soon after the dedication of the house of the Lord in 1836, Smith and Cowdery had a series of visions in which Old Testament figures, including Elijah, appeared and restored powers that augmented the new movement's idea of priesthood.[36]

Smith's restorationist lens magnified even the deepest pasts. An 1841 revelation explained that the practice of baptism for the dead—introduced the summer before—had been "instituted from before the foundation of the world."[37] As Smith envisioned a pretemporal frame for revealed teachings and practices, he continued to identify biblical antecedents and precedents for them, including the endowment, plural marriage, and radical ideas about the nature of God.[38] Smith also detected contemporary ideational resonances. In 1843, he taught that Presbyterians, Baptists, and Methodists all had some truth and that "one [of] the grand fundamental principles of Mormonism is to receive thruth [truth] let it come from where it may."[39] Smith often heard contemporary affinities as muffled echoes from ancient pasts.[40] His late efforts to restore past truths and purify present truths, which bespoke a restoration aimed at restoring relationships threatened by the vicissitudes of life, advanced an expansive restorationism.[41]

After Smith's death, Latter-day Saint narratives became more exclusionary. The expansiveness of Smith's restorationism encouraged some to articulate a Great Apostasy. In 1850, Orson Pratt continued to assert that "the whole Romish, Greek and Protestant ministry" was "destitute of authority from God."[42] Dismissing the Protestant appeal to the Bible, Pratt argued that "the history of what others enjoyed is a very different thing from actual possession and enjoyment for ourselves."[43] During the next few decades, Pratt used Smith's First Vision to narrate a "Universal Apostasy."[44] In the face of persecution, Pratt prioritized Smith's 1838–39 account. Smith, who had produced this account in response to outside pressures, described a vision in which Christ directed him to not join any church.[45] As the former religious associations of the first generation of Saints waned, and as Protestants attacked the church's polygamous practice, the First Vision became the touchstone for the claim to renewed revelation, which was the starting point for Latter-day Saint restorationism.[46]

The Great Apostasy narrative was given more definitive shape in the late nineteenth and early twentieth centuries, as Latter-day Saint writers reformulated Protestant-authored histories. In doing so, they depicted the Reformation as a precursor to the Restoration. While this mature narrative more fully embraced the old Protestant condemnation of Catholicism, it still saw deep corruption in Protestantism.[47] This narrative persisted throughout the twentieth century.

Late twentieth-century developments complicated this exclusionary view.[48] In 1978, the church's First Presidency declared that the "great religious leaders of the world . . . received a portion of God's light." In registering their belief that God "will give to all peoples sufficient knowledge to help them on their way to eternal salvation"[49]—an idea contained in the Book of Mormon[50]—the First Presidency broadened the

Saints' view of God's guidance. This message came amid the church's global expansion, which both contributed to and followed from the 1978 announcement ending the priesthood and temple ban for members of African descent. During these years, leaders made efforts to embrace and be embraced by other Christians, as indicated by the Book of Mormon's new subtitle, "Another Testament of Jesus Christ."[51]

A few decades after teaching that God speaks to other people, Latter-day Saint leaders began to emphasize that God continues to carry out the Restoration. In 2014, Dieter F. Uchtdorf, then a member of the First Presidency, stated that the "Restoration is an ongoing process."[52] This message has been reiterated by other leaders.[53] This might reflect the insight, yielded by historical research, that Smith's restoration was a process rather than an event.[54] Scholarship has contributed to shifting views of restoration and apostasy, and those shifting views have inspired further scholarship. Latter-day Saint scholars have begun to dismantle some apostasy narratives.[55] In turn, scholars have also provided new narratives of restoration.[56]

In April 2020, President Russell M. Nelson delivered a "Restoration Proclamation." In this proclamation, church leaders offered a brief narrative of Smith's vision, wherein he "learned that . . . Christ's New Testament Church was lost from the earth." The proclamation does not mention *apostasy*, nor does it indicate how the "Church was lost." It explains that "heavenly messengers came to instruct Joseph and re-establish the Church of Jesus Christ." In this narrative, apostasy is a passive development, while restoration is an active process whereby embodied biblical figures restored the "authority to baptize" and "the apostleship and keys of priesthood authority," including the "authority to join families together forever." In a statement that recalls early members' beliefs and follows late twentieth-century trends, the proclamation describes the Book of Mormon as "a companion scripture to the Bible" that "testifies that all human beings are sons and daughters of a loving Father in Heaven." Finally, church leaders affirm that the church "organized on April 6, 1830, is Christ's New Testament Church restored" and reaffirm the new emphasis that "the promised Restoration goes forward through continuing revelation."[57]

The church retains exclusive claims, but the most recent iteration of these claims has yielded less exclusionary understandings of apostasy and more expansive understandings of restoration, a concept that has recently come up for reexamination.[58] As the dialectics that produce these understandings proceed, the focus on revelation and authority will continue to shape Latter-day Saint views. But recent trends suggest a move toward greater flexibility, innovation, and openness surrounding the concepts of restoration and apostasy. Early and late narratives demonstrate that the Latter-day Saint commitment to an expansive restorationism does not necessitate a commitment to an expansive Great Apostasy.

RESPONSE TO JORDAN T. WATKINS

Thank you for your essay, Jordan. It's been a much better experience collaborating like this than I had thought it would be. Your essay underscores just how different the theological positions of our two traditions are. Even the way in which we responded to and interpreted the question of apostasy and restoration indicates our immense dissimilarities.

For instance, you make no mention of Community of Christ in this accounting. The mountain Saints have a tendency to imagine that they are the only expression of the Restoration and predictably give little regard for any group other than themselves. On the other hand, Community of Christ has always been a bit obsessed with the other church, with an eye constantly trained (albeit a benevolent one) upon Salt Lake City.

Your approach to the topic is rigorous, positivist, objective, and straightforward. Your essay is very well researched, and your use of endnotes is impressive. My essay is discursive, autoethnographic, feminist, indigenous, and highly subjective. Our respective methodologies once more glaringly indicate our different religious orientations. Yet, here we are, seeking a dialogical interaction with some goodwill. That's extraordinarily hopeful.

You give a thorough account of The Church of Jesus Christ of Latter-day Saints' early beginnings. Our respective traditions share that common story of Joseph Smith's formative revelations, and I thought it might be worth saying so. We have only fourteen years in common before Brigham went west, but this shared history is significant in that the opening account of Restoration history hasn't shaped just the mountain Saints but the prairie Saints as well. However, our respective evolving interpretations and trajectories related to apostasy and restoration eventually go in markedly different directions, and I'm left to wonder why.

You seem to be saying that Latter-day Saint understandings of restoration and apostasy are fixed and wholly dependent upon each other. This idea implies an obvious calculation that in order to fix something, it needs to be broken. An emphasis on legitimate authority is also clear, which suggests that the Latter-day Saints are determined that only they have the divine right to restore. I can see how the ideas of apostasy, restoration, and authority are conflated. Of course, I'm familiar with the rhetoric, but our conversations left me wondering, What is it about the Utah church that leans so heavily upon the question of authority? How has restoration become so dependent upon authority? Why does any one particular religious tradition bear the exclusive responsibility of restoration? Why can't the goal of restoration be shared across different churches, peoples, and cultures? Unless the point that you are making is that the reinstantiation of the Old Testament temple theology and its exclusive priesthood holders that serve in those rituals in the service of an exclusive, set-apart people *is* the Restoration—in which case, I would argue that the Latter-day Saints have held tenaciously to their identity as latter-day restorationists through the twinned ideas of apostasy and restoration. In consequence, I'm starting to think that Community of Christ is not a restorationist faith at all, except in the loosest possible interpretation. Members of Community of Christ are reformers. To restore is to painstakingly make something as it once was or even better. To reform is to break apart, unravel, and rebuild again, hopefully without the faulty parts.

You rightly point out that the Latter Day Saint movement offered spiritual freedom to Christian converts, which is certainly a part of our shared history. The push away from dogmatic constraint was a lure for many. You argue that there was a convert quest for legitimate religious authority, and I do take issue with that somewhat. I think the story of "legitimate authority" was written later and imposed upon a people who were largely after some fresh winds of the spirit away from a climate of dogmatic constraint in their own churches, whether Protestant or Catholic. My sense is that these early adherents were also captured by the idea of hope-filled immigration to the United States (in the case of the European converts) or social mobility and the promise of new possibilities in an age of terrible economic depression. I would argue that the legitimate authority discourse came after the fact to support the "one true church" doctrine of the Latter-day Saints.

I take issue somewhat with your seemingly innocent use of the idea of everlasting covenant and priesthood. In its earliest iterations, both were synonymous with the practice of plural marriage. The temple and the rituals of freemasonry were also triangulated into this development, particularly in Nauvoo. I can't see how any of these doctrines and early practices are innocent of the stain of polygamy.

Thank you for this dialogue. It has caused me to consider the possibility that the idea of restoration in the Latter-day Saint Church is based upon a theology that understands restoration as the return of religious practices that are drawn from a Jewish/Hebraic/Mosaic spiritual worldview—in which case, perhaps this is where we depart from each other. My growing sense is that the mountain Saints have developed as Old Testament restorationists and have brought together a bricolage of salvific propositions in order to furnish the tradition with something "better." The prairie Saints, on the other hand, have developed as New Testament reformationists. Sure, we keep that early "restoration" identity marker, but are we really restorationists?

RESPONSE TO GINA COLVIN

Gina, the essays you and I have written highlight distinctive and perhaps even contrasting approaches to the concepts of apostasy and restoration. The essays necessarily convey our subjective perspectives and do not reflect the spectrum of views and beliefs held by the communities that they represent, though some core differences do emerge in these accounts.

You provide an insightful, personal narrative of restoration by way of two apostasies. These apostasies include your own, at least according to some members in the Latter-day Saint Church, as well as your view of an apostasy of the Latter-day Saint Church itself. In your telling, you moved away from a church that "was in a state of apostasy" and toward "the larger body of Christ" that same church told you was apostate. In your narrative, apostasy functions not as a distant historical event that preceded a modern restoration but as a contemporary reality that shaped your own restorative move from one faith community to another.

Your faith transition powerfully informs your understanding of Latter-day Saint views of apostasy and restoration. Much of Latter-day Saint restorationism assumes and asserts a close relationship between past and present, and the Restoration present has often given shape to varied and evolving views of apostasy. In a similar yet distinct way, your past and present appear to have shaped your understanding of Latter-day Saint ideas about apostasy and restoration, which you tend to flatten and freeze. You present the Latter-day Saint views of apostasy and restoration as "a straightforward narrative" characterized by "simplicity." Consequently, in your passing statements on these views, you suggest that apostasy outweighs restoration. However, while the Latter-day Saint Church has embraced a robust view of apostasy from beginning to end, the concept of restoration has consistently given shape to the idea of apostasy. Your essay reveals little about how the concepts of apostasy and restoration have functioned in Latter-day Saint thought and instead conveys your experience and your narrative about that experience.

You trace the history of Community of Christ belief in apostasy and restoration, but more than that, you articulate how, in the process of giving up one faith tradition for another, you have embraced a new kind of restorationism. You describe your coreligionists as "restoration radicals" who "made more of restoration than apostasy." If you oversimplify the Latter-day Saint view, it's because you are more concerned with explaining the "irresistible" allure of a different restoration tradition. That allure resulted, in part, due to changes within the Reorganized Church that occurred during the second half of the twentieth century, which changes brought "the church more in line with traditional Christianity than with traditional Restoration movements." In this process, which perhaps has been echoed in your own conversion, the organization distinguished itself from the Latter-day Saint Church in ways that may have obscured its own past—including its own apostasy narratives—in favor of a new restoration present.

Your essay conveys your journey from apostasy to restoration, and in doing so it sheds light on theological developments within your faith tradition. You write of a belief in restoration as "reconciliation, renewal, and a refreshed theological spirit." And yet, despite this explanation, I remain somewhat unclear on what restoration means in this tradition that has set aside apostasy. You point to the salubrious move "to open up a dialogue with mainstream Christianity," but restoration seems unnecessary to this development. I'm left with this question: Does the Community of Christ adhere to restoration as an essential belief?

Even as I question the relevance of "restoration" for the Community of Christ, I still wonder about points of overlap with the Latter-day Saint Church on this issue. Toward the end of your essay, you characterize a "unique restoration theology, which enjoins all Saints to live in restorative, reconciling, and gracious relationship with one another, with the Divine, and with the earth." This characterization departs from the insistence on a restoration of past truths, practices, and powers in favor of a focus on relationships. This trimmed-down view of restoration can be seen as a clear departure from the earlier restorationisms resulting from Smith's ministry, but it does bear affinities with some of the teachings and practices that Smith introduced in Nauvoo, which Latter-day Saints continue to embrace. I am interested in the further articulation of the Community of Christ belief in restoration, or the negation of that belief, which might further highlight the differences between the two traditions, or, on the other hand, might point toward unsuspecting points of correspondence.

CONCLUSION

This exercise of intrareligious exchange has highlighted crucial distinctions in Latter-day Saint and Community of Christ conceptions of apostasy and restoration. The original breach between the mountain Saints and the prairie Saints has had lasting implications for the way in which our respective traditions have evolved. While both communities have maintained the original language of apostasy and restoration, we couldn't be more different in our interpretations of these concepts. In the Latter-day Saint tradition, these concepts have continuously evolved together in a kind of dialectic. While continuing to develop this binary, the Latter-day Saint Church has maintained an emphasis on authority even while moving away from an all-encompassing apostasy and toward a belief that God has inspired and continues to guide other prophets and peoples. In the Community of Christ tradition, apostasy has given way to a new kind of restoration, one that eschews a discourse of exclusivity in favor of a community that opens itself to other Christian conversations and communities. While our narratives about these developments underscore the different ways in which each faith tradition has responded to historical forces, the historical trajectories of both traditions have created the conditions to make this conversation possible. In other words, the very fact that we have been able to engage in this exchange from distinct perspectives and with contrasting methodologies, and that we have then been able to embrace the different narratives that resulted, indicates that the time is ripe for ongoing intrareligious dialogue. Developing a consciousness of the contextual factors that caused the differentiation could serve as a fresh starting place from which to host our future ecumenical conversations.

NOTES

1. Different forms of the term *Latter Day Saint* have been used by both Community of Christ and The Church of Jesus Christ of Latter-day Saints. In this chapter, the term *Latter Day Saint* with a capital *D* is used to denote the early movement before the split between the two churches. The hyphenated term *Latter-day Saints* with a lowercase *d* is used as shorthand for The Church of Jesus Christ of Latter-day Saints.

2. Hirini Kaa, *Te Hahi Mihinare: The Māori Anglican Church* (Wellington, NZ: Bridget Williams Books, 2020).

3. Keith Newman, *Beyond Betrayal: Trouble in the Promised Land: Restoring the Mission to Māori* (Auckland, NZ: Penguin, 2013).

4. Marjorie Newton, *Tiki and Temple: The Mormon Mission in New Zealand, 1854–1958* (Salt Lake City: Greg Kofford Books, 2012).

5. Peggy Fletcher Stack, "'Mormonism at Its Best'—Bishop Clears New Zealander Who Faced Possible Excommunication," *Salt Lake Tribune*, December 20, 2018.

6. Anthony Chvala-Smith, "Theological Analysis of Stewardship 2000" (unpublished manuscript, April 1997). This paper was written in response to the Latter-day Saint Presiding Bishopric's stewardship resource *Stand in Holy Places* (1997). Today, Tony would be very cautious about any form of restoring any pure past (email to author, August 25, 2021).

7. David G. Bromley, *Falling from the Faith: Causes and Consequences of Religious Apostasy* (Ann Arbor, MI: University Microfilms International, 1999).

8. Lester Bush, "Excommunication and Church Courts: A Note from the 'General Handbook of Instructions,'" *Dialogue* 14, no. 2 (1981): 74–98.

9. Colloquial terms referring to the Utah-based Latter-day Saint Church and the Missouri-based RLDS/Community of Christ Church, respectively.

10. William D. Russell, "Courage: A Liberal Journal Foreshadows RLDS Doctrinal Shifts," *John Whitmer Historical Association Journal* 28 (2008): 137–56.

11. Greg Prince, "Walking into the Heart of the Questions: An Interview with Grant McMurray," *Dialogue* (December 8, 2011), https://www.dialoguejournal.com/2011/12/walking-into-questions/.

12. Matthew Frizzell, "A Baby Boomer Transformation: The Current Generation of Leadership and the Remaking of the Reorganized Church," in *Theologies across the Generations*, ed. Ruth Ann Wood and Suzanne Trewhitt McLaughlin (Independence, MO: Graceland Press and Herald Publishing House, 2005), 56.

13. William D. Russell, "Beyond Literalism," *Dialogue* 19, no. 1 (Spring 1986): 57–68.

14. Frizzell, "Baby Boomer Transformation."

15. Walter Rauschenbusch, *A Theology for the Social Gospel* (London: Forgotten Books, 2017).

16. See Fredric Jameson, *The Cultural Turn: Selected Writings on the Postmodern, 1983–1998* (London: Verso, 1998).

17. Richard P. Howard, "An Analysis of Six Contemporary Accounts Touching Joseph Smith's First Vision," *Restoration Studies* 1 (1980): 95–117.

18. W. B. "Pat" Spillman, "Taking the Road More Travelled," *John Whitmer Historical Association Journal* 24 (2004): 135–48.

19. William J. Knapp, "Professionalizing Religious Education in the Church: The 'New Curriculum Controversy,'" *John Whitmer Historical Association Journal* 2 (1982): 47–59.

20. *Exploring the Faith: A Series of Studies in the Faith of the Church Prepared by a Committee on Basic Beliefs* (Independence, MO: Herald Publishing House, 1970).

21. Keith Wilson and Mitch McClellan, "Remaking the Reorganization: The Transformative Years of 1958 to 1970 in the RLDS Church," *John Whitmer Historical Association Journal* 32, no. 2 (Fall/Winter 2012): 88–104.

22. William D. Russell, "The Last Smith Presidents and the Transformation of the RLDS Church," *Journal of Mormon History* 34, no. 3 (2008): 46–84.

23. Neil J. Young, *We Gather Together: The Religious Right and the Problem of Interfaith Politics* (Oxford: Oxford University Press, 2015).

24. Shirley Erena Murray, "For Everyone Born," in *Community of Christ Sings* (Independence, MO: Herald Publishing House, 2013), 285–86.

25. See, for example, CofChrist I Nephi 4:32–34; LDS 1 Nephi 15:20; "Revelation, circa 7 March 1831 [Doctrine and Covenants 45]," The Joseph Smith Papers, https://www.josephsmithpapers.org/paper-summary/revelation-circa-7-march-1831-dc-45/1. On the restoration of Israel, see Grant Underwood, "Book of Mormon Usage in Early LDS Theology," *Dialogue* 17 (Autumn 1984): 39–41.

26. "Revelation, 16 April 1830 [Doctrine and Covenants 22]," p. 4, The Joseph Smith Papers, https://www.josephsmithpapers.org/paper-summary/revelation-16-april-1830-dc-22/1.

27. "Revelation, 1 November 1831-B [Doctrine and Covenants 1]," p. 126, The Joseph Smith Papers, https://www.josephsmithpapers.org/paper-summary/revelation-1-november-1831-b-dc-1/1.

28. On priesthood restoration as a process, see, for example, Michael Hubbard MacKay, *Prophetic Authority: Democratic Hierarchy and the Mormon Priesthood* (Urbana: University of Illinois Press, 2020).

29. See Christopher C. Jones and Stephen J. Fleming, "'Except among That Portion of Mankind': Early Mormon Conceptions of Apostasy," in *Standing Apart: Mormon Historical Consciousness and the Concept of Apostasy*, ed. Miranda Wilcox and John D. Young (New York: Oxford University Press, 2014), 66–71.

30. "Revelation, 7 December 1830 [Doctrine and Covenants 35]," p. 46, The Joseph Smith Papers, https://www.josephsmithpapers.org/paper-summary/revelation-7-december-1830-dc-35/1.

31. See Jones and Fleming, "'Except among That Portion of Mankind,'" 57–66.

32. Orson Pratt, *An Interesting Account of Several Remarkable Visions*, in *The Pamphlets of Orson Pratt*, comp. David Hammer (Salt Lake City: Eborn, 2017), 28–29.

33. See "Revelation, 22–23 September 1832 [Doctrine and Covenants 84]," The Joseph Smith Papers, https://www.josephsmithpapers.org/paper-summary/revelation-22-23-september-1832-dc-84/1.

34. See "Journal, November 12, 1835," pp. 30–35, The Joseph Smith Papers, https://www.josephsmithpapers.org/paper-summary/journal-1835-1836/31.

35. On the use of the Old Testament, see Jan Shipps, *Mormonism: The Story of a New Religious Tradition* (Urbana: University of Illinois Press, 1987), 67–85.

36. "Visions, 3 April 1836 [Doctrine and Covenants 110]," The Joseph Smith Papers, pp. 192–93, https://www.josephsmithpapers.org/paper-summary/visions-3 -april-1836-dc-110/1.

37. "Revelation, 19 January 1841 [Doctrine and Covenants 124]," p. 5, The Joseph Smith Papers, https://www.josephsmithpapers.org/paper-summary /revelation-19-january-1841-dc-124/5.

38. See "Discourse, 1 May 1842, as Reported by Willard Richards," The Joseph Smith Papers, https://www.josephsmithpapers.org/paper-summary/discourse-1-may -1842-as-reported-by-willard-richards/1; "Revelation, 12 July 1843 [Doctrine and Covenants 132]," The Joseph Smith Papers, https://www.josephsmithpapers .org/paper-summary/revelation-12-july-1843-dc-132/1; and "Discourse, 7 April 1844, as Reported by Thomas Bullock," The Joseph Smith Papers, https://www .josephsmithpapers.org/paper-summary/discourse-7-april-1844-as-reported -by-thomas-bullock/1.

39. "History, 1838–1856, volume E-1 [9 July 1843]," p. 1666, The Joseph Smith Papers, https://www.josephsmithpapers.org/paper-summary/history-1838-1856 -volume-e-1-1-july-1843-30-april-1844/36.

40. For example, while acknowledging the links between masonry and the endowment, Smith appears to have viewed masonry as a corrupted form of a purer ancient practice. See Heber C. Kimball to Parley P. Pratt, June 17, 1842, Parley P. Pratt Correspondence, 1842–1855, Church History Library, Salt Lake City.

41. See Samuel Morris Brown, *In Heaven as It Is on Earth: Joseph Smith and the Early Mormon Conquest of Death* (New York: Oxford University Press, 2012).

42. See Orson Pratt, *Divine Authenticity of the Book of Mormon*, in Hammer, *Pamphlets of Orson Pratt*, 285–86.

43. Pratt, *Divine Authenticity*, 381.

44. Orson Pratt, "Universal Apostasy, or the Seventeen Centuries of Darkness," in *A Series of Tracts on Mormon Doctrine*, in *Pamphlets*, 571–89.

45. "History, circa June 1939–circa 1841 [Draft 2]," The Joseph Smith Papers, https:// www.josephsmithpapers.org/paper-summary/history-circa-june-1839-circa -1841-draft-2/1.

46. See Steven C. Harper, *First Vision: Memory and Mormon Origins* (New York: Oxford University Press, 2019), 71–102.

47. See Eric R. Dursteler, "Historical Periodization in the LDS Great Apostasy Narrative," in *Standing Apart: Mormon Historical Consciousness and the Concept of Apostasy*, ed. Miranda Wilcox and John D. Young (New York: Oxford University Press, 2014), 55–76. See also Matthew Bowman, "James Talmage, B. H. Roberts, and Confessional History in a Secular Age," in *Standing Apart*, 77–92; and Miranda Wilcox, "Sacralizing the Secular in Latter-day Saint Salvation Histories (1890–1930)," *Journal of Mormon History* 46, no. 3 (July 2020): 23–59.

48. Even Bruce R. McConkie's language softened. See John G. Turner, *The Mormon Jesus: A Biography* (Cambridge: Belknap Press of Harvard University Press, 2016), 286–87.

49. Spencer W. Kimball, N. Eldon Tanner, and Marion G. Romney, "Statement of the First Presidency regarding God's Love for All Mankind," February 15, 1978.

50. See CofChrist II Nephi 12:64–72; LDS 2 Nephi 29:10–13.

51. See Boyd K. Packer, "Scriptures," *Ensign*, November 1982, 51–53.

52. Dieter F. Uchtdorf, "Are You Sleeping through the Restoration?," *Ensign*, May 2014, 59.

53. See Gary E. Stevenson, "The Ongoing Restoration," BYU Speeches, August 20, 2019; LeGrand R. Curtis Jr., "The Ongoing Restoration," *Ensign*, April 2020, 20–25; and Russell M. Nelson, "Hear Him," *Ensign*, May 2020, 88.

54. See, for example, Jonathan Stapley, *The Power of Godliness: Mormon Liturgy and Cosmology* (New York: Oxford University Press, 2018); and Michael Hubbard MacKay, "Event or Process? How 'the Chamber of Old Father Whitmer' Helps Us Understand Priesthood Restoration," *BYU Studies* 60, no. 1 (2021): 73–101.

55. See Miranda Wilcox and John D. Young, *Standing Apart: Mormon Historical Consciousness and the Concept of Apostasy* (New York: Oxford University Press, 2014).

56. See, for example, Terryl L. Givens, *Wrestling the Angel: The Foundations of Mormon Thought; Cosmos, God, Humanity* (New York: Oxford University Press, 2015), 23–41; and Nicholas J. Frederick and Joseph M. Spencer, "Remnant or Replacement? Outlining a Possible Apostasy Narrative," *BYU Studies* 60, no. 1 (2021): 105–27.

57. "The Restoration of the Fulness of the Gospel of Jesus Christ: A Bicentennial Proclamation to the World," ChurchofJesusChrist.org.

58. See Patrick Q. Mason, *Restoration: God's Call to the 21st-Century World* (Meridian, ID: Faith Matters Publishing, 2020), esp. 11–54.

SHARED
SACRED SPACE

Scott C. Esplin and Katherine Hill

Many chapters in this volume focus on doctrinal beliefs of The Church of Jesus Christ of Latter-day Saints and Community of Christ. While the two faiths have much in common theologically, it may be their history that most unites them. In their respective beginnings, they share a common heritage. Stories about individuals including Joseph and Emma Smith or locations like Kirtland and Nauvoo are familiar to members of both faiths. Furthermore, after the two churches took their divergent paths in the mid-1800s, their histories continued to intersect, as did their mutual interest in specific sacred spaces. Because of the overlap, however, the study, interpretation, and celebration of their common history has also significantly divided the faiths. Among the most frequent points of contact, and occasionally conflict, have been their sacred spaces and historic sites. The history of competing and sharing the sacred space of the Restoration may reveal as much about both faiths as does a study of their theological tenets.

Sacred Space in The Church of Jesus Christ of Latter-day Saints

SCOTT C. ESPLIN

Scott C. Esplin is a professor of church history and doctrine and
dean of Religious Education at Brigham Young University.

History and, by association, historical sites and sacred space are inseparable from the teachings and beliefs of The Church of Jesus Christ of Latter-day Saints because its truth claims are rooted in a belief in divine historical episodes. These generally center on the founding events of the church, including the theophany of Joseph Smith and his translation of the Book of Mormon. Professor Sara M. Patterson concludes that for Latter-day Saints, "place, material objects, and theological claims . . . [are] inextricably tied to one another."[1]

With this reliance upon history, The Church of Jesus Christ of Latter-day Saints seeks to leverage the advantage of being able to trace its story to identifiable, verifiable, and often surviving sacred spaces. However, with the exception of its temples, it does not generally ascribe salvific significance to worshipping in revered sacred space. Elder Bruce R. McConkie once emphatically wrote, "Neither shrines nor pilgrimages are a part of true worship as practiced by the true saints. . . . There is no thought that some special virtue will attach to worship by performing it at [historic sites]."[2] Instead, church leaders emphasize that its temples, meetinghouses, and homes are sacred sites, sanctified by the Spirit of the Lord that can dwell therein.[3] A Bible Dictionary entry for the church concludes, "A temple is literally a house of the Lord. . . . It is the most holy of any place of worship on the earth. Only the home can compare with the temple in sacredness."[4]

As indicated by these sources, temples occupy prime sacred space within Latter-day Saint theology and practice. This was true historically as well as in present practice. Joseph Smith taught, "What was the object of Gathering . . . the people of God in any age of the world[?]

The main object was to build unto the Lord an house whereby he Could reveal unto his people the ordinances of his house and glories of his kingdom & teach the people the ways of salvation."[5] Early members sacrificed to build the Kirtland and Nauvoo Temples in the 1830s and 1840s, and the Church of Jesus Christ continues to emphasize temple building to the present. Relocating to Utah, Latter-day Saints labored to construct three additional temples in the nineteenth century (St. George, Logan, and Manti). Over the past fifty years, the pace of temple construction has increased dramatically. At present, the church operates more than 160 temples, with as many as 80 others announced or under construction. Worthy members visit these structures as frequently as personal circumstances allow, receiving instruction and making sacred covenants, including being married for eternity. They also perform proxy ordinances such as baptisms for the dead and marriage sealings for deceased ancestors. The work performed in these sacred spaces, in the words of President Boyd K. Packer, are "the ultimate end of all we do in the Church," which "is to see that parents and children are happy at home and sealed together in the temple."[6]

In addition to its temples, the church also formally supports more than two dozen historic sites that its members, in informal ways, visit in droves, treating them as sacred spaces. These include sites in Palmyra, New York; Kirtland and Hiram, Ohio; Far West and Liberty, Missouri; and Nauvoo and Carthage, Illinois. Jennifer Lund, director of the Historic Sites division of the church, concludes, "For many people, these sites are sacred, evoking a sense of awe, reverence, and personal connection."[7] Because the operating temples of the church are only open to active members, they have limited impact on interfaith relations like those with members of Community of Christ.[8] At historic sites that host member and visitor alike, there is more frequent interaction because of the shared history between the faiths.

RIVAL INTERPRETATIONS AT HISTORIC SITES

The story of how the Church of Jesus Christ acquired and developed its public sacred sites and the interactions with Community of Christ that occurred as a result mirrors their relationship, alternating between contentious and cooperative. Throughout the twentieth century, The Church of Jesus Christ of Latter-day Saints slowly returned to the sites that were once central to it. In 1903, it purchased the Carthage Jail, the first historic structure acquired from the earlier Joseph Smith era of its history.[9] Through intermediaries and eventually as a church itself, the organization steadily secured additional historical sites, including the birthplace of Joseph Smith Jr. in Vermont (1905), the Smith family farm (1907) and Hill Cumorah (1923–28) in western New York, the John and Elsa Johnson Home (1956) and Newel K. Whitney Store (1965) in Ohio, a portion of the Independence temple lot (1904), the Far West temple site (1909), Liberty Jail (1939) and the property of Adam-ondi-Ahman (1944) in Missouri, and the temple lot (1937–62) as well as homes and buildings in Nauvoo (1930s–80s).[10] In many of these locations, missionaries were eventually stationed, tasked with recounting and interpreting history to visitors.

The church's emergence from what Kathleen Flake called its "mountain barrier" to "claim a place in America at large" placed it in direct interaction and competition with the Reorganized Church of Jesus Christ of Latter Day Saints, who had long maintained a religious presence in several of these locations.[11] Chief among them were Kirtland, where Community of Christ conducted tours and worshipped in the house of the Lord, and Nauvoo, where they guided visitors through the Smith home, mansion house, and family cemetery. Community of Christ reaction was swift to the return of the sister faith to these communities. The impact of the stream of visitors from both faiths was reflected by one Reorganized Church guide: "They desire to know what we teach and the main difference between us and the Utah church. We also have many visitors from the Utah people and we treat them kindly, and hope someday they will see the error of their ways and return to the true church."[12]

Beginning in the 1960s, the Church of Jesus Christ began robustly expanding the visitor experience at its sites. Commencing in Nauvoo, church leadership outlined a program of site acquisition and development that would "perpetuate in history the part played by the Mormon

Pioneers in the building of the West."[13] Over time, the vision of telling the Latter-day Saint story to interested visitors expanded beyond recounting participation in western settlement to encompass sites across the United States and include faith building and proselytizing goals as well. J. LeRoy Kimball, visionary founder of restored Nauvoo, summarized, "You are still telling the story in terms of history, but at the same time you are satisfying the desire of the brethren to preach the Gospel."[14]

Property acquisitions and expanded interpretive offerings, especially in Nauvoo, did not go unnoticed. Kenneth E. Stobaugh, former Community of Christ historical director, recalled that an aim in these years as a guide was "to spoil some Mormons' vacation," something he noted "unfortunately . . . was not a one-way street," as "similar episodes were taking place in the LDS section of Nauvoo as well."[15] Indeed, as an example, the Latter-day Saint director of Nauvoo projects counseled, "I think it is very important that we emphasize the Prophet's prediction that the saints would go to the Rocky Mountains in view of the fact that the Reorganites make the claim that he did not. This pins the label of authenticity upon the Utah Church."[16] Interpretive tension like this, followed by competitive construction programs, consumed Kirtland and Nauvoo as the two faiths sought to outbuild each other in rival restoration programs.

Sharing a Story

Competitive historic site interpretation dominated rival sites for decades throughout the twentieth century. However, eventually, "the apologetic curtain that divided" them came down. As Stobaugh described it, "Now . . . both LDS and RLDS churches are more kindly toward each other and strive to present historical information that is as accurate as possible."[17] Ironically, much of this came because of the sacred spaces and shared history that had sometimes divided the two faiths.

The détente developed, in part, through friendships established between scholars in historical associations like the Mormon History Association and John Whitmer Historical Association and, later, through the sharing of documents by scholars and church leaders.[18] Richard

Howard, historian emeritus for Community of Christ, described coming to the realization of "how useful it would be if scholars from Utah did not have to travel . . . to Mecca Midwest [Independence, Missouri] to do their research in our scriptural and historical sources, and scholars from here did not have to travel clear out to Mecca West [Salt Lake City, Utah] to study important sources on early Mormon history."[19] The faiths also began partnering at the overlapping historic sites themselves. In Nauvoo, for example, property transactions created clearer delineations between the property boundaries.[20] Later, family members from both faith traditions cooperated to beautify the Smith family cemetery, eventually forming the Joseph Smith Sr. and Lucy Mack Smith Family Foundation. At the dedication of the cemetery in 1991, Community of Christ president Wallace B. Smith (great-grandson of Joseph Smith Jr.) and Latter-day Saint apostle Elder M. Russell Ballard (great-great-grandson of Hyrum Smith) participated.[21] Two years later, Community of Christ leadership generously allowed Latter-day Saint leaders to hold a worship service in the Kirtland Temple, an example of the shared use of sacred space that continues to the present.[22]

In Nauvoo, the cooperation evident at historic sites was on public display in 2002 when The Church of Jesus Christ of Latter-day Saints dedicated the reconstructed Nauvoo Temple. At a wreath-laying ceremony in the Smith family cemetery, church presidents from both faiths met for the first time in more than a decade. "We are together on this day because we share an important slice of history," Community of Christ president Grant McMurray remarked. "We share a foundation in our respective faith journeys."[23]

SACRED SPACE IN COMMUNITY OF CHRIST

KATHERINE HILL

Katherine Hill is a member of Community of Christ and a professional historian who currently lives in Iceland.

Within the Community of Christ there are many sacred spaces, but places are made sacred not by where they are but by the presence of people seeking the sacred. As prophet-president Stephen M. Veazey put it in a 2018 challenge to the church, "Sacred community can be relatively uncomplicated and take place in many settings. It can happen in small groups, congregational groups, and online connections with occasional gatherings. It can happen in homes, storefronts, church buildings, and offices. It can occur at parks, on hiking trails, around dinner tables, in the Temple, and any combination of these."[24] With this in mind, this section will focus on Community of Christ reunion grounds and the Temple in Independence, Missouri.

REUNIONS

Reunions in Community of Christ are family camps that typically occur for a week in the summer. All ages are welcome, and each day church services are held in addition to Sunday school–style classes. Reunions also feature many recreational activities, including campfires where participants sing both secular and sacred songs. Although this is the general model of a reunion, there are many reunions that do not fit this description precisely. Reunions can happen any time of year and for any number of days at locations ranging from campgrounds to event centers. The defining hallmarks of a reunion are the sense of community and the intergenerational nature of these events.

Before 1883, Community of Christ had one church conference each year in either Kirtland, Ohio, or Plano, Illinois, and a second in southwestern Iowa. Church leaders recognized that this was leading to a disconnect in the church as part of the church went to one conference and the other part went to the other. Charles Derry proposed having a reunion in the western region in place of the second conference. This first official reunion took place in the fall of 1883. Reunions were so popular that the events immediately spread to other locations.[25]

The first reunions were primarily preaching focused, but over time Sunday school–type classes were incorporated and more and more recreation elements were added. In 1959 the church began putting out thematic and class materials that reunions all over the world could use each year. Reunions were not (and are not) required to use these materials, but the majority of reunions rely on these materials as a basis for camp planning.[26] As with most activities within Community of Christ, each area has its own method or flavor for activities, but a church member could attend a reunion in any part of the world and find familiar elements.

Today Community of Christ owns approximately three dozen campgrounds in the US and about a dozen internationally.[27] The campgrounds are used not only for reunions but also for youth camps in addition to being rented out for other events. Reunion grounds and reunion events (wherever they take place) are sacred events, and the places become sacred from the community experiences. Some people are so connected to the reunion grounds and the sacredness of the place that they further sanctify the grounds by being married there. In fact, any of the sacraments can be practiced at a reunion or camp.

THE TEMPLE

On April 1, 1968, President W. Wallace Smith (grandson of Joseph Smith Jr.) presented a new revelation to Community of Christ. The revelation concluded with directions for the church to start work on a temple: "The time has come for a start to be made toward building my temple in the Center Place. It shall stand on a portion of the plot of ground set apart for this purpose many years ago by my servant Joseph Smith, Jr. The shape and character of the building is to conform to ministries which will be carried out within its walls. These functions I will reveal through my servant the prophet and his counselors from time to time, as need for more specific direction arises" (CofChrist Doctrine and Covenants 149:6a).

The exact purposes of the temple were revealed when W. Wallace's son Wallace B. Smith was president of the church. On April 3, 1984, President Wallace B. Smith presented section 156 to the church. A portion of this revelation reads:

> The temple shall be dedicated to the pursuit of peace. It shall be for reconciliation and for healing of the spirit. It shall also be for a strengthening of faith and preparation for witness. By its ministries an attitude of wholeness of body, mind, and spirit as a desirable end toward which to strive will be fostered. It shall be the means for providing leadership education for priesthood and member. And it shall be a place in which the essential meaning of the Restoration as healing and redeeming agent is given new life and understanding, inspired by the life and witness of the Redeemer of the world. (CofChrist Doctrine and Covenants 156:5a–e)[28]

The pursuit of peace is practiced in the Temple through events such as the Community of Christ International Peace Award, given annually from 1993 to 2019, and the Community of Christ Peace Colloquy.[29] Each day in the sanctuary, a prayer for peace is offered for a particular country. These prayers are written and submitted by people from all over the world.

The artwork of the temple exemplifies peace. For example, outside on the temple grounds stands a statue representing Isaiah 2:4: "They shall beat their swords into plowshares and their spears into pruning hooks." In the atrium hang mobiles of paper cranes, and the door handles of the building have peace doves in flight.

The groundbreaking for the Community of Christ Temple was on April 6, 1990, and in April 1994 the dedication services were held. The Temple holds the world church administrative offices and the official archives for the church. The Temple is across the street from the Auditorium, and the two buildings are connected by an underground tunnel that allows the buildings to work in conjunction for hosting large gatherings like the World Conferences, which are held every three years. World Conferences are cherished events that allow people from all over the world to come together and share in community. Old friends across the globe reconnect, and many new national and international bonds of community form. Yes, World Conferences include business meetings, but the true spiritual power is in the sacred space that the Temple and Auditorium become through the gathered community.

The Temple is open for anyone who wants to visit. Any person can walk in and go on a tour of the building, request administration for the sick, or participate in a worship service (including participating in the sacrament of the Lord's Supper). Regardless of religious views or beliefs, all are welcome.

The sacraments of baptism, confirmation, blessing of children, and marriage are not practiced in either of the Community of Christ temples. Neither the Temple in Independence, Missouri, nor the Kirtland Temple has a baptismal font. Although only half of the sacraments are practiced in the two temples of the church, all eight sacraments are regularly practiced in local congregations and at reunions.[30]

TEMPLE SANCTUARY

There are two ways to enter the sanctuary in the Community of Christ Temple. There are grand doors that lead directly into the sanctuary up above the atrium, but these are rarely used by people entering for worship. The primary way to enter the sanctuary is to take the Worshiper's Path. This path provides a deep meditative experience and prepares all (no matter how many times they have traveled it before) to be ready for worship. The first phase of the Worshiper's Path is to enter through the sacred grove doorway of etched glass, which represents both the literal sacred grove that Joseph Smith Jr. entered and the metaphorical sacred grove of all seeking God. Directly through the doorway hangs a tapestry of the burning bush Moses encountered. Next is a depiction of the return of the prodigal son, with the father figure stretching out his arms to welcome his child back. Then the worshiper has a truly humbling experience of seeing the cross and then stepping through its shadow. Next is a sculpture, designed by a Muslim artist, of the tree of life. Continuing on the path leads to the ikebana flower arrangement. *Ikebana* is a Japanese flower arrangement style with Buddhist influences.[31] The ikebana arrangements represent "heaven, humanity, and earth."[32] Several florists have been specially trained to provide fresh ikebana arrangements. The "dark night of the soul" statues come next. These statues represent a person in states of despair, then turning to God. The first figure is huddled on the ground, the second on his knees clutching his chest, and the third is raising his arms in a worshipful manner. The final stop on the Worshiper's Path is a shallow waterfall fountain with the words from John 4:14: "Whoever drinks of the water I give . . . will never thirst."[33]

Like reading a scripture again, each journey on the Worshiper's Path is unique. Perhaps travelers need to be reminded to drink of the living water of Christ, or maybe they feel they are the prodigal child. Regardless of the journey that has brought him or her there, every traveler goes from the dimly lit and meditative Worshiper's Path into the bright light of the sanctuary. The sanctuary is the very center of the nautilus shape of the Temple.

Worshipers can exit the sanctuary through the peace doors embossed with the church peace seal onto the World Plaza—a map of the world created in bricks. Exiting onto the plaza metaphorically and literally has a person going outward into the world from his or her inner sacred journey.

The sacred space of the Temple pushes and encourages the people of Community of Christ as described in Doctrine and Covenants section 161: "Become a people of the Temple—those who see violence but proclaim peace, who feel conflict yet extend the hand of reconciliation, who encounter broken spirits and find pathways for healing. Fulfill the purposes of the Temple by making its ministries manifest in your hearts. It was built from your sacrifices and searching over many generations. Let it stand as a towering symbol of a people who knew injustice and strife on the frontier and who now seek the peace of Jesus Christ throughout the world" (CofChrist Doctrine and Covenants 161:2a–b).

John G. VanDerWalker II, Inland Northwest Mission Center president, explained how in Community of Christ "spaces become sacred through experiences that shape our lives and guide our actions. Historic buildings and places are treasured, congregational buildings are carefully cared for and maintained, and campgrounds are celebrated as holy ground."[34] Community of Christ has physical spaces that are considered sacred, but what truly makes a space sacred in Community of Christ are the experiences and community that are cultivated there.

RESPONSE TO KATHERINE HILL

As another of the many things that we share, The Church of Jesus Christ of Latter-day Saints and Community of Christ embrace similar views regarding sacred space. In her analysis, Katherine Hill emphasizes that within Community of Christ, space is sacralized by the people who occupy it and the experiences they create therein. True to their name, community development and seeking Christ are central to their view of place.

Latter-day Saints likewise highlight that space becomes sacred because of holy people and holy experiences. Elder Dennis B. Neuenschwander, a former member of the Presidency of the Seventy, taught, "Holy places have always been essential to the proper worship of God. For Latter-day Saints, such holy places include venues of historic significance, our homes, sacrament meetings, and temples. . . . The faith and reverence associated with them and the respect we have for what transpires or has transpired in them make them holy. The importance of holy places and sacred space in our worship can hardly be overestimated."[35]

Community of Christ places special emphasis on reunion grounds and reunion experiences. With the exception of youth camps, there is not a direct analog to reunions for Latter-day Saints. However, because reunions are "intergenerational," as Hill describes, Latter-day Saint historic sites may serve a comparative purpose. Church groups and families often visit these locations, seeking the "sense of community," spiritual uplift, and retrenchment evident in the reunion model. Parents and youth leaders take their children to the locations of earlier sacred experiences, hoping they will foster them anew in the rising generation. Elder Neuenschwander continues, "For Latter-day Saints, such holy places include venues of historic significance, our homes, sacrament meetings, and temples. . . . In holy places and in sacred space we find spiritual refuge, renewal, hope, and peace."[36] Furthermore, it is in these historic sites, especially in the temple cities of Kirtland and Nauvoo, where the two faiths most interact in sacred space.

The most obvious sacred space comparison between the two faiths is in the place of the temple within the respective theologies. While both operate temples, including placing them at the center of the respective church headquarters, they differ significantly in operation and theological significance. As Hill notes, Community of Christ operates two temples, both of which are open to public tours and participation in worship services. Sacraments like baptism, confirmation, and marriage, however, do not occur therein. This differs dramatically for Latter-day Saints, who limit access to their more than one hundred temples worldwide. Additionally, ordinances for both the living and the dead occur therein, with the theological import that entrance into the highest level of the celestial kingdom is conditioned on one of those ordinances (marriage) occurring in a house of the Lord (see LDS Doctrine and Covenants 124:39; 131:1–4).

Response to Scott C. Esplin

It is easy to see that temples are understood very differently theologically and practically in the two traditions. Community of Christ's temples are not necessary for salvation, and the church has no plans to build any more. The Temple, for Community of Christ, is a center place for gathering, connecting, and going out into the world to promote Christ's mission—the pursuit of peace, reconciliation, and healing of the spirit.

Scott Esplin highlighted historic sites as sacred space for the Church of Jesus Christ. This is an area where he noted that the two churches share much in common, but I would like to note some differences as well. The two churches have corporately solved many of their old disputes and now can work together peacefully, but it is worth mentioning that all tension has not come to an end on the individual level. Some of the disputes encountered at historical sites between members of the two churches are the result of Latter-day Saint individuals being upset that their church does not own, for instance, the Kirtland Temple. Other conflicts are from disagreements over how sites should be interpreted.

Before diving into the different viewpoints on interpretation of the sites, it is worth explaining staffing. The sites belonging to the Church of Jesus Christ are staffed by senior missionaries (usually retired couples serving six to eighteen months) and young missionaries (completing their eighteen- to twenty-four-month mission). Community of Christ sites are staffed by a few paid staff, but mostly retired volunteers, local volunteers, and, in the summer, a group of college-aged summer interns who receive a stipend and college credit. All staff at Latter-day Saint sites are Latter-day Saints and are missionaries, whereas the Community of Christ staff are not missionaries and are not necessarily members.

The Community of Christ interpretation in Nauvoo and Kirtland is historically focused. Guides are trained only to make statements for which they have a verifiable source and to honestly say, "I don't know," if they do not know the answer to a guest's question. Latter-day Saint sites use historical interpretation, but there is a missionary or faith-promoting message as well. Community of Christ guides might answer religious questions, but they do not bear testimony or directly promote a theological view. This difference in interpretation at times causes conflict. Latter-day Saint guests are at times confused by the lack of testimony in a Community of Christ site. Community of Christ guides are not out to ruin Latter-day Saint vacations, but many families leave having been confronted with the knowledge that what they thought was a fact was, in fact, folklore. As examples, Emma Smith did not regret staying in Nauvoo, and the Kirtland Temple plaster was made with already broken dishes, not ladies' finest china.

CONCLUSION

A historical and doctrinal thread regarding sacred space connects The Church of Jesus Christ of Latter-day Saints and Community of Christ. This thread includes the prominence of temples within faith practices, albeit with differences in access and function. Both utilize sacred spaces, including temples, recreation grounds, and historic sites, to build faith and foster community. Because of their mutual interest in several of the same historically sacred spaces, they interact in direct ways through site visits and a common desire to preserve, understand, and celebrate reminders of their past.

As with any relationship, the interactions at sacred spaces between the Church of Jesus Christ and Community of Christ are in constant need of being nourished. "Even though that relationship has significantly improved in recent years," one scholar of the faiths has noted, "unfounded rumors and hearsay still fuel misconceptions and hinder understanding between members of the two organizations."[37] Furthermore, from a practical standpoint, the turnover in site interpreters necessitates consistently forming new connections. David J. Howlett, a longtime student of the interactions between the faiths, rightly describes "a far more complicated story than a narrative of rivals becoming friends at Kirtland—a popular notion upheld by contemporary LDS and Community of Christ. Instead," Howlett continues, "the . . . changing proximities reveal ever-changing forms of contestation and new avenues of cooperation." The same may be said of the interactions and perspectives regarding historic sites among the faiths generally. While "deep differences persist," these historic sites are "contact zone[s] for trans denominational cooperation."[38]

Notes

1. Sara M. Patterson, *Pioneers in the Attic: Place and Memory along the Mormon Trail* (New York: Oxford University Press, 2020), xvi.

2. Bruce R. McConkie, *Mormon Doctrine*, 2nd ed. (Salt Lake City: Bookcraft, 1966), 574.

3. Gary E. Stevenson, "Sacred Homes, Sacred Temples," *Ensign*, May 2009, 101–3.

4. "Temple," Bible Dictionary (Salt Lake City: The Church of Jesus Christ of Latter-day Saints, 2013).

5. Joseph Smith, cited in *Wilford Woodruff Journal*, ed. Scott G. Kenney (Midvale, UT: Signature Books, 1983), 2:240 (June 11, 1843).

6. Boyd K. Packer, cited in "'Gathering Spirit' Still Continues," *Deseret News*, July 8, 2006.

7. Jennifer Lund, "Why Historic Sites?," February 1, 2020, https://history.Church ofJesusChrist.org/content/historic-sites/why-keep-historic-sites.

8. To be consistent with the rest of the volume, the authors use the current name of the church, Community of Christ, rather than Reorganized Church of Jesus Christ of Latter Day Saints, even when referring to events or activities conducted prior to the 2001 name change.

9. Scott C. Esplin, "Dark Tourism: Healing at Historic Carthage Jail," *Journal of Mormon History* 46, no. 1 (January 2020): 85–116.

10. Jennifer L. Lund, "Joseph F. Smith and the Origins of the Church Historic Sites Program," in *Joseph F. Smith: Reflections on the Man and His Times*, ed. Craig K. Manscill, Brian D. Reeves, Guy L. Dorius, and J. B. Haws (Provo, UT: Religious Studies Center, Brigham Young University; Salt Lake City: Deseret Book, 2013), 345; Cameron J. Packer, "A Study of the Hill Cumorah: A Significant Latter-day Saint Landmark in Western New York" (master's thesis, Brigham Young University, 2002); Lisle G. Brown, "Nauvoo's Temple Square," *BYU Studies* 41, no. 4 (2002): 5–45; Kenneth R. Mays, "A Man of Vision and Determination: A Photographic Essay and Tribute to Wilford C. Wood," *Mormon Historical Studies* 10, no. 1 (Spring 2009): 154–73; Scott C. Esplin, *Return to the City of Joseph: Modern Mormonism's Contest for the Soul of Nauvoo* (Urbana: University of Illinois Press, 2018).

11. Kathleen Flake, "Re-placing Memory: Latter-day Saint Use of Historical Monuments and Narrative in the Early Twentieth Century," *Religion and American Culture: A Journal of Interpretation* 13, no. 1 (Winter 2003): 80.

12. P. R. Burton, "Old Nauvoo," *Zion's Ensign* 32, no. 45 (November 4, 1920): 795.

13. "LDS Church Forms Corporation to Restore Historic Nauvoo," *Deseret News Telegram*, June 28, 1962, in Journal History of the Church, June 28, 1962, 4, Church History Library, Salt Lake City.

14. J. LeRoy Kimball to missionary couple, circa 1971, Nauvoo Restoration, Incorporated historical files, Nauvoo, IL.

15. Kenneth E. Stobaugh, "The Development of the Joseph Smith Historic Center in Nauvoo," *BYU Studies Quarterly* 32, nos. 1–2 (1992): 38; Kenneth E. Stobaugh, "Getting a Foothold Again: The Development of the Joseph Smith Historic Center in Nauvoo," UP S6100.1, Community of Christ Archives, Independence, MO.

16. J. LeRoy Kimball to missionary couple, circa 1971, Nauvoo Restoration, Incorporated historical files, Nauvoo, IL.

17. Stobaugh, "Development of the Joseph Smith Historic Center," 38–39.

18. William D. Russell, "The LDS Church and Community of Christ: Clearer Differences, Closer Friends," *Dialogue* 36, no. 4 (Winter 2003): 185.

19. Richard P. Howard, "The Beginning of the Sharing of Historical Sources between the LDS and the RLDS Churches, November 20, 1974," *John Whitmer Historical Association Journal* 36, no. 1 (Spring/Summer 2016): 162.

20. Esplin, *Return to the City of Joseph*, 116–17.

21. Lachlan Mackay, "A Brief History of the Smith Family Nauvoo Cemetery," *Mormon Historical Studies* 3, no. 2 (Fall 2002): 245.

22. David J. Howlett, *Kirtland Temple: The Biography of a Shared Mormon Sacred Space* (Urbana: University of Illinois Press, 2014), 199–204.

23. Stephen A. Martin, "Church Leaders Make Rare Joint Appearance," *Burlington Hawk Eye*, June 28, 2002.

24. Steve Veazey, "President's Challenge: Hope Rising," *Saints' Herald*, May/June 2018, 15.

25. Richard P. Howard, "Reunions: Part of Our Common Story," *Saints' Herald*, February 1973, 16.

26. Howard, "Reunions," 16–18.

27. "Campgrounds," Community of Christ, https://www.CofChrist.org/camp grounds.

28. Section 156 is famous in RLDS and Community of Christ circles for opening priesthood to women.

29. "International Peace Award," Community of Christ, https://www.CofChrist .org/international-peace-award.

30. The eight sacraments in Community of Christ are marriage, baptism, confirmation, Communion, evangelist blessing, laying on of hands for the sick, blessing of children, and ordination.

31. *Community of Christ: A People on the Move*, directed by Elray Henriksen (2019), https://www.youtube.com/watch?v=-zX4uGmYSUI.

32. Community of Christ, *The Worshiper's Path* (pamphlet).

33. *Community of Christ: A People on the Move*.

34. John G. VanDerWalker II, "Holy Spaces" (guiding document for Samish Island Board of Directors, Samish Island, WA, [2010s?]), 1.

35. Dennis B. Neuenschwander, "Holy Place, Sacred Space," *Ensign*, May 2003, 71.

36. Neuenschwander, "Holy Place, Sacred Space," 71–72.

37. Richard G. Moore, "LDS Misconceptions about the Community of Christ," *Mormon Historical Studies* 15, no. 1 (2014): 18.

38. Howlett, *Kirtland Temple*, 213, 216–17.

Zion

Maclane E. Heward and David J. Howlett

"To Meet the Lord and Enoch's Band": Latter-day Saint Perspectives on Zion

MACLANE E. HEWARD

Maclane E. Heward is a religious educator
at the Utah Valley Institute of Religion.

The quest for Zion is central to the purpose of The Church of Jesus Christ of Latter-day Saints. Latter-day Saint scholar Terryl Givens has recently summarized this purpose: "The church exists to create the kind of persons, in the kinds of relationships, that constitute the divine nature."[1] In this way, the church is not only seeking a future reunification with God but also a present union with God. This captures the essence of Zion.[2] "Zion-building is not *preparation* for heaven. It *is* heaven, in embryo."[3] Through covenants currently formalized in Latter-day Saint temples, individuals bind themselves directly to God in a "vertical dimension" of heaven. Similarly, individuals also covenant with God in temples to look horizontally to their fellowmen. This horizontal element of relatedness is Zion, a "divine society, centered on family relations but radiating far beyond."[4] The potential of Zion is the presence of God, for "Christ will reign [in Zion] personally ..."[5] This view of Zion became clear only after Joseph Smith's reception of the "prophecy of Enoch."[6]

JOSEPH SMITH'S VIEWS OF ZION

Joseph Smith's early use of the term Zion seems to parallel general Christian thought of his day. In essence, Zion was used by most American Christians as a metaphor for a gathering of heavenly people, or the work or kingdom of God.[7] Immediately after Smith received the "prophecy of Enoch," his usage of the word Zion was "energized ... in a powerful and unmistakable manner."[8] Smith and the church learned about a literal, not figurative, Zion. An actual society that became prepared to receive the Lord, for "Enoch and all his people walked with God, and he dwelt in the midst of Zion" (Moses 7:69). Significantly, Smith also learned about a latter-day Zion that would be established anticipatory to Christ's millennial reign.[9] This revelation seemed to drive Smith's "true prophetic task," which was to "replicate the city Enoch perfected."[10] Smith began immediately forging a society meant to welcome God—called Zion.

At the end of December 1830 and the beginning of January 1831, Smith received two revelations contextualized in Zion references and directing the Saints toward a purposeful gathering.[11] Within a few months, Smith had received additional information, directing the Saints to collect money and purchase land for their relocation, teach others, and gather to "the New Jerusalem, a land of peace, a city of refuge, a place of safety for the saints of the Most High God; and the glory of the Lord shall be there, . . . and it shall be called Zion" (LDS Doctrine and Covenants 45:66–67; CofChrist Doctrine and Covenants 45:12c–d). By the summer of 1831, the land of Zion was identified and dedicated, and individuals were instructed to "plant" themselves there (LDS Doctrine and Covenants 57:8, 11, 14; CofChrist Doctrine and Covenants 57:4a,

5a, 5c). In addition, this prophecy and the subsequent revelations also showed the foundational principles of a Zion society—namely, deep, transformative, sacrificial love for God and others.[12]

Smith's pursuit was thus to create a society that would partake of the divine nature. First, those inhabiting Zion must love God in word and deed, which, as happened with Enoch, may incur the displeasure of society.[13] Second, Zion demanded sacrificial love for others that both built community and oneness and prepared all for the presence of the Divine.[14] These commitments are currently well represented in church sacraments, particularly those performed in temples. Individuals covenant to live the laws of obedience, sacrifice, the gospel, chastity, and consecration. In essence, promises are made to obey God and sacrifice everything to support his work. Individuals are to dedicate their time, talents, and resources to bringing others to know God and build Zion.[15] Thus, the temple was located in the center of Zion geographically and in spiritual significance.[16]

THE TWO PHASES OF ZION: GATHERING AND CREATING LOCAL UNITS

There are two main phases in the history of the church as it relates to building Zion: gathering and creating local units worldwide. In the first twenty years of the church, the membership had gathered to several different locations—namely, Ohio, Missouri, Illinois, and then Utah Territory. Once in Utah, Brigham Young directed the building of hundreds of communities throughout the West. Throughout the nineteenth century, the call remained the same: "Come to Zion, come to Zion, and within her walls rejoice."[17] For the membership of the church, the call was consistent with the earlier revelations by Smith. Despite persecutions and through sacrifice, they were to obey God and his prophet by gathering to Zion, and they were to help others along that same trajectory.

Perhaps nothing illustrates the lived reality of the call to Zion like the organization of the Perpetual Emigrating Fund Company (PEF) in 1849, just two years after the church entered the valleys of the Rocky Mountains. The purpose of the PEF was to facilitate the gathering of poor and impoverished converts to Utah Territory. During its almost forty years of operation, possibly as many as thirty thousand Saints used the fund to facilitate their transoceanic and transcontinental immigration to the Intermountain West. By 1880, those that had used the PEF for their immigration had amassed an unpaid debt of over $1.5 million, and as part of the church's celebration of its fiftieth anniversary, the Twelve Apostles and the PEF Trustee in Trust proposed that half of the indebtedness be forgiven in order to free "the worthy poor" from "a burden which they have been unable, to honorably cast off."[18] Just seven years later the United States government put an end to the PEF with the passing of the Edmunds-Tucker Act in 1887.[19] The donation of the Saints' money, goods, and time to the fund exemplifies the principles of Zion as individuals showed a deep love for those they, in many situations, had not met but desired to gather in Zion.

In a speech given in 1878, George Q. Cannon began to lay the foundations of the next phase in Zion building: creating local units worldwide. After years of an isolationist stance that had arisen from persecution and marginalization, Cannon questioned a basic assumption when he indicated that "it is not the gathering of the people alone" for which the church must be engaged. The church must be about "teaching the world" and being the leaven for uplifting. Cannon went on to indicate that the church is a light to the rest of the nation in many ways, specifically mentioning the economic and political strength of the territory as examples.[20] Cannon stopped short of calling for church converts to remain in their native lands.

Beginning in the early years of the twentieth century, church leaders began to adjust their call for Saints and converts to gather to a Zion located in the Rocky Mountains. Leaders such as James Talmage in 1900 and the First Presidency in 1907 stated that Zion needed to be created in the stakes and branches located around the world. "The policy of the Church is not to entice or encourage people to leave their native lands," the First Presidency explained in 1907, "but to remain faithful and true in their allegiance to their governments, and to be good citizens."[21] This significant adjustment challenged Saints to adjust their view of Zion; instead of a call to gather to Utah, members ought to create Zion in their native lands.

The work of Zion continued as is exemplified with the development of the welfare program. This program was developed during the leadership of church president Heber J. Grant (1919 to 1945). During its inaugural year in 1936, Grant explained, "Our primary purpose [in establishing the church's welfare program] was to set up, in so far as it might be possible, a system . . . to help the people to help themselves."[22] Through time it became clear that the reach of the welfare program was much larger than just a myopic focus on church membership. In October 1945, US president Harry S. Truman called upon the church to determine how quickly supplies of food and clothing from the church's welfare program could be sent to those suffering the devastating effects of war in Europe. To Truman's surprise, church president George Albert Smith responded that supplies were already collected and ready for shipment.[23] In 1986, Presiding Bishop Robert D. Hales expressed the connection between Zion and the welfare system, saying, "When we think of welfare, let us think of the plan revealed by our Lord for the eternal welfare of our souls. It is a plan to build faith, love, compassion, self-reliance, and unity. When adopted to local needs throughout the world by vigorous priesthood leaders, the plan sanctifies both givers and receivers and prepares a Zion people."[24]

In the late 1970s, President Spencer W. Kimball asked that a talk by Elder Bruce R. McConkie of the Quorum of the Twelve Apostles be published in the church's *Ensign* magazine. The talk, "Come: Let Israel Build Zion," indicated that Zion is to be built in three different phases: first, setting up the kingdom, which McConkie indicated had already happened; second, the emphasis of creating and building up stakes in overseas areas, which is understood to be the current phase of the church; and finally, the return of the Lord, his reception by his earthly kingdom, Zion, and Zion's perfecting—a phase yet to begin.[25] Thus, anticipation of the divine presence remained central to the concept of Zion; the temple is still in the center of Zion. As President Gordon B. Hinckley announced and implemented in 1997, the church has been seeking "to take the temples to the people."[26] During President Russell M. Nelson's first four years of leadership (2018–21), the church announced the construction of an astounding eighty-three new temples.[27] Currently the church is calling upon its members to create Zion where they are and is attempting to put temples in their midst so that, through the vertical covenants of the temple, and the horizontal elements of Zion building, members are becoming one with the "divine nature."

"A Nucleus of Heaven"

Joseph Smith taught that the "great mission" of the Saints was to "organize a nucleus of Heaven."[28] The call to the church is essentially the same as it was in Smith's day. Instead of waiting for the Divine to place heaven upon us, we are seeking to create it. We have miles to go before we rest, but the pursuit enlivens those who are filled with the vision. President Nelson recently invited all young people to be a part of the gathering of souls to Zion. It is at the heart of the "greatest challenge, the greatest cause, and the greatest work on earth."[29]

The Abundant Song of Zion in Community of Christ

David J. Howlett

David Howlett is the Mellon Visiting Assistant Professor of Religion at Smith College and a World Church historian for Community of Christ.

As a six-year-old, I would listen to a cassette tape of a baritone singing traditional RLDS hymns. As my older sister smirked, I would muster my deepest child voice and sing, "Onward to Zion, Faithful and Strong! Zion the Beautiful beckons us on!" At age six, I did not know what Zion meant for the RLDS tradition, but I knew we sang of it—a lot.

Singing about Zion offers a resonant metaphor for understanding the presence of Zion theology in Community of Christ. In fact, Inez

Smith Davis, the midcentury chronicler of RLDS history, observed that "the Zionic ideal . . . comes singing up in every generation, over and over again, perhaps only to fade away in discordant notes. Our critics have missed more than all else this Zion-melody in their telling, perhaps because its notes have not been clear enough, but the fact remains that without it, the story [of the church] would scarcely be worth telling."[30] Smith Davis's apologetic history has limited utility in the contemporary Community of Christ, but her observation about the "Zion melody" provides an especially useful analogy for how doctrines can move across generations.

Going beyond an analogy about how a narrative moves and has influence, scholar Robert Orsi has theorized about how what he calls "abundant events" gain meaning beyond their initial conception. Orsi argues that "presence radiates out from the [abundant] event along a network of routes, a kind of capillary of presence, filling water, relics, images, things, and memories."[31] Orsi applies this term to a study of Marian apparitions, but other scholars have used his framework to understand other religious "events" and "narratives," such as Joseph Smith's gold plates.[32]

Through a synthesis of Orsi's theory and Smith Davis's analogy, I suggest that Community of Christ's Zion theology can be thought of as an abundant song. As such, Zion is a resonant, performed narrative not "exhausted by its source material," in Orsi's terms.[33] Instead, the abundant song of Zion resounds in places, media, objects, and memories far beyond its original performance. And as people share it, they create new variations on the abundant song, which, in turn, shape people, their aspirations, their relationships, and their church's official beliefs. But what exactly are these variations and themes within the abundant song of Zion in Community of Christ, past and present?

ZION AMONG THE EARLIEST RESTORATION SAINTS

In the era of the early American republic, many Protestants used "Zion" as a gloss to imbue something with holiness. This is the earliest sense that the original Latter Day Saints had when Joseph Smith first referred to the "cause of Zion," or God's holy cause.[34] Yet, by December 1830, Smith had greatly enlarged the meanings of the phrase when he revised a section of Genesis with Sidney Rigdon, his compatriot and scribe. In an act not unlike midrash (a filling in of the gaps of a biblical story), Smith expanded the story of Enoch in Genesis 5 from a few brief lines to a several-chapter saga in which the ancient prophet built a holy city in which "the Lord called his people Zion, for they were of one heart and one mind and dwelt in righteousness, and there were no poor among them" (CofChrist Doctrine and Covenants 36:2h–i; Moses 7:18). Zion, Enoch's holy city, was received by God into the heavens, where it was to await the last days when another holy city, the New Jerusalem, would be established on the earth. Enoch's city and the earthly New Jerusalem would then be united as one, marking the beginning of the Millennium, a thousand years of peace.

Smith, believing himself to be a prophet charged with restoring the ancient faith, felt that he had restored a lost part of the biblical text with his Zion story. While this might be historically untrue in the light of later historical-critical biblical scholarship, Smith's Zion narrative was part of a much larger Christian, Jewish, and Islamic speculative tradition on the prediluvian Enoch.[35] Smith's Zion narrative, too, had a life of its own, and, in this manner, it became historically real. That is, Smith's Zion story entered people's lives, and they subsequently acted on this narrative. Beyond his Genesis midrash, Smith added further details on the New Jerusalem in revelations included in the Book of Commandments and later Doctrine and Covenants. In 1831, he revealed that the city of Zion would be located in Independence, Jackson County, Missouri, and would include a temple complex (see CofChrist Doctrine and Covenants 57:1a–d; LDS Doctrine and Covenants 57:1–3).

Smith's revelations, poured onto an antebellum America awash in communal experiments, inspired ordinary Saints to move to Independence to build the holy city. Their subsequent attempts to organize a community were frustrated by Euro-American settlers who already lived in Jackson County. After an escalating religious and political conflict in 1833, the "old settlers" of Jackson County forced the Saints from the county by gunpoint. In the following years, the early

Restoration Saints moved their communal centers to places such as Far West, Missouri, and Nauvoo, Illinois.[36] After Smith's 1844 assassination and a subsequent leadership succession crisis, groups of Saints of the Nauvoo diaspora, like the Reorganized Church of Jesus Christ of Latter Day Saints, kept singing the song of Zion, and, in doing so, explored some of the most significant theological tensions and bold community-building attempts in the larger Restoration movement.

ZION IN THE REORGANIZATION

In the late nineteenth century, RLDS members sang from a hymnal titled *Zion's Praises*, but they debated how exactly those praises would be realized in the world. For example, one of the founders of the Reorganization, Jason Briggs, emphatically argued against gathering to a central community, while others started an Order of Enoch in Lamoni, Iowa, that made small steps toward a cooperative community. RLDS prophet Joseph Smith III, aware of the drawbacks of a mass movement back into Missouri and all-too-human imperfections of church members living in community, advocated for a policy of gradualism in creating a Zion community.[37] He canonized this decades-long approach when, in 1909, he counseled the church in a revelation not to withdraw from the world into their own communities. Instead, they were to live and act "honestly and honorably before God and in the sight of all men, using the things of this world in the manner designed of God, that the places where they occupy may shine as Zion, the redeemed of the Lord" (CofChrist Doctrine and Covenants 128:8c). Even with this nongeographical emphasis on personal holiness and living among other people rather than gathering to a central community, Smith moved the church headquarters from Illinois (1860) to Lamoni, Iowa (1880), and finally moved himself to Independence, Missouri (1910).

Securely headquartered in site for the future New Jerusalem, the next generation of RLDS members sang an efflorescent song of Zion that illuminated all areas of church life. Led by a prophet, F. M. Smith, who earned an MA in sociology and a PhD in social psychology, RLDS members attempted to take an eclectic mix of Protestant social gospel thought and social scientific insights and meld them with the nineteenth-century Zion narrative.[38] An official RLDS evangelistic flyer from the 1920s is illustrative of this synthesis, stating that the "[Reorganized] Latter Day Saint Program" proclaimed "Social reform by individual regeneration / Every man having opportunity to be his best; to do his best for the good of all / Love the dynamic / Righteousness the principle / Justice the basis of social relationship / To organize such men and women into the kingdom of God. / To provide all with suitable means which, with their talents, become their stewardships / Each one being brought to the task he is able best to perform, the product to be distributed so that none has less than is needed, and no one has more than he can use."[39] These points, the flyer proclaimed, constituted the "restored gospel." It is no wonder, then, that RLDS members in this era experimented with cooperative farms and cooperative grocery stores, wrote novels on Zion, preached tens of thousands of sermons on Zion, and wrote hymns of Zion. For example, F. M. Smith wrote the hymn "Onward to Zion!" in 1922 to the tune of Stephen Foster's "Beautiful Dreamer." It was an apt tune for a hymn from an era in which larger collectivist dreams felt like they could be real.

By the 1960s, the early twentieth-century song of Zion began to be revised as RLDS members sorted themselves into liberal and conservative camps, influenced by ecumenical Protestant theology or fundamentalist Protestant theology. Consequently, two distinct Zion theologies emerged. In the conservative version, Zion was decidedly centered on Independence and became a reality through personal holiness. Zion would happen when church members kept "all my commandments," a phrase from Smith's revised Enoch narrative. This Zion burned bright with last-days apocalyptic urgency, too.[40] In the progressive version, Zion became a process rather than simply a goal. Zion also became a "leavening influence" in the world rather than a "lighthouse," to use a popular analogy propounded by 1970s RLDS theologians. Zion as a leaven meant working with people of all goodwill for the kingdom of God, going hand in hand with progressive desires for ecumenism. Additionally, Zion as a leaven decentered Independence as the site of a holy city; the world became a place where Zion was manifest, regardless of geography.[41]

Nevertheless, in 1984, RLDS prophet Wallace B. Smith announced that the time had come to begin construction on the long-awaited temple in Independence. This temple, finished in 1994, was dedicated for "the pursuit of peace . . . [and] for reconciliation and for healing of the spirit" (CofChrist Doctrine and Covenants 156:5a). The progressive Zion, then, enacted a transformed millennialism in which the kingdom was "already and not yet," one that emphasized the justice theology of earlier generations, along with a new emphasis on peace. In a hymn from this era, one progressive RLDS apostle summed up this new emphasis on Zion:

> The cause of Zion celebrates the victory over fear,
> the witness of the kingdom's power, new life already here.
> Although fulfilment seems remote, the journey just begun,
> the kingdom has already come; the victory is won.
> The cause of Zion prophecies the future yet to be,
> when men and women everywhere shall walk in dignity.
> We now anticipate the day when pain and tears shall cease,
> when humankind shall live as one in righteousness and peace.[42]

Conservatives balked at this theology and largely left the RLDS Church in the late 1980s, leading to the normalization of the progressive, ecumenical song of Zion among church members by the 1990s.

ZION IN THE CONTEMPORARY COMMUNITY OF CHRIST

Zion has proved to be surprisingly resonant within the contemporary Community of Christ. Four key contemporary documents, developed by global working groups of Community of Christ leaders and approved by the First Presidency, have creatively revivified the song of Zion. First, in the Basic Beliefs statement, Community of Christ states, "'Zion' expresses our commitment to herald God's peaceable kingdom on Earth by forming Christ-centered communities in families, congregations, neighborhoods, cities, and throughout the world."[43] Similarly, the church's Enduring Principles document states that "the vision of

Zion is to promote God's reign on earth, as proclaimed by Jesus Christ, through the leavening influence of just and peaceful communities."[44] The "leaven" model for Zion, advocated in various forms since the nineteenth century, is further instantiated as a normative model for Zion.

In the church's Mission Initiatives document, Zion is seen as an eschatological symbol of hope, and its realization is equated with a coming restoration of "Christ's covenant of peace." This "hope of Zion will become reality when we live Christ's peace and generously share his peace with others." Furthermore, "God's ultimate vision" for Community of Christ will be fulfilled as it establishes "the Temple as a Center to Promote Peacemaking throughout the World," seeks "Justice, Create[s] Peacemakers around the World," and "Unite[s] with Others to Make Peace Around the World."[45] Here, Zion is tied to the Temple in Independence and its ministries of peacemaking and justice, along with a solidarity with all who work for peace.

Finally, *Community of Christ Sings*, the 2013 hymnal used in the English-speaking part of the church, added a core 150 songs used by the church around the world. One of these hymns, "Tiona Nehenehe," has been sung by French Polynesian Community of Christ members for generations. Roughly translated into English, the hymn reads, "Zion the beautiful, beloved homeland, saints in these days. Jesus will return, we will all go to Zion and we will all meet him there in Zion, the pure in heart."[46] The inclusion of this hymn in a contemporary Community of Christ hymnal does not represent a repristination of an earlier Zion theology. Rather, it represents how Zion has become indigenous and can mean multiple things in multiple places. Singing a hymn in a worshipping community, after all, is a cooperative endeavor, and the shared meaning of the words does not matter as much as the shared performance. Singing a hymn about Zion, then, seems like an apt image for how a diverse, global Community of Christ pragmatically strives for the peaceable kingdom of God.

CONCLUSION: SINGING A NEW SONG OF ZION

In the words of one Community of Christ theologian, Joseph Smith's experience is "illustrative, but not necessarily normative."[47] I would add that Joseph Smith's experience, at least around "Zion," is also generative. As such, Community of Christ theologians, leaders, and ordinary members have created new dimensions for talking about, expressing, and living Zion. They are all variations on themes first composed by Smith in the early Restoration church but have also taken on a life of their own, going beyond their author's original intent, as do all texts that achieve true influence in a larger culture.

As variations on a theme, Smith's pithy summation of the characteristics of Zion's people, along with his added revelations about a temple complex in Zion, helped Community of Christ generate an emphasis on peace and justice, ecumenism, and an expectation that such ministries will emanate from a temple in Independence, Missouri. Finally, Smith's story of "Enoch's people" who dwelt in the city of Zion continues to shape Community of Christ's conceptualization of itself as a people in covenant with God. True enough, Community of Christ folks are not the only covenant people or not even the most favored, but they are a people of God, nonetheless.

In these variations on themes, the Palmyra prophet's midrash-like narrative of Zion has gone beyond the bounds of antebellum American religious culture and been transformed into the abundant song sung by Community of Christ members, generation after generation. Smith's extrabiblical story could have constrained Community of Christ to a certain sectarian aloofness. Instead, Zion's abundant song, creatively rewritten by each generation, has gifted Community of Christ with a certain expansive theological imagination. This imagination sees salvation as social, seeks solidarity with those who work for justice and peace, and hopes for God's peaceable reign. And the song of Zion has verses yet to be written.

RESPONSE TO DAVID J. HOWLETT

David Howlett does a masterful job in describing Community of Christ's historical and theological relationship with Zion. The concept of Zion, its creation and implementation, has shaped both our pasts and our present lived religious experiences in profound and different ways. These differences present an opportunity for us to admire each other's views for their unique contributions to Joseph Smith's quest to create a divine society.

Zion, perhaps more than most other ecclesiastical or theological elements of our faiths, links us together more than it divides us. Patrick Mason has recently indicated that assertions of religious truth often fall into two distinct stances: exclusivism or relativism. Early revelations of Joseph Smith, suggests Mason, promote a third category: particularism.[48] Each faith has a particular melodic line to sing, to use David's musical analogy, to create the complete Zion song. This, I believe, is a helpful lens through which to view our different Zionic endeavors.

Some may argue that The Church of Jesus Christ of Latter-day Saints is spending too much of its energy looking back in our past and holding up Nauvoo theological developments. Some would say the church is stuck in a time when Joseph extended too far into theological wonderings. From a particularistic paradigm, there is another way of viewing the church. The temple ordinances, organized in Nauvoo but energized beginning at least by early 1831, can be seen as beautiful expressions of a selfless desire to grant all humankind the *opportunity* to dwell with God and family eternally. Seen in this light, one can embrace the concept of "holy envy" and simply appreciate the unique Latter-day Saint contribution to the collective body of Christ.

Some may think that Community of Christ has lost its historical and theological roots. Since the "past is all that makes the present coherent," Community of Christ has struggled, some may say, with coherency.[49] David has shown their relationship with history and theology as generated out of earlier expressions, making earlier concepts beautifully new. Community of Christ's emphasis on peace and justice and ecumenism, which emanates from their Temple in Independence, is a beautiful particular expression of a deep commitment to bring about God's peaceable reign. David has shown how the songs generated in Community of Christ can be sung with new meaning in a new context. Each religious expression stemming from Joseph Smith Jr. conveys different aspects of Zion and contributes uniquely to the overall work of God.

Edward Partridge, the first bishop of the church, arrived in Zion only to find that his imagined Zion was far different than the actual identified location. All the residents of Zion were informed that "it is not meet that I should command in all things. . . . Men should be anxiously engaged in a good cause and do many things of their own free will."[50] Our different contributions to Zion can be seen as our attempt to be anxiously engaged in God's work to bring about Zion. Partridge eventually caught the Zionic vision. He wrote, "Let Zion in her beauty rise; Her light begins to shine, Ere long her King will rend the skies, Majestic and divine. . . . Dear Lord prepare my heart, To stand with thee, on Zion's mount, And never more to part."[51] From these two essays on Zion, a few things seem clear. First, the songs of Zion have long captured our shared quest to create a heavenly society. Second, God will build Zion through our efforts. Third, those who catch the vision of Zion, as Partridge did, will focus on preparing their hearts to stand with God on Zion's mount, never more to part. Finally, though our Zionic expressions are divergent and our future expressions unknown, our particular contributions and our shared beginnings leave much for us to celebrate and encourage in each other.

RESPONSE TO MACLANE E. HEWARD

Maclane Heward provides an excellent historical overview of Zion theology in The Church of Jesus Christ of Latter-day Saints. As I reflect upon his work, I see a crucial historical disjuncture between Community of Christ and The Church of Jesus Christ of Latter-day Saints in terms of what Zion became, as well as a common interpretative strategy used by both traditions as they adapted the Enoch narrative in the wake of this disjuncture.

While it may be obvious to readers of this volume, the Nauvoo experience sent Community of Christ and The Church of Jesus Christ of Latter-day Saints on two different trajectories. Historian Roger Launius has shown how Joseph Smith III saw Nauvoo as a cautionary tale about trying to do too much too fast, as well as what happens when saints try to remove themselves from the evils of society. "In contrast to the Nauvoo approach to Zion, which sought to remove the saints from secular society," writes Launius, Joseph Smith III's "emphasis called for the church to be involved in the affairs of the world, in the hope that it would assist in changing it."[52]

As Maclane shows, Nauvoo's community-building endeavor became the model for nineteenth-century colonization of the Intermountain West. The doctrines developed in Nauvoo also became the theological foundation for the evolving church in which members made covenants at temples, uniting them to humans and divine figures in this world and the world to come. As temples began to dot the earth in the twentieth century, the concept of Zion also became decentered from Utah or a distant future Zion in Independence. Localized temples became the new gathering points to enact salvifically essential rituals. In contrast, a single temple in Community of Christ, the Independence Temple, served a symbolic function for church unity but had no salvifically essential role.

Both traditions have read back into Enoch's story the theology of their present. Smith's Enoch narrative was not intended to be a story about contemporary peace and justice theology and ecumenicism, but Community of Christ has made it so. Similarly, the Enoch narrative does not directly address the creation of a "heaven family" through temple rituals, a later Nauvoo-era theological concept that evolved in the Latter-day Saint tradition. Nonetheless, reading back into a story later realizations is exactly how narratives become living texts. At one level, I appreciate the sheer theological creativity of both traditions in doing so. At another level, I have to acknowledge that the text itself has gifted both traditions with affordances that channel this creativity along certain lines. To use an analogy from Hans-Georg Gadamer, in the interpretation of texts, our horizon meets the horizon of the text, and there is a fusion of horizons when this happens.[53] By allowing the Zion narrative to have its own voice, both traditions have been shaped by it in particular ways as their horizon has joined its horizon. In other words, there is not a simple reading into a text of whatever one wants; the text itself donates meaning too. Beyond this, a fusion of horizons seems to be an apt analogy for what the Enoch narrative itself implants as a hope within its readers—a fusion of heaven and earth within a concrete covenant community.

As I read Maclane's essay, I am left with admiration for some of the ways in which The Church of Jesus Christ of Latter-day Saints has concretely revivified Zion in the present. Maclane mentions the justice orientation of the Perpetual Emigrating Fund in the nineteenth century, and I see a similar gesture in the present by the church's Perpetual Education Fund. The former was centered on transporting people to a centralized geography to build Zion. The latter helps people be a leaven in the world wherever they live. In this way, while having very different histories, sacraments, and even ideas about the nature of God, The Church of Jesus Christ of Latter-day Saints and Community of Christ are not far away in terms of metaphor—taken from Jesus's parables—about what Zion is in the present; Zion for both can be seen as a God-sent leaven that grows within the elemental ingredients of our world.

CONCLUSION

We conclude our dialogue with four takeaways. First, what our two traditions have done with the Nauvoo-era church has greatly shaped what Zion theology became in our traditions. Here, we see our greatest divergences as traditions, in the forms of the rituals we practice, our theologies of God, and where we have lived as a people. Second, our relationship to the past also shapes Zion theology in very direct ways—Community of Christ seeing the past as generative, or a starting point, for being a living tradition, and the Church of Jesus Christ seeing the past as holding more of a normative status, part of what it means to be a church that preserves a restoration. Third, the narrative of Zion that Joseph Smith launched into the world in 1830 has been the most theologically significant text in our two churches over time. The Zion narrative shaped where people lived, their economic relationships, their theologies, their involvement in the wider world, and their aspirations as no other text did. As a shared text, the Zion narrative has been a song we sing together in the present and a common prayer for the future. Finally, if, as Terryl Givens suggests, Joseph Smith's mission was to establish a Zion community in the world, then although the Church of Jesus Christ and Community of Christ represent different particular expressions of Zion, their unique contributions evidence the continued flourishing of Joseph Smith's prophetic vision.

NOTES

1. Terryl L. Givens, *Feeding the Flock: The Foundations of Mormon Thought; Church and Praxis* (New York: Oxford, 2017), 34.

2. Prominent Christian theologian N. T. Wright said, "Heaven, in the Bible, is not a future destiny but the other, hidden, dimension of our ordinary life—God's dimension." N. T. Wright, *Surprised by Hope: Rethinking Heaven, the Resurrection, and the Mission of the Church* (New York: HarperCollins, 2008), 19. This description, according to Latter-day Saint scholar Robert L. Millet, resonates with Latter-day Saints as they see Zion and the gathering of Israel as a present endeavor. Robert L. Millet, "For Heaven's Sake: A Review of N.T. Wright's *Surprised by Hope*," *Religious Educator* 10, no. 3 (2009): 219–36.

3. Givens, *Feeding the Flock*, 34–35.

4. Givens, *Feeding the Flock*, 35.

5. "History, 1838–1856, volume C-1 [2 November 1838–31 July 1842]," p. 1285, The Joseph Smith Papers, https://www.josephsmithpapers.org/paper-summary/history-1838-1856-volume-c-1-2-november-1838-31-july-1842/459. For Joseph Smith, being in the presence of God was not just a future blessing but one available now in mortality. Smith promised those who were worthy and prepared that they could have this blessing in this life. "Minutes, circa 3–4 June 1831," p. 3, The Joseph Smith Papers, https://www.josephsmithpapers.org/paper-summary/minutes-circa-3-4-june-1831/1. See the historical introduction, in particular note 20. See also Anthony Sweat, *The Holy Invitation: Understanding Your Sacred Temple Endowment* (Salt Lake City: Deseret Book, 2017), 11–29.

6. "History, 1838–1856, volume A-1 [23 December 1805–30 August 1834]," pp. 80–81, The Joseph Smith Papers, https://www.josephsmithpapers.org/paper-summary/history-1838-1856-volume-a-1-23-december-1805-30-august-1834/86.

7. Givens, *Feeding the Flock*, 34–35. See also Terryl L. Givens, *The Prophecy of Enoch as Restoration Blueprint* (Logan: Utah State University Press, 2012), 11–12. Smith's early use of Zion can be seen in the following references: LDS Doctrine and Covenants 6:6; 11:6; 12:6; 14:6; 21:7; CofChrist Doctrine and Covenants 6:3a; 12:3a; 19:2d.

8. See Steven L. Olsen, "The Mormon Ideology of Place: Cosmic Symbolism of the City of Zion, 1830–1846" (PhD diss., University of Chicago, 1985), 26, cited in Reed M. Holmes, *Dreamers of Zion: Joseph Smith and George J. Adams; Conviction, Leadership and Israel's Renewal* (Portland, OR: Sussex Academic Press, 2012), 45.

9. This vision was received "to the joy of the little flock, which . . . numbered about seventy members." "History, 1838–1856, volume A-1 [23 December 1805–30 August 1834]," p. 81, The Joseph Smith Papers, https://www.josephsmithpapers.org/paper-summary/history-1838-1856-volume-a-1-23-december-1805-30-august-1834/87. The pattern of the development of Zion in the prophecy of Enoch is attempted by Joseph. The developed community progressed to the point that "Enoch and all his people walked with God" (Moses 7:69). The end of this revelation foretells a latter-day Zion receiving the Lord (Moses 7:60–67).

10. Givens, *Feeding the Flock*, 35.

11. One of these revelations began with God stating the following: "I am the same which have taken the Zion of Enoch into my own bosom" (LDS Doctrine and Covenants 38:4; CofChrist Doctrine and Covenants 38:1b).

12. Enoch's vision of humankind's sin and pain: "his heart swelled wide as eternity; and his bowels yearned" (Moses 7:41). This vision also illustrates the need for love between others, as those in Zion "were of one heart and one mind, and dwelt in righteousness; and there was no poor among them" (Moses 7:18). This seems to be suggested in a parable taught by Smith in a January 1831 revelation (LDS Doctrine and Covenants 38:24–27; CofChrist Doctrine and Covenants 38:5d–6a).

13. "Old Testament Revision, John Whitmer First Copy," p. [10], The Joseph Smith Papers, https://www.josephsmithpapers.org/paper-summary/old-testament-revision-john-whitmer-first-copy/14. The prophecy of Enoch reveals that, because of his teachings, "all men were offended because of him." It is clear from this passage that Enoch's first priority was not the acceptance of peers of society but of God. This allowed Enoch to walk with God.

14. "The Lord called his people Zion because they were of one heart and of one mind and dwelt in righteousness and there was no poor among them." This outcome grows out of a love and commitment for God and others. "Old Testament Revision 1," p. 16, The Joseph Smith Papers, https://www.josephsmithpapers.org/paper-summary/old-testament-revision-1/18.

15. *General Handbook: Serving in The Church of Jesus Christ of Latter-day Saints*, 27.2, ChurchofJesusChrist.org.

16. Aaron L. West, "Questions and Answers about the Temple Lot in Independence, Missouri," ChurchofJesusChrist.org.

17. Richard Smyth, "Come to Zion," *Millennial Star*, February 1861, 96. Richard Smyth penned the words of "Israel, Israel, God Is Calling," which first appeared in the *Millennial Star* in 1861.

18. Circular from the Twelve Apostles, April 16, 1880, Church History Library, Salt Lake City, 1, as cited in Emily Crumpton, "Perpetual Emigrating Fund Company," September 1, 2020, ChurchofJesusChrist.org.

19. Crumpton, "Perpetual Emigrating Fund Company."

20. George Q. Cannon, in *Journal of Discourses* (London: Latter-day Saints' Book Depot, 1880), 20:2–3. Speaking of the territorial solvency, Cannon said, "To-day it is conceded upon all sides, and the fact is not disputed by intelligent persons, that the Latter-day Saints, or, to speak more properly, the people of the Utah Territory, occupy a position superior to that of any other territory within the confines of the Union." Cannon reported that United States president Rutherford B. Hayes exclaimed, "Your position is certainly an enviable and unique one."

21. Givens, *Feeding the Flock*, 39.

22. Heber J. Grant, in Conference Report, October 1936, 3, as quoted in *Teachings of the Presidents of the Church: Heber J. Grant* (Salt Lake City: The Church of Jesus Christ of Latter-day Saints, 2011), 115.

23. Heather Wrigley, "Celebrating 75 Years of Welfare," *Ensign*, May 2011, 140.

24. Robert D. Hales, "Welfare Principles to Guide Our Lives: An Eternal Plan for the Welfare of Men's Souls," *Ensign*, May 1986, 30.

25. Bruce R. McConkie, "Come: Let Israel Build Zion," *Ensign*, May 1977, 115.

26. Gordon B. Hinckley, "Some Thoughts on Temples, Retention of Converts, and Missionary Service," *Ensign*, November 1997, 50. Brigham Young indicated that there would need to be thousands of temples for the purpose of the Restoration to be accomplished, and Elder McConkie indicated that temples would "dot the earth." See Givens, *Feeding the Flock*, 43.

27. "At the October 2021 General Conference, the Prophet Says the Church Will Build 13 More Temples," October 3, 2021, newsroom.ChurchofJesusChrist.org.

28. Benjamin Park, "Juvenile Instructor Heads to Calgary," juvenileinstructor.org, June 25, 2012.

29. Russell M. Nelson and Wendy W. Nelson, "Hope of Israel" (worldwide youth devotional, June 3, 2018), broadcasts.ChurchofJesusChrist.org.

30. Inez Smith Davis, *The Story of the Church: A History of the Church of Jesus Christ of Latter-Day Saints, and of Its Legal Successor, the Reorganized Church of Jesus Christ of Latter Day Saints* (Independence, MO: Herald Publishing House, 1934), 12.

31. Robert Orsi, "Abundant History: Marian Apparitions as Alternative Modernity," *Historically Speaking* 9, no. 7 (2008): 15. Orsi has extended these arguments in Robert A. Orsi, *History and Presence* (Cambridge, MA: Harvard University Press, 2016), 48–71.

32. Stephen Taysom, "Abundant Events or Narrative Abundance? Robert Orsi and the Academic Study of Mormonism," *Dialogue* 45, no. 4 (2012): 1–26.

33. Orsi, "Abundant History," 15.

34. Terryl Givens, *The Prophecy of Enoch as Restoration Blueprint* (Logan: Utah State University Press, 2012), 11.

35. John Reeves and Annette Yoshiko Reed, *Enoch from Antiquity to the Middle Ages*, vol. 1, *Sources from Judaism, Christianity, and Islam* (New York: Oxford University Press, 2018).

36. Patrick Q. Mason, *Mormonism and Violence: The Battles of Zion* (Cambridge: Cambridge University Press, 2019), 21–25.

37. Roger D. Launius, *Joseph Smith III: Pragmatic Prophet* (Urbana: University of Illinois Press, 1988), 168–89.

38. David J. Howlett, "The Death and Resurrection of the RLDS Zion: A Case Study in 'Failed Prophecy,' 1930–1970," *Dialogue* 40, no. 3 (2007): 115–16.

39. Photocopy of original in author's personal archives; original in Community of Christ Archives, file number misplaced.

40. Richard Price, *Saints at the Crossroads* (Independence, MO: Price Publishing, 1974), 139–43.

41. Duane E. Couey, "Zion as Process," in *Readings on Concepts of Zion*, ed. Paul A. Wellington (Independence, MO: Herald Publishing House, 1973), 114–23; Maurice L. Draper, "Zion, the Leaven," in *Readings on Concepts of Zion*, 204–8.

42. Geoffrey Spencer, "The Cause of Zion Summons Us," in *Community of Christ Sings* (Independence, MO: Herald Publishing House, 2013), 386.

43. "Basic Beliefs," Community of Christ, https://www.CofChrist.org/basic-beliefs.

44. "Enduring Principles," Community of Christ, https://www.CofChrist.org/enduring-principles.

45. "Mission Initiatives," Community of Christ, https://www.CofChrist.org/mission-initiatives.

46. "Tiona Nehenehe," in *Community of Christ Sings*, 382.

47. Anthony Chvala-Smith, email to David Howlett, February 27, 2021. Chvala-Smith made this statement in many settings, but he and I were unable to find it in print.

48. Patrick Mason, *Restoration: God's Call to the 21st-Century World* (Meridian, ID: Faith Matters, 2020), 42–48.

49. James Baldwin, "Collective Essays," *New York Times: On the Web*.

50. "Revelation, 1 August 1831 [Doctrine and Covenants 58]," p. 96, The Joseph Smith Papers, https://www.josephsmithpapers.org/paper-summary/revelation-1-august-1831-dc-58/3. For information regarding the argument between Partridge and Smith, see the historical introduction.

51. "Collection of Sacred Hymns, 1835, Page iii," pp. 86, 88, The Joseph Smith Papers, https://www.josephsmithpapers.org/paper-summary/collection-of-sacred-hymns-1835/88.

52. Roger D. Launius, "The Awesome Responsibility: Joseph Smith III and the Nauvoo Experience," in *Kingdom on the Mississippi Revisited: Nauvoo in Mormon History*, ed. Roger D. Launius and John E. Hallwas (Urbana: University of Illinois Press, 1996), 234.

53. Hans-Georg Gadamer, *Truth and Method*, 2nd ed. (New York: Continuum, 2004).

EPILOGUE

"The most difficult aspect of this process was also the most satisfying in the end. I found myself taking on a defensive or apologetic mode that felt counterproductive to the goal of the dialogue. It required me to sit with some difficult realities and seek for greater humility and understanding beyond what I thought I knew."

"Dialogue is always worthwhile and helpful when it's genuine. When authentically curious and informed people come together in a safe environment, rich and meaningful learning happens. . . . The dialogue enriched my own theological knowledge and thinking, as well as self-understanding."

"Often we are divided by a common language!"

"We immediately connected as mothers and were talking a lot about our own children and how they were viewed and seen as persons."

"Now I feel holy respect . . ."

These are a few of the statements made by authors when we met to discuss our experiences of dialogue with one another in the writing of this book. It has not been easy. For example, sometimes it felt frustrating for some when old stereotypes of each other surfaced. At the same time there was always kindness, civility, and patience as we quested to understand each other. Difficulties in our conversations are opportunities to go deeper and to understand better each other's sensitivities.

It is perhaps helpful to ask if our work together has been an "ecumenical dialogue" or an "interfaith dialogue." Christian churches often come together ecumenically to find common ground, enrich their understanding of the gospel, and partner with each in facing the issues of our time. The World Council of Churches is the largest umbrella ecumenical Protestant body. The National Council of Churches USA is a partner body of the World Council of Churches.

Interfaith dialogue is wider—it includes, for example, conversations between Muslims, Jews, Hindus, Buddhists, and Christians. The goal of interfaith dialogue is to create respect and mutual understanding. Sometimes partners come together in solidarity to address issues of mutual concern such as human rights, violence, racism, and so on.

Brigham Young University academics in conversation with Jewish academics is an example of interfaith dialogue. Community of Christ's membership in the USA of the National Council of Churches is an example of an ecumenical relationship.

Our dialogue in this book has been within the Latter Day Saint family of churches that goes back to the movement that began in the 1830s on the American frontier. Community of Christ and The Church of Jesus Christ of Latter-day Saints have perhaps fourteen years in common and nearly two hundred years apart. Our conversation has not been to bring our respective churches together into a close working relationship. We are not representatives of our churches seeking unity or merger. We have simply been people of goodwill seeking to understand each other accurately and fairly. Thus, this has been more of an interfaith dialogue than an ecumenical one but still a significant step of peacemaking and perhaps one day of even reconciliation. We share this book to draw you into the dialogue also.

Perhaps what we have experienced together in writing this book can be further illustrated in our shared history of early Latter Day Saint mission in the British Isles. The Ribble Valley in Lancashire, England, is sacred geography for all Restoration faiths and is as important as more familiar locations such as Palmyra, New York, or Kirtland, Ohio.[1] In the River Ribble at Preston, the first baptisms in the British Isles occurred in 1837. In December 2018, two members of our dialogue group and coeditors of this volume, Casey Paul Griffiths from The Church of Jesus Christ of Latter-day Saints and Andrew Bolton from Community of Christ, traveled together to the Ribble Valley, exploring this sacred place together. We stood in the spaces where the first Latter Day Saint missionaries proclaimed their message. We walked along the banks of the River Ribble where the first converts raced each other to the waters in their enthusiasm to be baptized first. We walked many of the same paths where the early Saints in this land shared their homes, their livelihood, and their hope for a restoration of the ancient faith of the apostles. As we walked through this special land, our differences melted away, and we felt only a shared heritage. We also help each other on our journeys. Casey and Andrew, for instance, were exploring the early Latter Day Saint history of Preston, Lancashire, and Casey helped Andrew discover the hospital Andrew was born in—a place Andrew had been searching for years to find.

The geography of the River Ribble is also a parable that illustrates our Latter-day Saint and Community of Christ dialogue since 2016. The estuary of the River Ribble, as it flows into the Irish Sea, is ten miles wide, but in its upper reaches in Yorkshire it is less than a yard in breadth and easy to step over from bank to bank. In our twelve dialogues in this book and earlier, we have found, unsurprisingly, that today the two churches are distinctly very different. In many ways they are as far apart as Lytham St Annes and Southport, towns north and south on the Ribble estuary. Understandings of divinity, Jesus Christ, Joseph Smith, Nauvoo, gender, sexual orientation, scripture, and common consent can seriously divide us. However, if we go "upstream" in our shared history, it is easier to cross over and find common stories that shape positively both our movements. For example, this includes the reality of spiritual experience exemplified by the First Vision, many sections of the Doctrine and Covenants, the Book of Mormon, the Kirtland Temple, concepts of revelation, sacred space, and the cause of Zion.

The story of the Ribble Valley in Lancashire adds also another dimension. The mountain Saints of the Great Basin and the prairie Saints[2] of the American Midwest are today both vigorous international churches. The arrival of the first missionaries in Canada (1833) and the British Isles (1837) served as only the beginning of a shared impulse to obey the command of Jesus to go into all the world and baptize (see Matthew 28:18–28). We are each deeply rooted in history and geography, but both churches also have a global consciousness that perhaps makes us more open and nuanced. Scholars contributing to this volume came from Canada, Iceland, the United Kingdom, Australia, New Zealand, and Germany, as well as Provo, Utah; Independence, Missouri; and elsewhere in the United States.

Discovering each other's understanding of sacred space has also become common ground and enriching conversation. This has also been a metaphor for our dialogue. As John Hull, professor emeritus of religious education at the University of Birmingham, once said, "I may not be particularly holy and you may not be very holy, but the space between us, as we talk, is holy ground." Dialogue is holy ground.

Respectful and sincere conversations break down stereotypes and simplistic and sometimes inaccurate understandings of "the other." Our dialogue has been characterized by candid exchanges and forthright, thoughtful expressions but also delightful humor, mutual courtesy, and good fellowship. We have eaten, teased, and laughed together. When things have been the most difficult and annoying, this is when dialogue has had to go deeper.

Our dialogue is far from over. Following are some other topics before us:

- Policy and implementing policy
- Joseph Smith Jr.
- Inner canon of scripture—what do we actually use?
- Hymnody
- Doctrine and theology
- Climate and stewardship
- Religion and science
- Globalization and becoming international movements

- Indigenous peoples / Native Americans
- Poverty

Authentic friendships have grown. We can be critical at times, but we have also enjoyed holy envy of each other's traditions. Holy respect has also grown for each other.

The Saints from both faiths find joy, meaning, and inspiration for discipleship in our temples. Today our temple traditions are symbolized by the Community of Christ Temple in Independence and the nearby Latter-day Saint temple in Kansas City. These temples are in or near Jackson County—a place of historical and future significance for both churches. These sacred spaces also connect with the great purpose of the Latter Day Saint movement: "Seek to bring forth and establish the cause of Zion" (LDS Doctrine and Covenants 6:6; CofChrist Doctrine and Covenants 6:3a). The cause of Zion means that all of the earth is to become redeemed sacred space. Zion is sacred space because of the presence of justice and the end of poverty and all violence and divisions between peoples (see Moses 7:18; CofChrist Doctrine and Covenants 36:2h–i). The triumph of Zion is the end of all "-ites" through conversion to the love of God in our hearts, modeled by the Redeemer of the world (see LDS 4 Nephi 1:15–17; CofChrist IV Nephi 1:17–20).

Through dialogue we seek that day when "oldest enemies" become trusting friends. Each of us has peace traditions, at times marginal or ignored, but then gloriously bubbling up into the light. The call to Zion and peace is clear for all of us in this inspired passage: "Blessed are they who shall seek to bring forth my Zion, . . . for they shall have the gift and power of the Holy Ghost. . . . And whoso shall publish peace, yea, tidings of great joy, how beautiful upon the mountains shall they be" (LDS 1 Nephi 13:37; CofChrist I Nephi 3:187, 189). Our dialogue and this book of conversations are a small but significant step on this journey.

Notes

1. See, for example, Matthew Lyman Rasmussen, *Mormonism and the Making of a British Zion* (Salt Lake City: University of Utah Press, 2016), 4–6.
2. "Mountain" and "prairie" Saints are terms used by Jan Shipps for The Church of Jesus Christ of Latter-day Saints and Community of Christ. See Jan Shipps,

"New History of the Prairie and Mountain Saints; Race and Gender," *Mormon Studies Podcast*, November 25, 2014, https://radiopublic.com/mormon-studies-podcast-Gm2Kya/s1!7a7cf.

INDEX

Y

Yale, Alfred H., 72

Young, Brigham
    and church following Joseph
        Smith's death, 2–3
    as custodian of Joseph's scriptural
        legacy, 39
    on Jesus Christ, 22
    and prophet-polity paradox, 89, 90
    on scripture and prophets, 40–41
    on temples, 212n26

Z

Zion
    in Church of Jesus Christ
        of Latter-day Saints, 102,
        193–98, 210n2
    in Community of Christ,
        198–206
    in Community of Christ versus
        Church of Jesus Christ of
        Latter-day Saints, 206–10
    evolution of conceptions of, 92
    interfaith dialogue on, 9
    Joseph Smith on, 194–95, 198,
        199–200, 205, 210
    and love for others, 211n12
    as sacred space, 219
    seeking, 18